Esther Singleton

Turrets, Towers, and Temples

The great buildings of the world, as seen and described by famous writers

Esther Singleton

Turrets, Towers, and Temples
The great buildings of the world, as seen and described by famous writers

ISBN/EAN: 9783337385828

Printed in Europe, USA, Canada, Australia, Japan

Cover: Foto ©ninafisch / pixelio.de

More available books at **www.hansebooks.com**

Turrets, Towers, and Temples

The Great Buildings of the World, as
Seen and Described by Famous Writers

EDITED AND TRANSLATED

By ESTHER SINGLETON

TRANSLATOR OF "THE MUSIC DRAMAS OF RICHARD WAGNER"

With Numerous Illustrations

NEW YORK
DODD, MEAD AND COMPANY
1904

Copyright, 1898,
BY DODD, MEAD AND COMPANY.

University Press:
JOHN WILSON AND SON, CAMBRIDGE, U.S.A.

Preface

IN making the selections for this book, which is thought to be the realization of a new idea, it has been my endeavour to bring together descriptions of several famous buildings written by authors who have appreciated the romantic spirit, as well as the architectural beauty and grandeur, of the work they describe.

It would be impossible to collect within the small boundaries of a single volume sketches and pictures of all the masterpieces of architecture, and a vast amount of interesting literature has had to be ignored. I have tried, however, to gather choice examples of as many different styles of architecture as possible and to give a description, wherever practicable, of each building's special object of veneration, such as the Christ of Burgos and the Cid's coffer in the same Cathedral; the Emerald Buddha at Wat Phra Kao, Bangkok; the statue of Our Lady at Toledo; the shrine of St. Thomas à Becket at Canterbury; etc., as well as the special feature for which any particular building is famous, such as the Court of Lions in the Alhambra; the Chapel of Henry VII. in Westminster Abbey; the Convent of the Escurial; the spiral stairway at Chambord; etc., and also a typical scene, like the dance *de los seises* in the Cathedral of Seville; and the celebration of Easter at St. Peter's.

Ruskin says: " It is well to have not only what men have thought and felt, but what their hands have handled and their strength wrought all the days of their life." It is also well to have what sympathetic authors have written about these massive and wonderful creations of stone which have looked down upon and outlived so many generations of mankind.

With the exception of the Mosque of Santa Sofia, all the translations have been made expressly for this book.

E. S.

NEW YORK, *May, 1898.*

Contents

ST. MARK'S, VENICE	1
JOHN RUSKIN.	
THE TOWER OF LONDON	11
WILLIAM HEPWORTH DIXON.	
THE CATHEDRAL OF ANTWERP	18
WILLIAM MAKEPEACE THACKERAY.	
THE TAJ MAHAL, AGRA	23
ANDRÉ CHEVRILLON.	
THE CATHEDRAL OF NOTRE-DAME, PARIS	28
VICTOR HUGO.	
THE KREMLIN, MOSCOW	38
THÉOPHILE GAUTIER.	
THE CATHEDRAL OF YORK	49
THOMAS FROGNALL DIBDIN.	
THE MOSQUE OF OMAR, JERUSALEM	56
PIERRE LOTI.	
THE CATHEDRAL OF BURGOS	65
THÉOPHILE GAUTIER.	
THE PYRAMIDS, GIZEH	71
GEORG EBERS.	
ST. PETER'S, ROME	76
CHARLES DICKENS.	

CONTENTS

THE CATHEDRAL OF STRASBURG 84
   VICTOR HUGO.

THE SHWAY DAGOHN RANGOON 92
   GWENDOLIN TRENCH GASCOIGNE.

THE CATHEDRAL OF SIENA 98
   JOHN ADDINGTON SYMONDS.

THE TOWN HALL OF LOUVAIN. 102
   GRANT ALLEN.

THE CATHEDRAL OF SEVILLE 105
   EDMONDO DE AMICIS.

WINDSOR CASTLE 110
   WILLIAM HEPWORTH DIXON.

THE CATHEDRAL OF COLOGNE 117
   ERNEST BRETON.

THE PALACE OF VERSAILLES 126
   AUGUSTUS J. C. HARE.

THE CATHEDRAL OF LINCOLN 132
   THOMAS FROGNALL DIBDIN.

THE TEMPLE OF KARNAK 137
   AMELIA B. EDWARDS.

SANTA MARIA DEL FIORE, FLORENCE 143
   CHARLES YRIARTE.

GIOTTO'S CAMPANILE, FLORENCE 147
   I. MRS. OLIPHANT.
   II. JOHN RUSKIN.

THE HOUSE OF JACQUES CŒUR, BOURGES 152
   AD. BERTY.

WAT PHRA KAO, BANGKOK 158
   CARL BOCK.

CONTENTS

THE CATHEDRAL OF TOLEDO 163
    THÉOPHILE GAUTIER.

THE CHÂTEAU DE CHAMBORD 170
    JULES LOISELEUR.

THE TEMPLES OF NIKKO 177
    PIERRE LOTI.

THE PALACE OF HOLYROOD, EDINBURGH 187
    DAVID MASSON.

SAINT-GUDULE, BRUSSELS 193
    VICTOR HUGO.

THE ESCURIAL, MADRID 195
    EDMONDO DE AMICIS.

THE TEMPLE OF MADURA 204
    JAMES FERGUSSON.

THE CATHEDRAL OF MILAN 209
    THÉOPHILE GAUTIER.

THE MOSQUE OF HASSAN, CAIRO 215
    AMELIA B. EDWARDS.

THE CATHEDRAL OF TRÈVES 221
    EDWARD AUGUSTUS FREEMAN.

THE VATICAN, ROME 225
    AUGUSTUS J. C. HARE.

THE CATHEDRAL OF AMIENS 234
    JOHN RUSKIN.

THE MOSQUE OF SANTA SOFIA, CONSTANTINOPLE . . . 242
    EDMONDO DE AMICIS.

WESTMINSTER ABBEY, LONDON 248
    ARTHUR PENRHYN STANLEY.

THE PARTHENON, ATHENS 257
    JOHN ADDINGTON SYMONDS.

CONTENTS

THE CATHEDRAL OF ROUEN 263
        THOMAS FROGNALL DIBDIN.

THE CASTLE OF HEIDELBERG 269
        VICTOR HUGO.

THE DUCAL PALACE, VENICE 278
        JOHN RUSKIN.

THE MOSQUE OF CORDOVA 286
        EDMONDO DE AMICIS.

THE CATHEDRAL OF THRONDTJEM 293
        AUGUSTUS J. C. HARE.

THE LEANING TOWER OF PISA 298
        CHARLES DICKENS.

THE CATHEDRAL OF CANTERBURY 301
        W. H. FREMANTLE.

THE ALHAMBRA, GRANADA 308
        THÉOPHILE GAUTIER.

Illustrations

		PAGE
ST. MARK'S . . . . *Italy* . . .		Frontis.
THE TOWER OF LONDON . . . . . *England* . .		Face 14
THE CATHEDRAL OF ANTWERP . . . *Belgium* . .		" 20
THE TAJ MAHAL . . . . *India* . . .		" 23
THE CATHEDRAL OF NOTRE DAME . . *France* . . .		" 30
THE KREMLIN . . . . *Russia* . . .		" 40
THE CATHEDRAL OF YORK . . . . *England* . .		" 49
THE MOSQUE OF OMAR . . . . . *Palestine* . .		" 58
THE CATHEDRAL OF BURGOS . . . *Spain* . . .		" 65
THE PYRAMIDS . . . . *Egypt* . . .		" 72
ST. PETER'S . . . . *Italy*		" 78
THE CATHEDRAL OF STRASBURG . . . *Germany* . .		" 86
THE SHWAY DAGOHN . . . . . . *Burmah* . .		" 94
THE CATHEDRAL OF SIENA . . . . *Italy*		" 98
THE TOWN HALL OF LOUVAIN . . . *Belgium* . .		" 103
THE CATHEDRAL OF SEVILLE . . . . *Spain* . . .		" 106
WINDSOR CASTLE . . . . *England* . .		" 110
THE CATHEDRAL OF COLOGNE . . . *Germany* . .		" 121
THE PALACE OF VERSAILLES . . . . *France* . . .		" 126
THE CATHEDRAL OF LINCOLN . . . *England* . .		" 132
THE TEMPLE OF KARNAK . . . . *Egypt* . . .		" 139
SANTA MARIA DEL FIORE . . . . . *Italy*		" 144
GIOTTO'S CAMPANILE . . . . . . *Italy*		" 147
THE HOUSE OF JACQUES CŒUR . . . *France* . . .		" 155
WAT PHRA KAO . . . . *Siam* . . .		" 159
THE CATHEDRAL OF TOLEDO . . . *Spain* . . .		" 164
THE CHÂTEAU DE CHAMBORD . . . *France* . . .		" 172

		PAGE
THE TEMPLES OF NIKKO	*Japan*	Face 178
THE PALACE OF HOLYROOD	*Scotland*	" 187
SAINT-GUDULE	*Belgium*	" 193
THE ESCURIAL	*Spain*	" 195
THE TEMPLE OF MADURA	*India*	" 204
THE CATHEDRAL OF MILAN	*Italy*	" 213
THE MOSQUE OF HASSAN	*Egypt*	" 216
THE CATHEDRAL OF TRÈVES	*Germany*	" 221
THE VATICAN	*Italy*	" 225
THE CATHEDRAL OF AMIENS	*France*	" 234
THE MOSQUE OF SANTA SOFIA	*Turkey*	" 242
WESTMINSTER ABBEY	*England*	" 248
THE PARTHENON	*Greece*	" 257
THE CATHEDRAL OF ROUEN	*France*	" 265
THE CASTLE OF HEIDELBERG	*Germany*	" 269
THE DUCAL PALACE	*Italy*	" 280
THE MOSQUE OF CORDOVA	*Spain*	" 288
THE CATHEDRAL OF THRONDTJEM	*Norway*	" 293
THE LEANING TOWER OF PISA	*Italy*	" 298
THE CATHEDRAL OF CANTERBURY	*England*	" 301
THE ALHAMBRA	*Spain*	" 310

Turrets, Towers, and Temples.

ST. MARK'S.

JOHN RUSKIN.

A YARD or two farther, we pass the hostelry of the Black Eagle, and, glancing as we pass through the square door of marble, deeply moulded, in the outer wall, we see the shadows of its pergola of vines resting on an ancient well, with a pointed shield carved on its side; and so presently emerge on the bridge and Campo San Moisè, whence to the entrance into St. Mark's Place, called the Bocca di Piazza (mouth of the square), the Venetian character is nearly destroyed, first by the frightful façade of San Moisè, which we will pause at another time to examine, and then by the modernizing of the shops as they near the piazza, and the mingling with the lower Venetian populace of lounging groups of English and Austrians. We will push fast through them into the shadow of the pillars at the end of the "Bocca di Piazza," and then we forget them all; for between those pillars there opens a great light, and, in the midst of it, as we advance slowly, the vast tower of St. Mark seems to lift itself visibly forth from the level field of chequered stones;

and, on each side, the countless arches prolong themselves into ranged symmetry, as if the rugged and irregular houses that pressed together above us in the dark alley had been struck back into sudden obedience and lovely order, and all their rude casements and broken walls had been transformed into arches charged with goodly sculpture and fluted shafts of delicate stone.

And well may they fall back, for beyond those troops of ordered arches there rises a vision out of the earth, and all the great square seems to have opened from it in a kind of awe, that we may see it far away; — a multitude of pillars and white domes, clustered into a long, low pyramid of coloured light; a treasure-heap, it seems, partly of gold, and partly of opal and mother-of-pearl, hollowed beneath into five great vaulted porches, ceiled with fair mosaic, and beset with sculpture of alabaster, clear as amber and delicate as ivory, — sculpture fantastic and involved, of palm leaves and lilies, and grapes and pomegranates, and birds clinging and fluttering among the branches, all twined together into an endless network of buds and plumes; and, in the midst of it, the solemn forms of angels, sceptred, and robed to the feet, and leaning to each other across the gates, their figures indistinct among the gleaming of the golden ground through the leaves beside them, interrupted and dim, like the morning light as it faded back among the branches of Eden, when first its gates were angel-guarded long ago. And round the walls of the porches there are set pillars of variegated stones, jasper and porphyry, and deep-green serpentine spotted with flakes of snow, and marbles, that half refuse and half yield to the sunshine, Cleopatra-like, "their bluest veins to kiss"— the shadow, as it steals back from them, revealing line after line of azure undulation, as a receding tide leaves the waved sand; their capitals rich with interwoven tracery, rooted knots of herbage, and drifting leaves of acanthus and vine, and mystical signs, all beginning and ending in the Cross; and above them, in the broad archivolts, a continuous chain of language and of life — angels, and the signs of heaven, and the labours of men, each in its appointed season upon the earth; and above these, another range of glittering pinnacles, mixed with white arches edged with scarlet flowers,—a confusion of delight, amidst which the breasts of the Greek horses are seen blazing in their breadth of golden strength, and the St. Mark's Lion, lifted on a blue field covered with stars, until at last, as if in ecstasy, the crests of the arches break into a marble foam, and toss themselves far into the blue sky in flashes and wreaths of sculptured spray, as if the breakers on the Lido shore had been frost-bound before they fell, and the sea-nymphs had inlaid them with coral and amethyst.

Between that grim cathedral of England and this, what an interval! There is a type of it in the very birds that haunt them; for, instead of the restless crowd, hoarsevoiced and sable-winged, drifting on the bleak upper air, the St. Mark's porches are full of doves, that nestle among the marble foliage, and mingle the soft iridescence of their living plumes, changing at every motion with the tints, hardly less lovely, that have stood unchanged for seven hundred years.

And what effect has this splendour on those who pass beneath it? You may walk from sunrise to sunset, to and fro, before the gateway of St. Mark's, and you will not see an eye lifted to it, nor a countenance brightened by it. Priest and layman, soldier and civilian, rich and poor, pass by it alike regardlessly. Up to the very recesses of the porches, the meanest tradesmen of the city push their counters; nay, the foundations of its pillars are themselves the seats — not "of them that sell doves" for sacrifice, but of vendors of toys and caricatures. Round the whole square in front of the church there is almost a continuous line of cafés, where the idle Venetians of the middle classes lounge, and read empty journals; in its centre the Austrian bands play during the time of vespers, their martial music jarring with the organ notes, — the march drowning the miserere, and the sullen crowd thickening around them, — a crowd which, if it had its will, would stiletto every soldier that pipes to it. And in the recesses of the porches, all day long, knots of men of the lowest classes, unemployed and listless, lie basking in the sun like lizards; and unregarded children, — every heavy glance of their young eyes full of desperation and stony depravity, and their throats hoarse with cursing, — gamble, and fight, and snarl, and sleep, hour after hour, clashing their bruised *centesimi* upon the marble ledges of the church porch. And the images of Christ and His angels look down upon it continually. . . . Let us enter the church itself. It is lost in still deeper twilight, to which the eye must be accustomed for some moments before the form of the building can be traced; and then there opens before us a vast cave hewn out into the form of a Cross, and divided into shadowy aisles by many pillars. Round the domes of its roof the light enters only through narrow apertures like large stars; and here and there a ray or two from some far-away casement wanders into the darkness, and casts a narrow phosphoric stream upon the waves of marble that heave and fall in a thousand colours along the floor. What else there is of light is from torches or silver lamps, burning ceaselessly in the recesses of the chapels; the roof sheeted with gold, and the polished walls covered with alabaster, give back at every curve and angle some feeble gleaming to the flames; and the glories round the heads of the sculptured saints flash out upon us as we pass them, and sink again into the gloom. Under foot and over head, a continual succession of crowded imagery, one picture passing into another, as in a dream; forms beautiful and terrible mixed together; dragons and serpents, and ravening beasts of prey, and graceful birds that in the midst of them drink from running fountains and feed from vases of crystal; the passions and the pleasures of human life symbolized together, and the mystery of its redemption; for the mazes of interwoven lines and changeful pictures lead always at last to the Cross, lifted and carved in every place and upon every stone; sometimes with the serpent of eternity wrapt round it, sometimes with doves beneath its arms, and sweet herbage growing forth from its feet; but conspicuous most of all on the great rood that crosses the church before the altar, raised in bright blazonry against the shadow of the apse. And although in the recesses of the aisles and chapels, when the mist of the incense hangs heavily, we may see continually a figure traced in faint lines upon their marble, a woman standing with her eyes raised to heaven, and the inscription above her, " Mother of God," she is not here the presiding deity. It is the Cross that is first seen, and always, burning in the centre of the temple; and every dome and hollow of its roof has the figure of Christ in the utmost height of it, raised in power, or returning in judgment.

Nor is this interior without effect on the minds of the people. At every hour of the day there are groups collected before the various shrines, and solitary worshippers scattered through the darker places of the church, evidently in prayer both deep and reverent, and, for the most part, profoundly sorrowful. The devotees at the greater number of the renowned shrines of Romanism may be seen murmuring their appointed prayers with wandering eyes and unengaged gestures; but the step of the stranger does not disturb those who kneel on the pavement of St. Mark's; and hardly a moment passes, from early morning to sunset, in which we may not see some half-veiled figure enter beneath the Arabian porch, cast itself into long abasement on the floor of the temple, and then rising slowly with more confirmed step, and with a passionate kiss and clasp of the arms given to the feet of the crucifix, by which the lamps burn always in the northern aisle, leave the church as if comforted. . . .

It would be easier to illustrate a crest of Scottish mountain, with its purple heather and pale harebells at their fullest and fairest, or a glade of Jura forest, with its floor of anemone and moss, than a single portico of St. Mark's. . . .

The balls in the archivolt project considerably, and the interstices between their interwoven bands of marble are filled with colours like the illuminations of a manuscript; violet, crimson, blue, gold, and green alternately: but no green is ever used without an intermixture of blue pieces in the mosaic, nor any blue without a little centre of pale green; sometimes only a single piece of glass a quarter of an inch square, so subtle was the feeling for colour which was thus to be satisfied. The intermediate circles have golden stars set on an azure ground, varied in the same manner; and the small crosses seen in the intervals are alternately blue and subdued scarlet, with two small circles of white set in the golden ground above and beneath them, each only about half an inch across (this work, remember, being on the outside of the building, and twenty feet above the eye), while the blue crosses have each a pale green centre. . . .

The third cupola, that over the altar, represents the witness of the Old Testament to Christ; showing him enthroned in its centre and surrounded by the patriarchs and prophets. But this dome was little seen by the people; their contemplation was intended to be chiefly drawn to that of the centre of the church, and thus the mind of the worshipper was at once fixed on the main groundwork and hope of Christianity — " Christ is risen," and " Christ shall come." If he had time to explore the minor lateral chapels and cupolas, he could find in them the whole series of New Testament history, the events of the Life of Christ, and the Apostolic miracles in their order, and finally the scenery of the Book of Revelation;

but if he only entered, as often the common people do to this hour, snatching a few moments before beginning the labour of the day to offer up an ejaculatory prayer, and advanced but from the main entrance as far as the altar screen, all the splendour of the glittering nave and variegated dome, if they smote upon his heart, as they might often, in strange contrast with his reed cabin among the shallows of the lagoon, smote upon it only that they might proclaim the two great messages — "Christ is risen," and "Christ shall come." Daily, as the white cupolas rose like wreaths of sea-foam in the dawn, while the shadowy campanile and frowning palace were still withdrawn into the night, they rose with the Easter Voice of Triumph — "Christ is risen;" and daily, as they looked down upon the tumult of the people, deepening and eddying in the wide square that opened from their feet to the sea, they uttered above them the sentence of warning, — "Christ shall come."

And this thought may surely dispose the reader to look with some change of temper upon the gorgeous building and wild blazonry of that shrine of St. Mark's. He now perceives that it was in the hearts of the old Venetian people far more than a place of worship. It was at once a type of the Redeemed Church of God, and a scroll for the written word of God. It was to be to them, both an image of the Bride, all glorious within, her clothing of wrought gold; and the actual Table of the Law and the Testimony, written within and without. And whether honoured as the Church or as the Bible, was it not fitting that neither the gold nor the crystal should be spared in the adornment of it; that, as the symbol of the Bride, the building of the wall thereof should be of jasper, and the foundations of it garnished with all manner of precious stones; and that, as the channel of the World, that triumphant utterance of the Psalmist should be true of it — " I have rejoiced in the way of thy testimonies, as much as in all riches "? And shall we not look with changed temper down the long perspective of St. Mark's Place towards the sevenfold gates and glowing domes of its temple, when we know with what solemn purpose the shafts of it were lifted above the pavement of the populous square? Men met there from all countries of the earth, for traffic or for pleasure; but, above the crowd swaying forever to and fro in the restlessness of avarice or thirst of delight, was seen perpetually the glory of the temple, attesting to them, whether they would hear or whether they would forbear, that there was one treasure which the merchantmen might buy without a price, and one delight better than all others, in the word and the statutes of God. Not in the wantonness of wealth, not in vain ministry to the desire of the eyes or the pride of life, were those marbles hewn into transparent strength, and those arches arrayed in the colours of the iris. There is a message written in the dyes of them, that once was written in blood; and a sound in the echoes of their vaults, that one day shall fill the vault of heaven, — " He shall return, to do judgment and justice." The strength of Venice was given her, so long as she remembered this: her destruction found her when she had forgotten this; and it found her irrevocably, because she forgot it without excuse. Never had city a more glorious Bible. Among the nations of the North, a rude and shadowy sculpture filled their temples with confused and hardly legible imagery; but, for her the skill and the treasures of the East had gilded every letter, and illumined every page, till the Book-Temple shone from afar off like the star of the Magi.

Stones of Venice (London, 1851-'3).

THE TOWER OF LONDON.

WILLIAM HEPWORTH DIXON.

HALF a mile below London Bridge, on ground which was once a bluff, commanding the Thames from St. Saviour's Creek to St. Olave's Wharf, stands the Tower; a mass of ramparts, walls, and gates, the most ancient and most poetic pile in Europe.

Seen from the hill outside, the Tower appears to be white with age and wrinkled by remorse. The home of our stoutest kings, the grave of our noblest knights, the scene of our gayest revels, the field of our darkest crimes, that edifice speaks at once to the eye and to the soul. Grey keep, green tree, black gate, and frowning battlement, stand out, apart from all objects far and near them, menacing, picturesque, enchaining; working on the senses like a spell; and calling us away from our daily mood into a world of romance, like that which we find painted in light and shadow on Shakespeare's page.

Looking at the Tower as either a prison, a palace, or a court, picture, poetry, and drama crowd upon the mind; and if the fancy dwells most frequently on the state prison, this is because the soul is more readily kindled by a human interest than fired by an archaic and official fact. For one man who would care to see the room in which a council met or a court was held, a hundred men would like to see the chamber in which Lady Jane Grey was lodged, the cell in which Sir Walter Raleigh wrote, the tower from which Sir John Oldcastle escaped. Who would not like to stand for a moment by those steps on which Ann Boleyn knelt; pause by that slit in the wall through which Arthur De la Pole gazed; and linger, if he could, in that room in which Cranmer, Latimer and Ridley, searched the New Testament together?

The Tower has an attraction for us akin to that of the house in which we were born, the school in which we were trained. Go where we may, that grim old edifice on the Pool goes with us; a part of all we know, and of all we are. Put seas between us and the Thames, this Tower will cling to us like a thing of life. It colours Shakespeare's page. It casts a momentary gloom over Bacon's story. Many of our books were written in its vaults; the Duke of Orleans' " Poesies," Raleigh's " Historie of the World," Eliot's " Monarchy of Man," and Penn's " No Cross, No Crown."

Even as to the length of days, the Tower has no rival among palaces and prisons; its origin, like that of the Iliad, that of the Sphinx, that of the Newton Stone, being lost in the nebulous ages, long before our definite history took shape. Old writers date it from the days of Cæsar; a legend taken up by Shakespeare and the poets, in favour of which the name of Cæsar's Tower remains in popular use to this very day. A Roman wall can even yet be traced near some parts of the ditch. The Tower is mentioned in the Saxon Chronicle, in a way not incompatible with the fact of a Saxon stronghold having stood upon this spot. The buildings as we have them now in block and plan were commenced by William the Conqueror; and the series of apartments in Cæsar's tower, — hall, gallery, council-chamber, chapel, — were built in the early Norman reigns, and used as a royal residence by all our Norman kings. What can Europe show to compare against such a tale?

Set against the Tower of London — with its eight hundred years of historic life, its nineteen hundred years of traditional fame — all other palaces and prisons appear like things of an hour. The oldest bit of palace in Europe, that of the west front of the Burg in Vienna, is of the time of Henry the Third. The Kremlin in Moscow, the Doge's Palazzo in Venice, are of the Fourteenth Century. The Seraglio in Stamboul was built by Mohammed the Second. The oldest part of the Vatican was commenced by Borgia, whose name it bears. The old Louvre was commenced in the reign of Henry the Eighth; the Tuileries in that of Elizabeth. In the time of our Civil War Versailles was yet a swamp. Sans Souci and the Escurial belong to the Eighteenth Century. The Serail of Jerusalem is a Turkish edifice. The palaces of Athens, of Cairo, or Tehran, are all of modern date.

Neither can the prisons which remain in fact as well as in history and drama — with the one exception of St. Angelo in Rome — compare against the Tower. The Bastile is gone; the Bargello has become a museum; the Piombi are removed from the Doge's roof. Vincennes, Spandau, Spilberg, Magdeburg, are all modern in comparison with a jail from which Ralph Flambard escaped so long ago as the year 1100, the date of the First Crusade.

Standing on Tower Hill, looking down on the dark lines of wall — picking out keep and turret, bastion and ballium, chapel and belfry — the jewel-house, the armoury, the mounts, the casemates, the open leads — the Bye-ward gate, the Belfry, the Bloody tower — the whole edifice seems alive with story; the story of a nation's highest splendour, its deepest misery, and its darkest shame. The soil beneath your feet is richer in blood than many a great battlefield; for out upon this sod has been poured, from generation to generation, a stream of the noblest life in our land. Should you have come to this spot alone, in the early day, when the Tower is noisy with martial doings, you may haply catch, in the hum which rises from the ditch and issues from the wall below you — broken by roll of drum, by blast of bugle, by tramp of soldiers — some echoes, as it were, of a far-off time; some hints of a May-day revel; of a state execution; of a royal entry. You may catch some sound which recalls the thrum of a queen's virginal, the cry of a victim on the rack, the laughter of a bridal feast. For all these sights and sounds — the dance of love and the dance of death — are part of that gay and tragic memory which clings around the Tower.

From the reign of Stephen down to that of Henry of Richmond, Cæsar's tower (the great Norman keep, now called the White tower) was a main part of the royal palace; and for that large interval of time, the story of the White tower is in some sort that of our English society as well as of our English kings. Here were kept the royal

THE TOWER OF LONDON.

wardrobe and the royal jewels; and hither came with their goodly wares, the tiremen, the goldsmiths, the chasers and embroiderers, from Flanders, Italy, and Almaigne. Close by were the Mint, the lions' dens, the old archery-grounds, the Court of King's Bench, the Court of Common Pleas, the Queen's gardens, the royal banqueting-hall; so that art and trade, science and manners, literature and law, sport and politics, find themselves equally at home.

Two great architects designed the main parts of the Tower; Gundul the Weeper and Henry the Builder; one a poor Norman monk, the other a great English king. . . .

Henry the Third, a prince of epical fancies, as Corffe, Conway, Beaumaris, and many other fine poems in stone attest, not only spent much of his time in the Tower, but much of his money in adding to its beauty and strength. Adam de Lamburn was his master mason; but Henry was his own chief clerk of the works. The Water gate, the embanked wharf, the Cradle tower, the Lantern, which he made his bedroom and private closet, the Galleyman tower, and the first wall, appear to have been his gifts. But the prince who did so much for Westminster Abbey, not content with giving stone and piles to the home in which he dwelt, enriched the chambers with frescoes and sculpture, the chapels with carving and glass; making St. John's chapel in the White tower splendid with saints, St. Peter's church on the Tower Green musical with bells. In the Hall tower, from which a passage led through the Great hall into the King's bedroom in the Lantern, he built a tiny chapel for his private use — a chapel which served for the devotion of his successors until Henry the Sixth was stabbed to death before the cross. Sparing neither skill nor gold to make the great fortress worthy of his art, he sent to Purbeck for marble, and to Caen for stone. The dabs of lime, the spawls of flint, the layers of brick, which deface the walls and towers in too many places, are of either earlier or later times. The marble shafts, the noble groins, the delicate traceries, are Henry's work. Traitor's gate, one of the noblest arches in the world, was built by him; in short, nearly all that is purest in art is traceable to his reign. . . .

The most eminent and interesting prisoner ever lodged in the Tower is Raleigh; eminent by his personal genius, interesting from his political fortune. Raleigh has in higher degree than any other captive who fills the Tower with story, the distinction that he was not the prisoner of his country, but the prisoner of Spain.

Many years ago I noted in the State Papers evidence, then unknown, that a very great part of the second and long imprisonment of the founder of Virginia was spent in the Bloody tower and the adjoining Garden house; writing at this grated window; working in the little garden on which it opened; pacing the terrace on this wall, which was afterwards famous as Raleigh's Walk. Hither came to him the wits and poets, the scholars and inventors of his time; Johnson and Burrell, Hariot and Pett; to crack light jokes; to discuss rabbinical lore; to sound the depths of philosophy; to map out Virginia; to study the shipbuilder's art. In the Garden house he distilled essences and spirits; compounded his great cordial; discovered a method (afterwards lost) of turning salt water into sweet; received the visits of Prince Henry; wrote his political tracts; invented the modern warship; wrote his History of the World. . . .

The day of Raleigh's death was the day of a new English birth. Eliot was not the only youth of ardent soul who stood by the scaffold in Palace Yard, to note the matchless spirit in which the martyr met his fate, and walked away from that solemnity — a new man. Thousands of men in every part of England who had led a careless life became from that very hour the sleepless enemies of Spain. The purposes of Raleigh were accomplished, in the very way which his genius had contrived. Spain held the dominion of the sea, and England took it from her. Spain excluded England from the New World, and the genius of that New World is English.

The large contest in the new political system of the world, then young, but clearly enough defined, had come to turn upon this question — Shall America be mainly Spanish and theocratic, or English and free? Raleigh said it should be English and free. He gave his blood, his fortune, and his genius, to the great thought in his heart; and, in spite of that scene in Palace Yard, which struck men as the victory of Spain, America is at this moment English and free.

Her Majesty's Tower (London, 1869).

THE CATHEDRAL OF ANTWERP.

WILLIAM MAKEPEACE THACKERAY.

I WAS awakened this morning with the chime which the Antwerp Cathedral clock plays at half hours. The tune has been haunting me ever since, as tunes will. You dress, eat, drink, walk, and talk to yourself to their tune; their inaudible jingle accompanies you all day; you read the sentences of the paper to their rhythm. I tried uncouthly to imitate the tune to the ladies of the family at breakfast, and they say it is "the shadow dance of *Dinorah*." It may be so. I dimly remember that my body was once present during the performance of that opera, while my eyes were closed, and my intellectual faculties dormant at the back of the box; howbeit, I have learned that shadow dance from hearing it pealing up ever so high in the air at night, morn, noon.

How pleasant to lie awake and listen to the cheery peal, while the old city is asleep at midnight, or waking up rosy at sunrise, or basking in noon, or swept by the scudding rain which drives in gusts over the broad places, and the great shining river; or sparkling in snow, which dresses up a hundred thousand masts, peaks, and towers; or wrapped round with thunder — cloud canopies, before which the white gables shine whiter; day and night the kind little carillon plays its fantastic melodies overhead. The bells go on ringing. *Quot vivos vocant, mortuos plangunt, fulgura frangunt;* so on to the past and future tenses, and for how many nights, days, and years! While the French were pitching their *fulgura* into Chassé's citadel, the bells went on ringing quite cheerfully. While the scaffolds were up and guarded by Alva's soldiery, and regiments of penitents, blue, black, and grey, poured out of churches and convents, droning their dirges, and marching to the place of the Hôtel de Ville, where heretics and rebels were to meet their doom, the bells up yonder were chanting at their appointed half hours and quarters, and rang the *mauvais quart d'heure* for many a poor soul. This bell can see as far away as the towers and dikes of Rotterdam. That one can call a greeting to St. Ursula's at Brussels, and toss a recognition to that one at the town hall of Oudenarde, and remember how, after a great struggle there a hundred and fifty years ago, the whole plain was covered with flying French chivalry — Burgundy, and Berri, and the Chevalier of St. George flying like the rest. "What is your clamour about Oudenarde?" says another bell (Bob Major *this* one must be). "Be still thou querulous old clapper! *I* can see over to Hougoumont and St. John. And about forty-five years since, I rang all through one Sunday in June, when there was such a battle going on in the cornfields there as none of you others ever heard tolled of. Yes, from morning service until after vespers, the French and English were all at it, ding-dong!" And then calls of business intervening, the bells have to give up their private jangle, resume their professional duty, and sing their hourly chorus out of *Dinorah*.

What a prodigious distance those bells can be heard! I was awakened this morning to their tune, I say. I have been hearing it constantly ever since. And this house whence I write, Murray says, is two hundred and ten miles from Antwerp. And it is a week off; and there is the bell still jangling its shadow dance out of *Dinorah*. An audible shadow, you understand, and an invisible sound, but quite distinct; and a plague take the tune!

Who has not seen the church under the bell? Those lofty aisles, those twilight chapels, that cumbersome pulpit with its huge carvings, that wide grey pavement flecked with various light from the jewelled windows, those famous pictures between the voluminous columns over the altars which twinkle with their ornaments, their votive little silver hearts, legs, limbs, their little guttering tapers, cups of sham roses, and what not? I saw two regiments of little scholars creeping in and forming square, each in its appointed place, under the vast roof, and teachers presently coming to them. A stream of light from the jewelled windows beams slanting down upon each little squad of children, and the tall background of the church retires into a greyer gloom. Pattering little feet of laggards arriving echo through the great nave. They trot in and join their regiments, gathered under the slanting sunbeams. What are they learning? Is it truth? Those two grey ladies with their books in their hands in the midst of these little people have no doubt of the truth of every word they have printed under their eyes. Look,

THE CATHEDRAL OF ANTWERP.

through the windows jewelled all over with saints, the light comes streaming down from the sky, and heaven's own illuminations paint the book! A sweet, touching picture indeed it is, that of the little children assembled in this immense temple, which has endured for ages, and grave teachers bending over them. Yes, the picture is very pretty of the children and their teachers, and their book — but the text? Is it the truth, the only truth, nothing but the truth? If I thought so, I would go and sit down on the form *cum parvulis*, and learn the precious lesson with all my heart.

But I submit, an obstacle to conversions is the intrusion and impertinence of that Swiss fellow with the baldric — the officer who answers to the beadle of the British islands — and is pacing about the church with an eye on the congregation. Now the boast of Catholics is that their churches are open to all; but in certain places and churches there are exceptions. At Rome I have been into St. Peter's at all hours: the doors are always open, the lamps are always burning, the faithful are forever kneeling at one shrine or the other. But at Antwerp it is not so. In the afternoon you can go to the church and be civilly treated, but you must pay a franc at the side gate. In the forenoon the doors are open, to be sure, and there is no one to levy an entrance fee. I was standing ever so still, looking through the great gates of the choir at the twinkling lights, and listening to the distant chants of the priests performing the service, when a sweet chorus from the organ-loft broke out behind me overhead, and I turned round. My friend the drum-major ecclesiastic was down upon me in a moment. "Do not turn your back to the altar during divine service," says he, in very intelligible English. I take the rebuke, and turn a soft right-about face, and listen a while as the service continues. See it I cannot, nor the altar and its ministrants. We are separated from these by a great screen and closed gates of iron, through which the lamps glitter and the chant comes by gusts only. Seeing a score of children trotting down a side aisle, I think I may follow them. I am tired of looking at that hideous old pulpit, with its grotesque monsters and decorations. I slip off to the side aisle; but my friend the drum-major is instantly after me — almost I thought he was going to lay hands on me. "You must n't go there," says he; "you must n't disturb the service." I was moving as quietly as might be, and ten paces off there were twenty children kicking and chattering at their ease. I point them out to the Swiss. "They come to pray," says he. "*You* don't come to pray; you —" "When I come to pay," says I, "I am welcome," and with this withering sarcasm I walk out of church in a huff. I don't envy the feelings of that beadle after receiving point blank such a stroke of wit.

Roundabout Papers (London, 1863).

THE TAJ MAHAL.

THE TAJ MAHAL.

ANDRÉ CHEVRILLON.

IT is well known that the Taj is a mausoleum built by the Mogul Shah-Jehan to the Begum Mumtaz-i-Mahal. It is a regular octagon surmounted by a Persian dome, which is surrounded by four minarets. The building, erected upon a terrace which dominates the enclosing gardens, is constructed of blocks of the purest white marble, and rises to a height of two hundred and forty-three feet. We step from the carriage before a noble portico of red sandstone, pierced by a bold arch and covered with white arabesques. After passing through this arch, we see the Taj looming up before us eight hundred metres distant. Probably no masterpiece of architecture calls forth a similar emotion.

At the back of a marvellous garden and with all of its whiteness reflected in a canal of dark water, sleeping inertly among thick masses of black cypress and great clumps of red flowers, this perfect tomb rises like a calm apparition. It is a floating dream, an aërial form without weight, so perfect is the balance of the lines, and so pale, so delicate the shadows that float across the virginal and translucent stone. These black cypresses which frame it, this verdure through the openings of which peeps the blue sky, and this sward bathed in brilliant sunlight and on which the sharply-cut silhouettes of the trees are lying,—all these real objects render more unreal the delicate vision, which seems to melt away into the light of the sky. I walk towards it along the marble bank of the dark canal, and the mausoleum assumes sharper form. On approaching you take more delight in the surface of the octagonal edifice. This consists of rectangular expanses of polished marble where the light rests with a soft, milky splendour. One would never imagine that so simple a thing as surface could be so beautiful when it is large and pure. The eye follows the ingenious and graceful scrolls of great flowers, flowers of onyx and turquoise, incrusted with perfect smoothness, the harmony of the delicate carving, the marble lace-work, the balustrades of a thousand perforations,—the infinite display of simplicity and decoration.

The garden completes the monument, and both unite to form this masterpiece of art. The avenues leading to the Taj are bordered with funereal yews and cypresses, which make the whiteness of the far-away marble appear even whiter. Behind their slender cones thick and massive bushes add richness and depth to this solemn vegetation. The stiff and sombre trees, standing out in relief from this waving foliage, rise up solemnly with their trunks half-buried in masses of roses, or are surrounded by clusters of a thousand unknown and sweet-scented flowers which are blossoming in great masses in this solitary garden. He must have been an extraordinary artist who conceived this place. Sweeps of lawn, purple-chaliced flowers, golden petals, swarms of humming bees, and diapered butterflies give light and joy to the gloom of the burial-ground. This place is both luminous and solemn; it contains the amorous and religious delights of the Mussulman paradise, and the poem in trees and flowers unites with the poem in marble to sing of splendour and peace.

The interior of the mausoleum is at first as dark as night, but through this darkness a grille of antique marble is faintly gleaming, a mysterious marble-lace, which drapes the tombs, and which seems to wind and unwind forever, shedding on the splendour of the vault a yellow light, which seems to be ancient, and to have rested there for ages. And the pale web of marble wreathes and wreathes until it loses itself in the darkness.

In the centre are the tombs of the lovers; two small sarcophagi upon which a mysterious light falls, but whence it comes no one knows. There is nothing more. They sleep here in the silence, surrounded by perfect beauty which celebrates their love that has lasted even through death, and which is still isolated from everything by the mysterious marble-lace which enfolds them and which floats above them like a dream.

Very high overhead, as if through a thick vapour, we see the dome loom through the shadows, although its entire outlines are not perceptible; its walls seem made of mist, and its marble blocks appear to have no solidity. Everything is aërial here, nothing is substantial or real: this is a world of shadowy visions. Even sounds are unearthly. A note sung under this vault is echoed above our heads in an invisible region. First, it is as clear as the voice of Ariel, then it grows fainter and fainter until it dies away and then is re-echoed very far above, but glorified, spiritualized, and multiplied indefinitely as if repeated by a distant company, a choir of unseen angels who soar with it aloft until all is lost save a faint murmur which never ceases to vibrate over the tomb of the beloved, as if it were the very soul of a musician.

I have seen the Taj again; this time at noon. Under the vertical sun the melancholy phantom has vanished, the sweet sadness of the mausoleum has gone. The great marble table on which it stands is blinding. The light, reflected back and forth from the immense surfaces of white marble, is increased a hundred-fold in intensity, and some of the sides are like burning plaques. The incrustations seem to be sparks of magic fire; their hundreds of red flowers gleam like burning coals. The religious texts and the hieroglyphs, inlaid with black marble, stand out as if traced by the lightning-finger of a savage god. All the mystical rows of lotus and lilies unfolding in relief, which just now had the softness of yellowed ivory, spring forth like flames. — I retrace my steps, passing out of the entrance, and for an instant I have a dazzling view of the lines and incandescent surfaces of the building with its unchanging virgin whiteness. — Indeed, this severe simplicity and intensity of light give it something of a Semitic character: we think of the flaming and chastening sword of the Bible. The minarets lift themselves into the blue like pillars of fire.

I wander outside in the fresh air under the shadows of the leafy arches until twilight. This garden is the conception of one of the faithful who wished to glorify Allah.

It is the home of religious delight : — " No one shall enter the garden of God unless he is pure of heart," is the Arabian text graven over the entrance-gate. Here are flower-beds, which are masses of velvet, — unknown blooms resembling heaps of purple moss. The trunks of the trees are entwined with blue convolvulus, and flowers like great red stars gleam through the dark foliage. Over these flowers a hundred thousand delicate butterflies hover in a perpetual cloud. Many pretty creatures, little striped squirrels and numerous birds, green parrots and parrots of more brilliant plumage, disport themselves here, making a little world, happy and secure, for guards, dressed in white muslin, menace with long pea-shooters the crows and vultures and protect them from everything that would bring mischief or cruelty into this peaceful place.

On the surface of the still waters lilies and lotus are sleeping, their stiff leaves pinked out and resting heavily upon the dark mirror.

Through the blackness of the boughs English meadows are revealed, bathed in brilliant sunlight, and spaces of blue sky, across which a triangle of white storks is sometimes seen flying, and, at certain moments, the far-away vision of the phantom tomb seems like the melancholy spectre of a virgin. — How calm, how superb this solitude, charged with voluptuousness at once solemn and enervating! Here dwell the beauty, the tenderness, and the light of Asia, dreamed of by Shelley.

Dans l'Inde (Paris, 1891).

THE CATHEDRAL OF NOTRE-DAME.

VICTOR HUGO.

MOST certainly, the Cathedral of Notre-Dame is still a sublime and majestic edifice. But, despite the beauty which it preserves in its old age, it would be impossible not to be indignant at the injuries and mutilations which Time and man have jointly inflicted upon the venerable structure without respect for Charlemagne, who laid its first stone, and Philip Augustus, who laid its last.

There is always a scar beside a wrinkle on the face of this aged queen of our cathedrals. *Tempus edax homo edacior*, which I should translate thus: Time is blind, man is stupid.

If we had leisure to examine one by one, with the reader, the various traces of destruction imprinted on the old church, Time's work would prove to be less destructive than men's, especially *des hommes de l'art*, because there have been some individuals in the last two centuries who considered themselves architects.

First, to cite several striking examples, assuredly there are few more beautiful pages in architecture than that façade, exhibiting the three deeply-dug porches with their pointed arches; the plinth, embroidered and indented with twenty-eight royal niches; the immense central rose-window, flanked by its two lateral windows, like the priest by his deacon and sub-deacon; the high and frail gallery of open-worked arches, supporting on its delicate columns a heavy platform; and, lastly, the two dark and massive towers, with their slated pent-houses. These harmonious parts of a magnificent whole, superimposed in five gigantic stages, and presenting, with their innumerable details of statuary, sculpture, and carving, an overwhelming yet not perplexing mass, combine in producing a calm grandeur. It is a vast symphony in stone, so to speak; the colossal work of man and of a nation, as united and as complex as the Iliad and the *romanceros* of which it is the sister; a prodigious production to which all the forces of an epoch contributed, and from every stone of which springs forth in a hundred ways the workman's fancy directed by the artist's genius; in one word, a kind of human creation, as strong and fecund as the divine creation from which it seems to have stolen the two-fold character: variety and eternity.

And what I say here of the façade, must be said of the entire Cathedral; and what I say of the Cathedral of Paris, must be said of all the Mediæval Christian churches. Everything in this art, which proceeds from itself, is so logical and well-proportioned that to measure the toe of the foot is to measure the giant.

Let us return to the façade of Notre-Dame, as it exists to-day when we go reverently to admire the solemn and mighty Cathedral, which, according to the old chroniclers, was terrifying: *quæ mole sua terrorem incutit spectantibus.*

That façade now lacks three important things: first, the

flight of eleven steps, which raised it above the level of the ground; then, the lower row of statues which occupied the niches of the three porches; and the upper row [1] of the twenty-eight ancient kings of France which ornamented the gallery of the first story, beginning with Childebert and ending with Philip Augustus, holding in his hand " *la pomme impériale.*"

Time in its slow and unchecked progress, raising the level of the city's soil, buried the steps; but whilst the pavement of Paris like a rising tide has engulfed one by one the eleven steps which formerly added to the majestic height of the edifice, Time has given to the church more, perhaps, than it has stolen, for it is Time that has spread that sombre hue of centuries on the façade which makes the old age of buildings their period of beauty.

But who has thrown down those two rows of statues? Who has left the niches empty? Who has cut that new and bastard arch in the beautiful middle of the central porch? Who has dared to frame that tasteless and heavy wooden door carved *à la Louis XV.* near Biscornette's arabesques? The men, the architects, the artists of our day.

And when we enter the edifice, who has overthrown that colossal Saint Christopher, proverbial among statues as the *grand' salle du Palais* among halls, or the *flèche* of Strasburg among steeples? And those myriads of statues that peopled all the spaces between the columns of the nave and choir, kneeling, standing, on horseback, men,

---

[1] The outside of Notre-Dame has been restored since Victor Hugo wrote his famous romance. — E. S.

THE CATHEDRAL OF NOTRE-DAME.

women, children, kings, bishops, warriors, in stone, wood, marble, gold, silver, copper, and even wax, — who has brutally swept them away? It was not Time!

And who has substituted for the old Gothic altar, splendidly overladen with shrines and reliquaries, that heavy marble sarcophagus with its angels' heads and clouds, which seems to be a sample from the Val-de-Grâce or the Invalides? Who has so stupidly imbedded that heavy stone anachronism in Hercanduc's Carlovingian pavement? Is it not Louis XIV. fulfilling the vow of Louis XIII.?

And who has put cold white glass in the place of those richly-coloured panes, which made the astonished gaze of our ancestors pause between the rose of the great porch and the pointed arches of the apsis? What would an under-chorister of the Sixteenth Century say if he could see the beautiful yellow plaster with which our vandal archbishops have daubed their Cathedral? He would remember that this was the colour with which the executioner brushed the houses of traitors; he would remember the Hôtel du Petit-Bourbon, all besmeared thus with yellow, on account of the treason of the Constable, "yellow of such good quality," says Sauval, "and so well laid on that more than a century has scarcely caused its colour to fade;" and, imagining that the holy place had become infamous, he would flee from it.

And if we ascend the Cathedral without stopping to notice the thousand barbarities of all kinds, what has been done with that charming little bell-tower, which stood over the point of intersection of the transept, and which, neither less frail nor less bold than its neighbour, the steeple of the Sainte-Chapelle (also destroyed), shot up into the sky, sharp, harmonious, and open-worked, higher than the other towers? It was amputated by an architect of good taste (1787), who thought it sufficient to cover the wound with that large plaster of lead, which looks like the lid of a pot.

This is the way the wonderful art of the Middle Ages has been treated in all countries, particularly in France. In this ruin we may distinguish three separate agencies, which have affected it in different degrees; first, Time which has insensibly chipped it, here and there, and discoloured its entire surface; next, revolutions, both political and religious, which, being blind and furious by nature, rushed wildly upon it, stripped it of its rich garb of sculptures and carvings, shattered its tracery, broke its garlands of arabesques and its figurines, and threw down its statues, sometimes on account of their mitres, sometimes on account of their crowns; and, finally, the fashions, which, ever since the anarchistic and splendid innovations of the Renaissance, have been constantly growing more grotesque and foolish, and have succeeded in bringing about the decadence of architecture. The fashions have indeed done more harm than the revolutions. They have cut it to the quick; they have attacked the framework of art; they have cut, hacked, and mutilated the form of the building as well as its symbol; its logic as well as its beauty. And then they have restored, a presumption of which time and revolutions were, at least, guiltless. In the name of *good taste* they have insolently covered the wounds of Gothic architecture with their paltry gew-gaws of a day, their marble ribbons, their metal pompons, a veritable leprosy of oval ornaments, volutes, spirals, draperies, garlands, fringes, flames of stone, clouds of bronze, over-fat Cupids, and bloated cherubim, which begin to eat into the face of art in Catherine de' Medici's oratory, and kill it, writhing and grinning in the boudoir of the Dubarry, two centuries later.

Therefore, in summing up the points to which I have called attention, three kinds of ravages disfigure Gothic architecture to-day: wrinkles and warts on the epidermis, — these are the work of Time; wounds, bruises and fractures, — these are the work of revolutions from Luther to Mirabeau; mutilations, amputations, dislocations of members, *restorations*, — these are the Greek and Roman work of professors, according to Vitruvius and Vignole. That magnificent art which the Vandals produced, academies have murdered. To the ravages of centuries and revolutions, which devastated at least with impartiality and grandeur, were added those of a host of school architects, patented and sworn, who debased everything with the choice and discernment of bad taste; and who substituted the *chicorées* of Louis XV. for the Gothic lacework, for the greater glory of the Parthenon. It is the ass's kick to the dying lion. It is the old oak crowning itself with leaves for the reward of being bitten, gnawed, and devoured by caterpillars.

How far this is from the period when Robert Cenalis, comparing Notre-Dame de Paris with the famous Temple of Diana at Ephesus, so highly extolled by the ancient heathen, which has immortalized Erostratus, found the

Gaulois cathedral "*plus excellente en longueur, largeur, hauteur, et structure.*"

Notre-Dame de Paris is not, however, what may be called a finished, defined, classified monument. It is not a Roman church, neither is it a Gothic church. This edifice is not a type. Notre-Dame has not, like the Abbey of Tournus, the solemn and massive squareness, the round and large vault, the glacial nudity, and the majestic simplicity of those buildings which have the circular arch for their generative principle. It is not, like the Cathedral of Bourges, the magnificent product of light, multiform, tufted, bristling, efflorescent Gothic. It is out of the question to class it in that ancient family of gloomy, mysterious, low churches, which seem crushed by the circular arch; almost Egyptian in their ceiling; quite hieroglyphic, sacerdotal, and symbolic, charged in their ornaments with more lozenges and zigzags than flowers, more flowers than animals, more animals than human figures; the work of the bishop more than the architect, the first transformation of the art, fully impressed with theocratic and military discipline, which takes its root in the Bas-Empire, and ends with William the Conqueror. It is also out of the question to place our Cathedral in that other family of churches, tall, aërial, rich in windows and sculpture, sharp in form, bold of mien; *communales* and *bourgeois*, like political symbols; free, capricious, unbridled, like works of art; the second transformation of architecture, no longer hieroglyphic, immutable, and sacerdotal, but artistic, progressive, and popular, which begins with the return from the Crusades and ends with Louis XI. Notre-Dame de Paris is not pure Roman, like the former, nor is it pure Arabian, like the latter.

It is an edifice of the transition. The Saxon architect had set up the first pillars of the nave when the Crusaders introduced the pointed arch, which enthroned itself like a conqueror upon those broad Roman capitals designed to support circular arches. On the pointed arch, thenceforth mistress of all styles, the rest of the church was built. Inexperienced and timid at the beginning, it soon broadens and expands, but does not yet dare to shoot up into steeples and pinnacles, as it has since done in so many marvellous cathedrals. You might say that it feels the influence of its neighbours, the heavy Roman pillars.

Moreover, these edifices of the transition from the Roman to the Gothic are not less valuable for study than pure types. They express a *nuance* of the art which would be lost but for them. This is the engrafting of the pointed upon the circular arch.

Notre-Dame de Paris is a particularly curious specimen of this variety. Every face and every stone of the venerable structure is a page not only of the history of the country, but also of art and science. Therefore to glance here only at the principal details, while the little Porte Rouge attains almost to the limits of the Gothic delicacy of the Fifteenth Century, the pillars of the nave, on account of their bulk and heaviness, carry you back to the date of the Carlovingian Abbey of Saint-Germain des Près, you would believe that there were six centuries between that doorway and those pillars. It is not only the hermetics who find in the symbols of the large porch a satisfactory compendium of their science, of which the church of Saint-Jacques de la Boucherie was so complete an hieroglyphic. Thus the Roman Abbey, the philosophical church, the Gothic art, the Saxon art, the heavy, round pillar, which reminds you of Gregory VII., the hermetic symbols by which Nicholas Flamel heralded Luther, papal unity and schism, Saint-Germain des Près and Saint-Jacques de la Boucherie; all are melted, combined, amalgamated in Notre-Dame. This central and generatrix church is a sort of chimæra among the old churches of Paris; it has the head of one, the limbs of another, the body of another, — something from each of them.

I repeat, these hybrid structures are not the least interesting ones to the artist, the antiquary, and the historian. They show how far architecture is a primitive art, inasmuch as they demonstrate (what is also demonstrated by the Cyclopean remains, the pyramids of Egypt, and the gigantic Hindu pagodas), that the grandest productions of architecture are social more than individual works; the offspring, rather, of nations in travail than the inspiration of men of genius; the deposit left by a people; the accumulation of ages; the residuum of the successive evaporations of human society; in short, a species of formation. Every wave of time superimposes its alluvion, every generation deposits its stratum upon the building, every individual lays his stone. Thus build the beavers; thus, the bees; and thus, men. The great symbol of architecture, Babel, is a beehive.

Great buildings, like great mountains, are the work of centuries. Often the fashions in art change while they are being constructed, *pendent opera interrupta*; they are continued quietly according to the new art. This new art takes the edifice where it finds it, assimilates with it, develops it according to its own fancy, and completes it, if it is possible. The result is accomplished without disturbance, without effort, without reaction, following a natural and quiet law. It is a graft which occurs unexpectedly, a sap which circulates, a vegetation which returns. Certes, there is material for very large books and often a universal history of mankind, in those successive solderings of various styles at various heights upon the structure. The man, the artist, and the individual efface themselves in these vast anonymous masses; human intelligence is concentrated and summed up in them. Time is the architect; the nation is the mason.

Notre Dame de Paris (Paris, 1831).

THE KREMLIN.

THÉOPHILE GAUTIER.

THE Kremlin, always regarded as the Acropolis, the Holy Place, the Palladium, and the very heart of Russia, was formerly surrounded by a palisade of strong oaken stakes — similar to the defence which the Athenian citadel had at the time of the first invasion of the Persians. Dmitri-Donskoi substituted for this palisade crenellated walls, which, having become old and dilapidated, were rebuilt by Ivan III. Ivan's wall remains to-day, but in many places there are restorations and repairs. Thick layers of plaster endeavour to hide the scars of time and the black traces of the great fire of 1812 which was only able to lick this wall with its tongues of flame. The Kremlin somewhat resembles the Alhambra. Like the Moorish fortress, it stands on the top of a hill which it encloses with its wall flanked by towers: it contains royal dwellings, churches, and squares, and among the ancient buildings a modern Palace whose intrusion we regret as we do the Palace of Charles V. amid the delicate Saracenic architecture which it seems to crush with its weight. The tower of Ivan Veliki is not without resemblance to the tower of the Vela; and from the Kremlin, as from the

Alhambra, a beautiful view is to be enjoyed, a panorama of enchantment which the fascinated eye will ever retain.

It is strange that when seen from a distance the Kremlin is perhaps even more Oriental than the Alhambra itself whose massive reddish towers give no hint of the splendour within. Above the sloping and crenellated walls of the Kremlin and among the towers with their ornamented roofs, myriads of cupolas and globular bell-towers gleaming with metallic light seem to be rising and falling like bubbles of glittering gold in the strong blaze of light. The white wall seems to be a silver basket holding a bouquet of golden flowers, and we fancy that we are gazing upon one of those magical cities which the imagination of the Arabian story-tellers alone can build — an architectural crystallization of the *Thousand and One Nights!* And when Winter has sprinkled these strange dream-buildings with its powdered diamonds, we fancy ourselves transported into another planet, for nothing like this has ever met our gaze.

We entered the Kremlin by the Spasskoi Gate which opens upon the Krasnaia. No entrance could be more romantic. It is cut through an enormous square tower, placed before a kind of porch. The tower has three diminishing stories and is crowned with a spire resting upon open arches. The double-headed eagle, holding the globe in its claws, stands upon the sharp point of the spire, which, like the story it surmounts, is octagonal, ribbed, and gilded. Each face of the second story bears an enormous dial, so that the hour may be seen from every point of the compass. Add for effect some patches of snow laid on the jutting masonry like bold dashes of pigment, and you will have a faint idea of the aspect presented by this queenly tower, as it springs upward in three jets above the denticulated wall which it breaks. . . .

Issuing from the gate, we find ourselves in the large court of the Kremlin, in the midst of the most bewildering conglomeration of palaces, churches, and monasteries of which the imagination can dream. It conforms to no known style of architecture. It is not Greek, it is not Byzantine, it is not Gothic, it is not Saracen, it is not Chinese: it is Russian; it is Muscovite. Never did architecture more free, more original, more indifferent to rules, in a word, more romantic, materialize with such fantastic caprice. Sometimes it seems to resemble the freaks of frostwork. However, its leading characteristics are the cupolas and the golden-bulbed bell-towers, which seem to follow no law and are conspicuous at the first glance.

Below the large square where the principal buildings of the Kremlin are grouped and which forms the plateau of the hill, a circular road winds about the irregularities of the ground and is bordered by ramparts flanked with towers of infinite variety: some are round, some square, some slender as minarets, some massive as bastions, and some with machicolated turrets, while others have retreating stories, vaulted roofs, sharply-cut sides, open-worked galleries, tiny cupolas, spires, scales, tracery, and all conceivable endings. The battlements, cut deeply through the wall and notched at the top like an arrow, are alternately plain and pierced with little barbicans. We will ignore the strategic value of this defence, but from a poetic standpoint it satisfies the imagination and gives the idea of a formidable citadel.

Between the rampart and the platform bordered by a balustrade gardens extend, now powdered with snow, and a picturesque little church lifts its globular bell-towers. Beyond, as far as the eye can reach, lies the immense and wonderful panorama of Moscow to which the crest of the saw-toothed wall forms an admirable foreground and frame for the distant perspective which no art could improve. . . .

The Kremlin contains within its walls many churches, or cathedrals, as the Russians call them. Exactly like the Acropolis, it gathers around it on its narrow plateau a large number of temples. We will visit them one by one, but we will first pause at the tower of Ivan Veliki, an enormous octagon belfry with three retreating stories, upon the last of which there rises from a zone of ornamentation a round turret finished with a swelling dome, fire-gilt with ducat-gold, and surmounted by a Greek cross resting upon the conquered crescent. Upon each side of each story little arches are cut so that the brazen body of a bell may be seen.

In this place there are thirty-three bells, among which is said to be the famous alarm-bell of Novgorod, whose reverberations once called the people to the tumultuous deliberations in the public square. One of these bells weighs not less than a hundred and ninety-three tons, and is such a monster of metal that beside it the great bell of Notre-Dame of which Quasimodo was so proud, would be nothing more than the tiny hand-bell used at Mass. . . .

Let us enter one of the most ancient and characteristic cathedrals of the Kremlin, the first one built of stone, the

Cathedral of the Assumption (*Ouspenskosabor*). It is not the original edifice founded by Ivan Kalita. That crumbled away after a century and a half of existence and was rebuilt by Ivan III. Notwithstanding its Byzantine style and archaic appearance, the present Cathedral dates only from the Fifteenth Century. One is astonished to learn that it is the work of Fioraventi, an architect of Bologna, whom the Russians called Aristotle because of his astounding knowledge. One would imagine it the work of some Greek architect from Constantinople whose head was filled with memories of Santa Sofia and models of Greco-Oriental architecture. The Assumption is almost square and its great walls soar with a surprising pride and strength. Four enormous pillars, large as towers and massive as the columns of the Palace of Karnak, support the central cupola, which rests on a flat roof in the Asiatic style, flanked by four similar cupolas. This simple arrangement produces a magnificent effect and these massive pillars contribute, without any heaviness, a fine balance and extraordinary stability to the Cathedral.

The interior of the church is covered with Byzantine paintings on a gold background. The pillars themselves are embellished with figures arranged in zones as in the Egyptian temples and palaces. Nothing could be more strange than this decoration where thousands of figures surround you like a mute assemblage, ascending and descending the entire length of the walls, walking in files in Christian panathenæa, standing alone in poses of hieratic rigidity, bending over to the pendentives, and draping the temple with a human tapestry swarming with motionless beings. A strange light, carefully disposed, contributes greatly to the disquieting and mysterious effect. In these ruddy and fawn-coloured shadows the tall savage saints of the Greek calendar assume a formidable semblance of life; they look at you with fixed eyes and seem to threaten you with their hands outstretched for benediction. . . . The interior of St. Mark's at Venice, with its suggestion of a gilded cavern, gives the idea of the Assumption; only the interior of the Muscovite church rises with one sweep towards the sky, while the vault of St. Mark's is strangely weighed down like a crypt. The *iconostase*, a lofty wall of silver-gilt with five rows of figures, is like the façade of a golden palace, dazzling the eye with fabled magnificence. In the filigree framework of gold appear in tones of bistre the dark heads and hands of the Madonnas and saints. The rays of their aureoles are set with precious stones, which, as the light falls upon them, scintillate and blaze with celestial glory; the images, objects of peculiar veneration, are adorned with breastplates of precious stones, necklaces, and bracelets, starred with diamonds, sapphires, rubies, emeralds, amethysts, pearls, and turquoises; the madness of religious extravagance can go no further.

It is in the Cathedral of the Assumption that the coronation of the Czar takes place. The platform for this occasion is erected between the four pillars which support the cupola and faces the *iconostase*.

The tombs of the Metropolitans of Moscow are placed in rows along the sides of the walls. They are oblong: as they loom up in the shadows, they make us think of trunks packed for the great voyage of eternity. . . .

At the side of the new palace and very near these churches a strange building is seen, of no known style of architecture, neither Asiatic nor Tartar, and which for a secular building is much what Vassili-Blagennoi is for a religious edifice, — the perfectly realized chimæra of a sumptuous, barbaric, and fantastic imagination. It was built under Ivan III. by the architect Aleviso. Above its roof several towers, capped with gold and containing within them chapels and oratories, spring up with a graceful and picturesque irregularity. An outside staircase, from the top of which the Czar shows himself to the people after his coronation, gives access to the building and produces by its ornamented projection a unique architectural effect. It is to Moscow what the Giants' Stairway is to Venice. It is one of the curiosities of the Kremlin. In Russia it is known as the Red Stairway (*Krasnoi-Kriltosi*). The interior of the Palace, the residence of the ancient Czars, defies description; one would say that its chambers and passages have been excavated according to no determined plan in some curious block of stone, for they are so strangely entangled, so winding and complicated, and so constantly changing their level and direction that they seem to have been ordered at the caprice of an extravagant fancy. We walk through them as in a dream, sometimes stopped by a grille which opens mysteriously, sometimes forced to follow a narrow dark passage in which our shoulders almost touch both walls, sometimes having no other path than the toothed ledge of a cornice from which the copper plates of the roofs and the globular belfries are visible, constantly ascending, descending without knowing where we are, seeing beyond us through the golden trellises the gleam of a lamp flashing back from the golden filigree-work of the shrines, and emerging after this intramural journey into a hall with a rich and riotous wildness of ornamentation, at the end of which we are surprised at not seeing the Grand Kniaz of Tartary seated cross-legged upon his carpet of black felt.

Such for example is the hall called the Golden Chamber, which occupies the entire Granovitaïa Palata (the Facet Palace), so called doubtless on account of its exterior being cut in diamond facets. The Granovitaïa Palata adjoins the old palace of the Czars. The golden vaults of this hall rest upon a central pillar by means of surbased arches from which thick bars of elliptical gilded iron go across from one arc to another to prevent their spreading. Several paintings here and there make sombre spots upon the burnished gold splendour of the background.

Upon the string-courses of the arches legends are written in old Sclavonic letters — magnificent characters which lend themselves with as much effect for ornamentation as the Cufic letters on Arabian buildings. Richer, more mysterious, and yet more brilliant decorations than these of the Golden Chamber cannot be imagined. A romantic person would like to see a Shakespearian play acted here.

Certain vaulted halls of the old Palace are so low that a man who is a little above the average height cannot stand upright in them. It is here, in an atmosphere overcharged with heat, that the women, lounging on cushions in Oriental style, spend the hours of the long Russian winter in gazing through the little windows at the snow sparkling on the golden cupolas and the ravens whirling in great circles around the bell-towers.

These apartments with their motley wall-decorations of palms, foliage, and flowers, recalling the patterns of Cashmere, make us imagine these to be Asiatic harems transported to the polar frosts. The true Muscovite taste, perverted later by a badly-understood imitation of Western art, appears here in all its primitive originality and intensely barbaric flavour.

I have frequently observed that the progress of civilization seems to deprive nations of the true sense of architecture and decoration. The ancient edifices of the Kremlin prove once again how true is this assertion, which appears paradoxical at first. An inexhaustible fantasy presides over the decoration of these mysterious rooms where the gold, the green, the blue, and the red mingle with a rare happiness and produce the most charming effects. This architecture, without the least regard for symmetry, rises like a honeycomb of soap-bubbles blown upon a plate. Each little cell takes its place adjoining its neighbour, arranging its own angles and facets until the whole glitters with colours diapered with iris. This childish and bizarre comparison will give you a better idea than anything else of the aggregation of these palaces, so fantastic, yet so real.

It is in this style that we wish they had built the new Palace, an immense building in good modern taste and which would have a beauty elsewhere, but none whatever in the centre of the old Kremlin. The classic architecture with its long cold lines seems more wearisome and solemn here among these palaces with their strange forms, their gaudy colours, and this throng of churches of Oriental style darting towards the sky a golden forest of cupolas, domes, pyramidal spires, and bulbous bell-towers.

When looking at this Muscovite architecture you could easily believe yourself in some chimerical city of Asia, fancying the cathedrals mosques, and the bell-towers minarets, if it were not for the sober façade of the new Palace which leads you back to the unpoetic Occident and its unpoetic civilization: a sad thing for a romantic barbarian of the present day. We enter the new Palace by a stairway of monumental size closed at the top by a magnificent grille of polished iron which is opened to allow the visitor to pass. We find ourselves under the large vault of a domed hall where sentinels are perpetually on guard: four effigies clothed from head to foot in antique and curious Sclavonic armour These knights have a noble air; they are surprisingly life-like; we could easily believe that hearts are beating beneath their coats of mail. Mediæval armour disposed in this way always gives me an involuntary shiver. It so faithfully suggests the external form of a man who has vanished forever.

From this rotunda lead two galleries which contain priceless riches: the treasure of the Caliph Haroun-al Raschid, the wells of Aboul-Kasem, and the Green Vaults of Dresden united could not show such an accumulation of marvels, and here historic association is added to the material value. Here, sparkling, gleaming, and sportively flashing their prismatic light, are diamonds, sapphires, rubies, and emeralds — all the precious stones which Nature has hidden in the depths of her mines — in as much profusion as if they were mere glass. They glitter like constellations in crowns, they flash in points of light from the ends of sceptres, they fall like sparkling raindrops upon the Imperial insignias and form arabesques and cyphers until they nearly hide the gold in which they are set. The eye is dazzled and the mind can hardly calculate the sums that represent such magnificence.

Voyage en Russie (Paris, 1866).

THE CATHEDRAL OF YORK.

THE CATHEDRAL OF YORK.

THOMAS FROGNALL DIBDIN.

LET us go immediately to the Cathedral — the deepening tones of whose tenor bell seem to hurry us on to the spot. Gentle reader, on no account visit this stupendous edifice — this mountain of stone — for the first time from the Stonegate (Street) which brings you in front of the south transept. Shun it — as the shock might be distressing; but, for want of a better approach, wend your steps round by Little Blake Street, and, at its termination, swerve gently to the left, and place yourself full in view of the *West Front*. Its freshness, its grandeur, its boldness and the numerous yet existing proofs of its ancient richness and variety, will peradventure make you breathless for some three seconds. If it should strike you that there is a want of the subdued and mellow tone of antiquity, such as we left behind at Lincoln, you must remember that nearly all this front has undergone a recent scraping and repairing in the very best possible taste — under the auspices of the late Dean Markham, who may be said to have loved this Cathedral with a holy love. What has been done, under his auspices, is admirable; and a pattern for all future similar doings.

Look at those towers — to the right and left of you. How airy, how elegant, what gossamer-like lightness, and yet of what stability! It is the decorative style of architecture, in the Fourteenth Century, at which you are now gazing with such untiring admiration. Be pleased to pass on (still outside) to the left, and take the whole range of its northern side, including the Chapter-House. Look well that your position be far enough *out* — between the house of the residing prebendary and the deanery — and then, giving rein to your fancy, gaze, rejoice, and revel in every expression of admiration and delight! — for it has *no equal:* at least, not in Germany and France, including Normandy. What light and shade! — as I have seen it, both beneath the sun and moon, on my first visit to the house of the prebendal residentiary — and how lofty, massive, and magnificent the Nave! You catch the Chapter-House and the extreme termination of the choir, connecting one end of the Cathedral with the other, at the same moment — comprising an extent of some 550 feet! You are lost in astonishment, almost as much at the conception, as at the completion of such a building.

Still you are disappointed with the central Tower, or Lantern; the work, in great part, of Walter Skirlaw, the celebrated Bishop of Durham, — a name that reflects honour upon everything connected with it. Perhaps the upper part only of this tower was of his planning — towards the end of the Fourteenth Century. It is sadly disproportionate with such a building, and should be lifted up one hundred feet at the least. . . .

After several experiments, I am of the opinion that you

should enter the *interior* at the spot where it is usually entered; and which, from the thousand pilgrim-feet that annually visit the spot, may account for the comparatively worn state of the pavement;— I mean the *South Transept.* Let us enter alone, or with the many. Straight before you, at the extremity of the opposite or northern transept, your eyes sparkle with delight on a view of the stained-glass lancet windows. How delicate — how rich — how chaste — how unrivalled! All the colours seem to be intertwined, in delicate fibres, like Mechlin lace. There is no glare: but the tone of the whole is perfectly bewitching. You move on. A light streams from above. It is from the Lantern, or interior summit of the Great Tower, upon which you are gazing. Your soul is lifted up with your eyes: and if the diapason harmonies of the organ are let loose, and the sweet and soft voices of the choristers unite in the Twelfth Mass of Mozart — you instinctively clasp your hands together and exclaim, " *This must be Heaven!* "

Descend again to earth. Look at those clustered and colossal bases, upon which the stupendous tower is raised. They seem as an Atlas that for some five minutes would sustain the world. Gentle visitor, I see you breathless, and starting back. It is the Nave with its " storied windows richly dight," that transports you; so lofty, so wide, so simple, so truly grand! The secret of this extraordinary effect appears to be this. The pointed arches that separate the nave from the side aisles, are at once spacious and destitute of all obtruding ornaments; so that you catch very much of the side aisles with the nave; and on the left, or south aisle, you see some of the largest windows in the kingdom, with their *original stained glass*, a rare and fortunate result — from the fanatical destruction of the Sixteenth and Seventeenth Centuries; and for which you must laud the memory of General Lord Fairfax, Cromwell's son-in-law: who showed an especial tenderness towards this Cathedral.

"Breathe a prayer for his soul and pass on"

to the great window at the extremity of the nave. To my eye the whole of this window wants simplicity and grandeur of effect. Even its outside is too unsubstantial and playful in the tracery, for my notion of congruity with so immense a Cathedral. The stained glass is decidedly second-rate. The colour of the whole interior is admirable and worthy of imitation.

But where is *The Choir*, that wonder of the world? — "Yet more wondrous grown" from its phœnix-like revival from an almost all devouring flame?[1] You must retrace your steps — approach the grand screen — throwing your eye across the continued roof of the nave; and, gently drawing a red curtain aside, immediately under the organ, you cannot fail to be ravished with the most marvellous sight before you. Its vastness, its unspeakable and

[1] I scarcely know how to trust myself with the mention of that most appalling, unprecedented, act of a one-third madman and two-thirds rogue — Jonathan Martin by name — who set fire to the choir of York Minster: a fire which was almost miraculously stopt in its progress towards the destruction of the entire Cathedral. This had been a result which Martin would have rejoiced to have seen effected. This horrid deed, at the very thought of which the heart sickens, took place on the 2d of February, 1829.

indescribable breadth, grandeur, minuteness, and variety of detail and finish — the clustering stalls, the stupendous organ, the altar, backed by a stone Gothic screen, with the interstices filled with plate-glass — the huge outspreading eastern window behind, with its bespangled stained-glass, describing two hundred scriptural subjects — all that you gaze upon, and all that you feel is so much out of everyday experience, that you scarcely credit the scene to be of this world. To add to the effect, I once saw the vast area of this choir filled and warmed by the devotion of a sabbath afternoon. Sitting under the precentor's stall, I looked up its almost interminable pavement where knees were bending, responses articulated, and the organ's tremendous peal echoing from its utmost extremity. Above the sunbeams were streaming through the chequered stained-glass — and it was altogether a scene of which the recollection is almost naturally borne with one to the grave. . . .

This Cathedral boasts of two transepts, but the second is of very diminutive dimensions: indeed, scarcely amounting to the designation of the term. But these windows are most splendidly adorned with ancient stained-glass. They quickly arrest the attention of the antiquary; whose bosom swells, and whose eyes sparkle with delight, as he surveys their enormous height and richness. That on the southern side has a sort of mosaic work or dove-tailed character, which defies adequate description — and is an admirable *avant-propos* to the CHAPTER HOUSE: — the Chapter House! — that glory of the Cathedral — that wonder of the world! . . .

Doubtless this Chapter House is a very repertory of all that is curious and grotesque, and yet tasteful, and of most marvellous achievement. You may carouse within it for a month — but it must be in the hottest month of the year; and when you are tired of the "cool tankard," you may feast upon the pages of Britton and Halfpenny. . . . But the "world of wonders" exhibited in the shape of grotesque and capricious ornaments within this "House," is responded to by ornaments to the full as fanciful and extravagant within the Nave and Choir. What an imagination seems to have been let loose in the designer engaged! Look at what is before you! Those frisky old gentlemen are sculptured at the terminating point, as corbels, of the arches on the *roof of the nave:* and it is curious that, in the bottom corbel, the figure to the left is a sort of lampoon, or libellous representation of the clergy: the bands and curled hair are decisive upon this point. . . . When I pace and repace the pavement of this stupendous edifice — when I meditate within this almost unearthly HOUSE OF GOD — when I think of much of its departed wealth and splendour,[1] as well as of its present durability and

---

[1] I gather the following from the abridged English version (1693) of *Dugdale's Monasticon* as quoted by Drake. Where is even the Protestant bosom that does not heave heavily as it reads it? "To this Cathedral did belong abundance of jewels, vessels of gold and silver, and other ornaments; rich vestments and books, — amongst which were ten mitres of great value, and one small mitre set with stones for the '*Boy Bishop*.' One silver and gilt pastoral staff, many pastoral rings, amongst which one for the bishop of the boys. Chalices, viols, pots, basons, candlesticks, thuribles, holy-water pots, crosses of silver — one of which weighed eight pounds, six ounces.

grandeur — a spirit within me seems to say, that *such* an achievement of human skill and human glory should perish only with the crumbling fragments of a perishing world. Altogether it looks as if it were built for the day of doom.

" A Bibliographical, Antiquarian, and Picturesque Tour of the Northern Counties of England and in Scotland" (London, 1838).

Images of gold and silver; relicts in cases extremely rich; great bowls of silver; an unicorn's horn; a table of silver and gilt, with the image of the Virgin enamelled thereon, weighing nine pounds, eight ounces, and a half. Several Gospellaries and Epistolaries, richly adorned with silver, gold, and precious stones. Jewels, affixed to shrines and tombs, of an almost inestimable value. Altar cloths and hangings, very rich; copes of tissue, damask, and velvet, white, red, blue, green, black, and purple. Besides this, there was a great treasure, deposited in the common chest in gold chains, collars of the Order of the Garter, with large sums of old gold and silver."

THE MOSQUE OF OMAR.

PIERRE LOTI.

I AM enchanted to-day by the spell of Islam, by the newly-risen sun, by the Spring which warms the air.

Moreover, we will direct our steps this morning towards the holy spot of the Arabs, towards the Mosque of Omar, accounted marvellous and honoured throughout the world. — Jerusalem, city sacred to Christians and Jews, is also, after Mecca, the most sacred Mohammedan city. — The French consul-general and Father S——, a Dominican, celebrated for his Biblical erudition, gladly accompanied us, and a janizary of the consulate preceded us, without whom even the approaches of the Mosque would have been forbidden.

We walked along the narrow streets, gloomy notwithstanding the sunlight, and between the old windowless walls, made of the *débris* of all epochs of history and into which Hebraic stones and Roman marbles are fitted here and there. As we advanced towards the sacred quarter everything became more ruined, more devastated, more dead, — infinite desolation, which even surrounded the Mosque, the entrances to which are guarded by Turkish sentinels who prohibit passage to Christians.

THE MOSQUE OF OMAR

Thanks to the janizary, we clear this zone of fanatics, and then, by a series of little dilapidated doors, we pass into a gigantic court, a kind of melancholy desert where the grass pushes up between the stones as it does in a meadow where no human foot ever treads : — this is *Harâm es Sherif* (The Sacred Enclosure). In the centre, and very far from us, there rises a solitary and surprising edifice, all blue, but of a blue so exquisite and rare that it seems to be some old enchanted palace made of turquoise; this is the Mosque of Omar, the marvel of all Islam.

How wild and magnificent is the solitude that the Arabs have succeeded in preserving around their Mosque of blue!

On each of its sides, which are at least five hundred metres long, this square is hemmed in with sombre buildings, shapeless by reason of decay, incomprehensible by reason of restorations and changes made at various epochs of ancient history : at the base are Cyclopean rocks, remnants of the walls of Solomon ; above, the *débris* of Herod's citadel, the *débris* of the *prætorium* where Pontius Pilate was enthroned and whence Christ departed for Calvary ; then the Saracens, and, after them, the Crusaders, left everything in a confused heap, and, finally, the Saracens, again having become the masters of this spot, burned or walled-up the windows, raised their minarets at hap-hazard, and placed at the top of the buildings the points of their sharp battlements.

Time, the leveller, has thrown over everything a uniform colour of old reddish terra-cotta, and given to all the buildings the same vegetation, the same decay, the same dust. This bewildering chaos of bits and fragments, formidable in its hoary age, speaks the nothingness of man, the decay of civilizations and races, and bestows infinite sadness upon this little desert beyond which rises in its solitude the beautiful blue palace surmounted by its cupola and crescent, — the marvellous and incomparable Mosque of Omar.

As we advance through this desert broken by large white stones and grass, giving it the feeling of a cemetery, the casing of the blue Mosque becomes more defined: we seem to see on its walls jewels of many colours and brilliantly cut, equally divided into pale turquoise and a deep *lapis-lazuli*, with a little yellow, a little white, a little green, and a little black, soberly combined in very delicate arabesques.

Among some cypresses, nearly sapless, several very ancient and dying olives, a series of secondary edicules more numerous towards the centre of the great court, lead to the Mosque, the great wonder of the square. Dotted about are some little marble *mihrabs*, some light arches, some little triumphal arches, and a kiosk with columns, which also seems covered with blue jewels. Yet here in this immense square, which centuries have rendered so desert-like, so melancholy, and so forsaken, Spring has placed amid the stones her garlands of daisies, buttercups, and wild peonies.

Coming nearer, we perceive that these elegant and frail little Saracen buildings are composed of the *débris* of Christian churches and antique temples; the columns and the

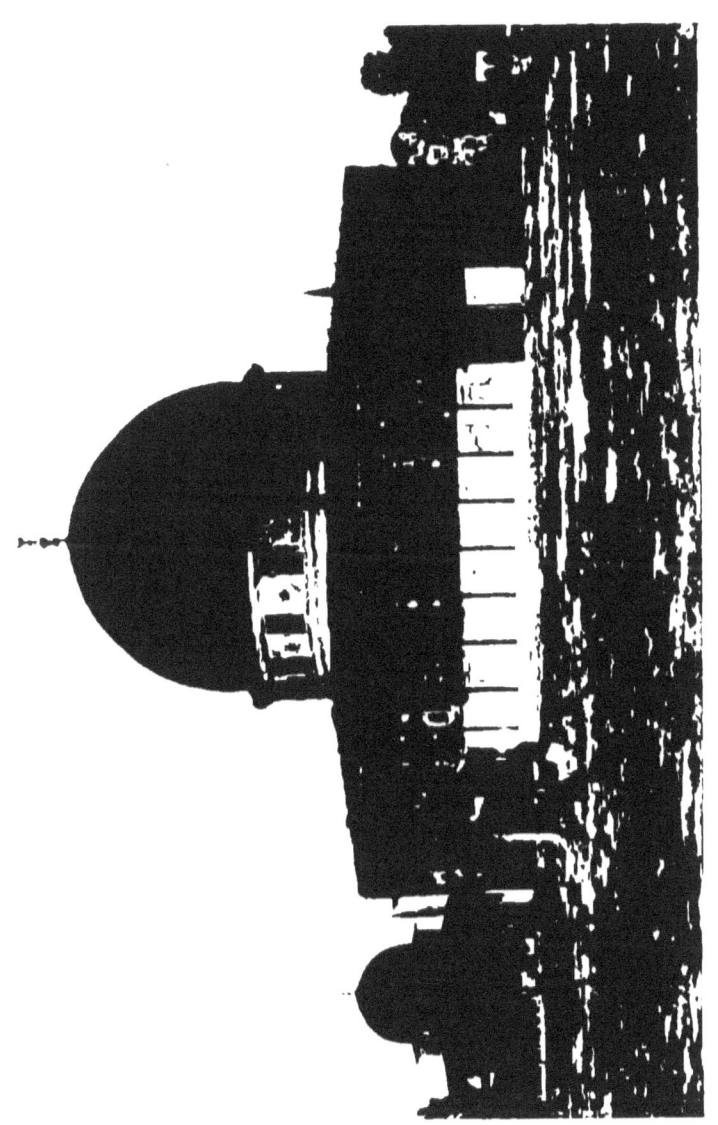

THE MOSQUE OF OMAR.

marble friezes have all vanished, torn away from a chapel of the Crusaders, from a basilica of the Greek Emperors, from a temple of Venus, or from a synagogue. If the general arrangement is Arab, calm and stamped with the grace of Aladdin's palace, the detail is full of instruction regarding the frailty of religions and empires; this detail perpetuates the memory of great exterminating wars, of horrible sacks, of days when blood ran here like water and when the wholesale slaughtering "did not end until the soldiers were weary with killing."

In all this conglomeration only that blue kiosk, neighbour of the blue Mosque, can tell its companion of Jerusalem's terrible past. Its double row of marble columns is like a museum of *débris* from all countries; we see Greek, Roman, Byzantine, or Hebraic capitals, others of an undetermined age, of a wild style almost unknown.

Now the tranquillity of death has settled over all; the remnants of so many various sanctuaries at enmity have been grouped, in honour of the God of Islam, in an unexpected harmony, and this will perhaps continue until they crumble into dust. When one recalls the troublous past it is strange to find this silence, this desolation, and this supreme peace in the centre of a court whose white stones are invaded by the daisies and weeds of the field.

Let us enter this mysterious mosque surrounded by death and the desert. At first it seems dark as night: we have a bewildering sense of fairy-like splendour. A very faint light penetrates the panes, which are famed throughout the Orient and which fill the row of little windows above; we fancy that the light is passing through flowers and arabesques of precious stones regularly arranged, and this is the illusion intended by the inimitable glass-workers of old. Gradually, as our eyes grow accustomed to the dim light, the walls, arches, and vaults seem to be covered with some rich embroidered fabric of raised mother-of-pearl and gold on a foundation of green. Perhaps it is an old brocade of flowers and leaves, perhaps precious leather from Cordova, or perhaps something even more beautiful and rare than either, which we shall recognize presently when our eyes have recovered from the blinding effect of the sun on the flags outside and have adjusted themselves to the dusk of this most holy sanctuary. The mosque, octagonal in form, is supported within by two concentric rows of pillars, the first octagonal, and the second circular, sustaining the magnificent dome.

Each column with its gilded capital is composed of a different and priceless material : one of violet marble veined with white; another of red porphyry; another of that marble, for centuries lost, known as *antique verde*. The entire base of the walls, as high as the line where the green and gold embroideries begin, is cased with marble. Great slabs cut lengthwise are arranged in symmetrical designs like those produced in cabinet-work by inlaid woods.

The little windows placed close to the dome, from which altitude falls the reflected light as though from jewels, are all of different colours and designs; one is shaped like a daisy and composed of ruby glass; another of delicate arabesques of sapphire mingled with the yellow of the topaz; and a third of emerald sprinkled with rose.

What makes the beauty of these, as of all Arabian windows, is that the various colours are not separated, like ours, by lines of lead, but the framework of the window is a plate of thick stucco pierced with an infinite number of little holes, ever changing with the light; the effect is always some new and beautiful design; the pieces of transparent blue, yellow, rose, or green, are inserted deep in the thickness of the setting so that they seem to be surrounded by a kind of nimbus caused by the reflected light along the sides of the thick apertures, and the result is a deep and soft glow over all, and through this light gleam and sparkle the pearl, and precious stones.

Now we begin to distinguish what we supposed was tapestry over the masonry: it consists of marvellous mosaics covering everything and simulating brocades and embroideries, but far more beautiful and durable than any woven tissue, for its lustre and diaper-work have been preserved through long centuries because it is formed of almost imperishable matter, — myriads of fragments of marble, with mother-of-pearl and gold. Throughout the whole, green and gold predominate. The designs are numbers of strange vases holding stiff and symmetrical bouquets: conventional foliage of a bygone period, dream-flowers fashioned in ancient days. Above these are antique vine-branches composed of an infinite variety of green marbles, stems of archaic rigidity bearing grapes of gold and clusters of pearl. Here and there, to break the monotony of the green, twin-petals of great, red flowers, shaded with minute fragments of pink marble and porphyry, are thrown upon a background of gold.

In the glow of colour streaming through the windows all the splendours of Oriental tales seem to be revealed, vibrating through the twilight and silence of this sanctuary which is always open and surrounded by the spacious courtyard in which we stroll alone. Little birds, quite at home in the mosque, fly in and out of the open, bronze doors, and alight on the porphyry cornices and on the pearl and gold, and are benevolently regarded by the two or three venerable and white-bearded officials who are praying in the shadowy recesses. On the marble pavement are spread several antique Persian and Turkish rugs of the most delicate, faded hues.

On entering this circular mosque its vast centre is invisible, as it is surrounded by a double screen. The first is of wood, finely carved in the style of the Mozarabians; the second, of Gothic iron-work, placed there by the Crusaders when they used it temporarily as a Christian fane. Mounting some marble steps, our eyes at last rest upon this jealously-guarded interior.

Considering all the surrounding splendour, we now expect even more marvellous riches to be revealed, but we are awed by an apparition of quite a different nature, — a vague and gloomy shape seems to have its abode amid the shadows of this gorgeous precinct; a mass, as yet undefined, seems to surge through the semi-darkness like a great, black, solidified wave.

This is the summit of Mount Moriah, sacred alike to the Israelites, Mussulmans, and Christians; this is the threshing-floor of Ornan the Jebusite, where King David saw the Destroying Angel holding in his hand the destroy-

THE MOSQUE OF OMAR. 63

ing sword stretched out over Jerusalem (2 Samuel xxiv. 16; 1 Chronicles xxi. 15).

Here David built an altar of burnt-offering and here his son Solomon raised the Temple, levelling the surroundings at great cost, but preserving the irregularities of this peak because the foot of the angel had touched it. " Then Solomon began to build the house of the Lord at Jerusalem in Mount Moriah, where the Lord appeared unto David his father, in the place that David had prepared in the threshing-floor of Ornan the Jebusite " (2 Chronicles iii. 1).

We know through what scenes of inconceivable magnificence and desolating fury this mountain of Moriah passed during the ages. The Temple that crowned it, razed by Nebuchadnezzar, rebuilt on the return from the captivity in Babylon, and again destroyed under Antonius IV., was again rebuilt by Herod: it saw Jesus pass by; His voice was heard upon its summit.

Therefore, each of those mighty edifices which cost the ransom of an empire, and whose almost superhuman foundations are still found buried in the earth, confound the imagination of us moderns. After the destruction of Jerusalem by Titus, a Temple of Jupiter was erected under Hadrian's reign, replacing the Temple of the Saviour. Later, the early Christians, to spite the Jews, kept this sacred peak covered with *débris* and dirt, and it was the Caliph Omar who piously caused it to be cleared as soon as he had conquered Palestine; and finally, his successor, the Caliph Abd-el-Melek, about the year 690, enclosed it with the lovely Mosque that is still standing.

With the exception of the dome, restored during the

Twelfth and Fourteenth Centuries, the Crusaders found it in its present condition, already ancient and bearing the same relation to them that the Gothic cathedrals do to us, for it was clothed with the same fadeless embroideries of gold and marble and with its glistening brocades which are almost imperishable. Converting it into a church, they placed their marble altar in the centre on David's rock. On the fall of the Franks, Saladin, after long purifications by sprinklings of rose-water, restored it to the Faith of Allah.

Inscriptions of gold in old Cufic characters above the friezes speak of Christ after the Koran, and their deep wisdom is such as to sow disquietude in Christian souls: " O ye who have received the scriptures, exceed not the just bounds of your religion. Verily Christ Jesus is the son of Mary, the apostle of God, and his Word which he conveyed unto Mary. Believe then in God and in his Apostle, but say not there is a Trinity, forbear this, it will be better for you. God is but one. It is not meet that God should have a son. When He decreeth a thing He only saith unto it: 'Be'; and it is." (Sura iv. 19.)

A dread Past, crushing to our modern puerility, is evoked by this black rock, this dead and mummified mountain peak, on which the dew of Heaven never falls, which never produces a plant, nor a spray of moss, but which lies like the Pharaohs in their sarcophagi, and which, after two thousand years of troubles, has now been sheltered for thirteen centuries beneath the brooding of this golden dome and these marvellous walls raised for it alone.

Jérusalem (Paris, 1895).

THE CATHEDRAL OF BURGOS.

THE CATHEDRAL OF BURGOS.

THÉOPHILE GAUTIER.

NOTWITHSTANDING that Burgos was for so long a time the first city of Castile, it is not very Gothic in appearance; with the exception of a street where there are several windows and doors of the Renaissance, ornamented with coats of arms and their supporters, the houses do not date further back than the beginning of the Seventeenth Century, and are exceedingly commonplace; they are old, but not antique. But Burgos has her Cathedral, which is one of the most beautiful in the world; unfortunately, like all the Gothic cathedrals, it is shut in by a number of ignoble buildings which prevent you from appreciating the structure as a whole and grasping the mass at a glance. The principal porch looks upon a square, in the centre of which is a beautiful fountain surmounted by a delightful statue of Christ, the target for all the ruffians of the town who have no better pastime than throwing stones at its sculptures. The magnificent porch, like an intricate and flowered embroidery of lace, has been scraped and rubbed as far as the first frieze by I don't know what Italian prelates, — some important amateurs in architecture, who were great admirers of plain walls and ornamentation in *good taste*, and who, having pity for those poor barbarian architects who would not follow the Corinthian order and had no appreciation of Attic grace and the triangular fronton, wished to arrange the Cathedral in the Roman style. Many people are still of this opinion in Spain, where the so-called Messidor style flourishes in all its purity, and, exactly as was the case in France before the Romantic School brought the Middle Ages into favour again and caused the beauty and meaning of the cathedrals to be understood, prefer all kinds of abominable edifices, pierced with innumerable windows and ornamented with Pæstumian columns, to the most florid and richly-carved Gothic cathedrals. Two sharp spires cut in saw-teeth and open-worked, as if pierced with a punch, festooned, embroidered, and carved down to the last details like the bezel of a ring, spring towards God with all the ardour of faith and transport of a firm conviction. Our unbelieving campaniles would not dare to venture into the air with only stone-lace and ribs as delicate as gossamer to support them. Another tower, sculptured with an unheard-of wealth, but not so high, marks the spot where the transept intersects the nave, and completes the magnificence of the outline. A multitude of statues of saints, archangels, kings, and monks animates the whole mass of architecture, and this stone population is so numerous, so crowded, and so swarming, that surely it must exceed the population of flesh and blood inhabiting the town. . . .

The choir, which contains the stalls, called *silleria*, is enclosed by iron grilles of the most wonderful *repoussé* work; the pavement, according to the Spanish custom, is covered with immense mats of spartium, and each stall has, moreover, its own little mat of dry grass, or rushes. On raising your head you see a kind of dome, formed by the interior of the tower of which we have already spoken; it is a gulf of sculptures, arabesques, statues, little columns, ribs, lancets, and pendentives — enough to give you a vertigo. If you looked at it for two years, you would not see it all. It is as crowded together as the leaves of a cabbage, and fenestrated like a fish-slice; it is as gigantic as a pyramid and as delicate as a woman's ear-ring, and you cannot understand how such a piece of filigree-work has remained suspended in the air for so many centuries. What kind of men were those who made these marvellous buildings, whose splendours not even fairy palaces can surpass? Is the race extinct? And we, who are always boasting of our civilization, are we not decrepit barbarians in comparison? A deep sadness always oppresses my heart when I visit one of these stupendous edifices of the Past; I am seized with utter discouragement and my one desire is to steal into some corner, to place a stone beneath my head, and, in the immobility of contemplation, to await death, which is immobility itself. What is the use of working? Why should we tire ourselves? The most tremendous human effort will never produce anything equal to this. Ah well! even the names of these divine artists are forgotten, and to find any trace of them you must ransack the dusty archives in the convent! . . .

The sacristy is surrounded by a panelled wainscot, forming closets with flowered and festooned columns in rich taste; above the wainscot is a row of Venetian mirrors whose use I do not understand; certainly they must only be for ornament as they are too high for any one to see himself in them. Above the mirrors are arranged in chronological order, the oldest nearest the ceiling, the portraits of all the bishops of Burgos, from the first to the one now occupying the episcopal chair. These portraits, although they are oil, look more like pastels, or distemper, which is due to the fact that in Spain pictures are never varnished, and, for this lack of precaution, the dampness has destroyed many masterpieces. Although these portraits are, for the most part, imposing, they are hung too high for one to judge of the merit of the execution. There is an enormous buffet in the centre of the room and enormous baskets of spartium, in which the church ornaments and sacred vessels are kept. Under two glass cases are preserved as curiosities two coral trees, whose branches are much less complicated than the least arabesque in the Cathedral. The door is embellished with the arms of Burgos in relief, sprinkled with little crosses, gules.

Juan Cuchiller's room, which we next visited, is not at all remarkable in the way of architecture, and we were hastening to leave it when we were asked to raise our eyes and look at a very curious object. This was a great chest fastened to the wall by iron clamps. It would be hard to imagine a box more patched, more worm-eaten, or more dilapidated. It is surely the oldest chest in the world; an inscription in black-letter — *Cofre del Cid* — gives, at once, as you will readily believe, an enormous importance to these four boards of rotting wood. If we may believe the old chronicle, this chest is precisely that of the famous Ruy Diaz de Bivar, better known under the name of the

Cid Campeador, who, once lacking money, exactly like a simple author, notwithstanding he was a hero, had this filled with sand and stones and carried to the house of an honest Jewish usurer who lent money on this security, the Cid Campeador forbidding him to open the mysterious coffer until he had reimbursed the borrowed sum. . . .

The need of the real, no matter how revolting, is a characteristic of Spanish Art: idealism and conventionality are not in the genius of these people completely deficient in æsthetic feeling. Sculpture does not suffice for them; they must have their statues coloured, and their madonnas painted and dressed in real clothes. Never, according to their taste, can material illusion be carried too far, and this terrible love of realism makes them often overstep the boundaries which separate sculpture from wax-works.

The celebrated Christ, so revered at Burgos that no one is allowed to see it unless the candles are lighted, is a striking example of this strange taste: it is neither of stone, nor painted wood, it is made of human skin (so the monks say), stuffed with much art and care. The hair is real hair, the eyes have eye-lashes, the thorns of the crown are real thorns, and no detail has been forgotten. Nothing can be more lugubrious and disquieting than this attenuated, crucified phantom with its human appearance and deathlike stillness; the faded and brownish-yellow skin is streaked with long streams of blood, so well imitated that they seem to trickle. It requires no great effort of imagination to give credence to the legend that it bleeds every Friday. In the place of folded, or flying drapery, the Christ of Burgos wears a white skirt embroidered in gold, which falls from the waist to the knees; this costume produces a peculiar effect, especially to us who are not accustomed to see our Lord attired thus. At the foot of the Cross three ostrich eggs are placed, a symbolical ornament of whose meaning I am ignorant, unless they allude to the Trinity, the principle and germ of everything.

We went out of the Cathedral dazzled, overwhelmed, and satiated with *chefs d'œuvre*, powerless to admire any longer, and only with great difficulty we threw a glance upon the arch of Fernan Gonzalez, an attempt in classical architecture made by Philip of Burgundy at the beginning of the Renaissance.

Voyage en Espagne (Paris, new ed., 1865).

THE PYRAMIDS.

GEORG EBERS.

EARLY in the morning our carriage, drawn by fast horses, rattles across the Nile on the iron bridge which joins Cairo to the beautiful island of Gezirah. The latter, with its castle and the western tributary of the river which ripples by it, are soon left behind. Beneath the shade of acacias and sycamore-trees runs the well-kept and level highway. On our left lie the castle and the high-walled, vice-regal gardens of Gizeh; the dewy green fields, intersected by canals, rejoice the eye, and a tender blue mist veils the west. The air has that clearness and aromatic freshness which is only offered by an Egyptian winter's morning. For a moment the enveloping curtain of cloud lifts from the horizon, and we see the prodigious Pyramids standing before us with their sharp triangles, and the misty curtain falls; to the right and left we sometimes see buffaloes grazing, sometimes flocks of silvery herons, sometimes a solitary pelican within gun-shot of our carriage; then half-naked peasants at their daily labour and pleasing villages some distance from the road. Two large, whitish eagles now soar into the air. The eye follows their flight, and, in glancing upwards, perceives how the mist has gradually disappeared, how brightly dazzling is the blue of the sky, and how the sun is at last giving out the full splendour of his rays. . . .

We stand before the largest of these works of man, which, as we know, the ancients glorified as "wonders of the world." It is unnecessary to describe their form for everybody knows the stereometrical figure to which their name has been given, and this is not the place to print a numerical estimate of their mass. Only by a comparison with other structures present in our memory can any idea of their immensity be realized; and, consequently, it may be said here that while St. Peter's in Rome is 131 metres high (430 feet), the Great Pyramid (of Cheops), with its restored apex would be 147 metres (482 feet), and is thus 16 metres (52 feet) taller; therefore, if the Pyramid of Cheops were hollow, the great Cathedral of Rome could be placed within it like a clock under a protecting glass-shade. Neither St. Stephen's Cathedral in Vienna, nor the Munster of Strasburg reaches the height of the highest Pyramid; but the new towers of the Cathedral of Cologne exceed it. In one respect no other building in the world can be compared with the Pyramids, and that is in regard to the mass and weight of the materials used in their construction. If the tomb of Cheops were razed, a wall could be built with its stones all around the frontiers of France. If you fire a good pistol from the top of the great Pyramid into the air, the ball falls halfway down its side. By such comparisons they who have not visited Egypt may form an idea of the dimensions of these amazing structures; he who stands on the sandy ground and raises his eyes to the summit, needs no such aids.

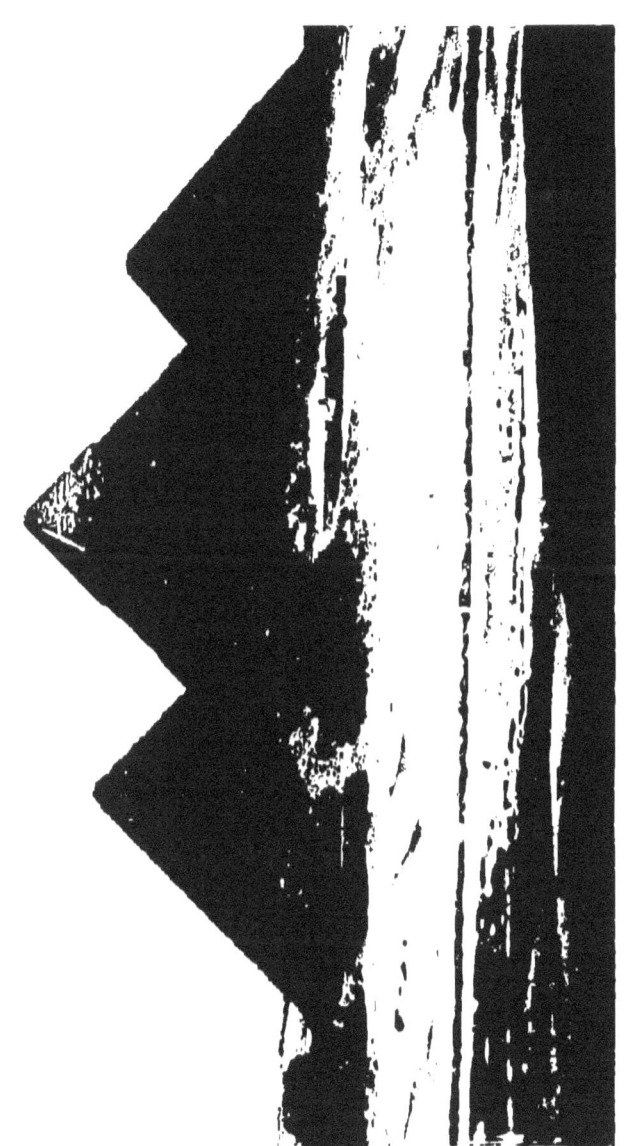

THE PYRAMIDS.

THE PYRAMIDS.

We get out of the carriage on the north side of the Pyramid of Cheops. In the sharply-defined triangular shadows women are squatted, offering oranges and various eatables for sale; donkey-boys are waiting with their grey animals; and travellers are resting after having accomplished the ascent. This work now lies before us, and if we were willing to shirk it, there would be many attacks on our indolence, for from the moment we stepped from our carriage, we have been closely followed by a ragged, brown, and sinewy crowd, vehemently offering their services. They call themselves *Bedouin* with great pride, but they have nothing in common with the true sons of the desert except their faults. Nevertheless, it is not only prudent but necessary to accept their assistance, although the way up can scarcely be mistaken.

We begin the ascent at a place where the outside stone casing of the Pyramid has fallen away, leaving the terrace-like blocks of the interior exposed; but the steps are unequal and sometimes of considerable height; some of them are half as high as a man. Two or three lads accompany me; one jumps up first with his bare feet, holds my hands, and drags me after him; another follows the climber, props his back, and thrusts and pushes him forwards; while a third grabs his side beneath his arm, and lifts him. Thus, one half-scrambles up himself and is half-dragged up, while the nimble lads give the climber no rest, if he wants to stop for breath or to wipe the drops of moisture from his brow. These importunate beggars never cease shouting and clamouring for *baksheesh*, and are so persistently annoying that they seem to want us to forget the gratitude we owe them for their aid.

At length we reach our destination. The point of the Pyramid has long since crumbled away, and we stand on a tolerably spacious platform. When our gasping breath and throbbing pulses have partially recovered and we have paid and got rid of the *Bedouin*, who torment us to exchange our money for sham antiquities, we look down upon the vast landscape, and the longer we gaze and absorb this distant view, the more significant and the more incomparable it appears. Fertility and sterility, life and death, lie nowhere in such close mingling as here. There in the east flows the broad Nile covered with lateen sails, and like emerald tapestry are the fields and meadows, gardens and groves of palm-trees, spread along its shores. The villages, hidden under the trees, look like birds' nests among green boughs, and at the foot of the Mokattam mountain, which is now shining with golden light and which at sunset will reflect the rosy and violet afterglow, rise the thousand mosques of the city of the Caliphs, overtopped by the citadel and by those slenderest of all minarets which grace the Mausoleum of Mohammed Ali, an unmistakable feature of Cairo, visible from the farthest distance. Gardens and trees encircle the city like a garland around some lovely head. Nowhere is there to be found a more beautiful picture of prosperity, fertility, and life. The silver threads of the canals crossing the entire luxuriant valley appear to be some shining fluid. Unclouded is the sky, and yet light shadows fall across the fields. These are flocks of birds which find plenty of food and drink here. How vast is the bounty of God! How beautiful and rich is the earth!

The *Bedouin* have left us. We stand alone on the summit. All is still. Not a sound reaches us from far or near. Turning now to the west, the eye can see nothing but pyramids and tombs, rocks and sand in countless number. Not a blade, not a bush can find nutriment in this sterile ground. Yellow, grey, and dull brown cover everything, far and wide, in unbroken monotony.

Only here and there a white object is shining amidst the dust. It is the dried skeleton of some dead animal. Silent and void, the enemy to everything that has life — the desert — stretches before us. Where is its end? In days, weeks, months the traveller would never reach it, even if he escaped alive from the choking sand. Here, if anywhere, Death is king; here, where the Egyptians saw the sun vanish every day behind the wall of the Libyan mountains, begins a world which bears the same comparison to the fruitful lands of the East as a corpse does to a living man happy in the battle and joy of life. A more silent burial-place than this desert exists nowhere on this earth; and so tomb after tomb was erected here, and, as if to preserve the secret of the dead, the desert has enveloped tombs and bodies with its veil of sand. Here the terrors of infinity are displayed. Here at the gate of the future life, where eternity begins, man's work seems to have eluded the common destiny of earthly things and to have partaken of immortality.

" Time mocks all things, but the Pyramids mock Time " is an Arabian proverb which has been repeated thousands of times.

Cicerone durch das alte und neue Ægypten (Stuttgart und Leipzig, 1886).

SAINT PETER'S.

CHARLES DICKENS.

WHEN we were fairly off again, we began, in a perfect fever, to strain our eyes for Rome; and when, after another mile or two, the Eternal City appeared, at length, in the distance, it looked like — I am half afraid to write the word — like LONDON!!! There it lay, under a thick cloud, with innumerable towers, and steeples, and roofs of houses, rising up into the sky, and, high above them all, one Dome. I swear, that keenly as I felt the seeming absurdity of the comparison, it was so like London, at that distance, that if you could have shown it me in a glass, I should have taken it for nothing else.

We entered the Eternal City at about four o'clock in the afternoon, on the thirtieth of January, by the Porta del Popolo, and came immediately — it was a dark, muddy day, and there had been heavy rain — on the skirts of the Carnival. We did not, then, know that we were only looking at the fag-end of the masks, who were driving slowly round and round the Piazza, until they could find a promising opportunity for falling into the stream of carriages, and getting, in good time, into the thick of the festivity; and coming among them so abruptly, all travel-stained and weary, was not coming very well prepared to enjoy the scene. . . .

Immediately on going out next day we hurried off to St. Peter's. It looked immense in the distance but distinctly and decidedly small, by comparison, on a near approach. The beauty of the Piazza in which it stands, with its clusters of exquisite columns and its gushing fountains — so fresh, so broad, and free and beautiful — nothing can exaggerate. The first burst of the interior, in all its expansive majesty and glory: and most of all, the looking up into the Dome: is a sensation never to be forgotten. But, there were preparations for a Festa; the pillars of stately marble were swathed in some impertinent frippery of red and yellow; the altar, and entrance to the subterranean chapel: which is before it, in the centre of the church : were like a goldsmith's shop, or one of the opening scenes in a very lavish pantomime. And though I had as high a sense of the beauty of the building (I hope) as it is possible to entertain, I felt no very strong emotion. I have been infinitely more affected in many English cathedrals when the organ has been playing, and in many English country churches when the congregation have been singing. I had a much greater sense of mystery and wonder in the Cathedral of San Mark, at Venice. . . .

On Sunday the Pope assisted in the performance of High Mass at St. Peter's. The effect of the Cathedral on my mind, on that second visit, was exactly what it was at first, and what it remains after many visits. It is not religiously impressive or affecting. It is an immense edifice, with no one point for the mind to rest upon; and it tires itself with wandering round and round. The very purpose of the place is not expressed in anything you see there, unless you examine its details — and all examination of details is incompatible with the place itself. It might be a Pantheon, or a Senate House, or a great architectural trophy, having no other object than an architectural triumph. There is a black statue of St. Peter, to be sure, under a red canopy; which is larger than life, and which is constantly having its great toe kissed by good Catholics. You cannot help seeing that: it is so very prominent and popular. But it does not heighten the effect of the temple as a work of art; and it is not expressive — to me, at least — of its high purpose.

A large space behind the altar was fitted up with boxes, shaped like those at the Italian Opera in England, but in their decoration much more gaudy. In the centre of the kind of theatre thus railed off was a canopied dais with the Pope's chair upon it. The pavement was covered with a carpet of the brightest green; and what with this green, and the intolerable reds and crimsons, and gold borders of the hangings, the whole concern looked like a stupendous Bonbon. On either side of the altar was a large box for lady strangers. These were filled with ladies in black dresses and black veils. The gentlemen of the Pope's guard, in red coats, leather breeches, and jack-boots, guarded all this reserved space, with drawn swords that were very flashy in every sense; and, from the altar all down the nave, a broad lane was kept clear by the Pope's Swiss Guard, who wear a quaint striped surcoat, and striped tight legs, and carry halberds like

ST. PETER'S.

those which are usually shouldered by those theatrical supernumeraries, who never *can* get off the stage fast enough, and who may be generally observed to linger in the enemy's camp after the open country, held by the opposite forces, has been split up the middle by a convulsion of Nature.

I got upon the border of the green carpet, in company with a great many other gentlemen attired in black (no other passport is necessary), and stood there, at my ease, during the performance of mass. The singers were in a crib of wire-work (like a large meat-safe or bird-cage) in one corner; and sung most atrociously. All about the green carpet there was a slowly-moving crowd of people: talking to each other: staring at the Pope through eye-glasses: defrauding one another, in moments of partial curiosity, out of precarious seats on the bases of pillars: and grinning hideously at the ladies. Dotted here and there were little knots of friars (Francescani, or Cappuccini, in their coarse brown dresses and peaked hoods), making a strange contrast to the gaudy ecclesiastics of higher degree, and having their humility gratified to the utmost, by being shouldered about, and elbowed right and left, on all sides. Some of these had muddy sandals and umbrellas, and stained garments: having trudged in from the country. The faces of the greater part were as coarse and heavy as their dress; their dogged, stupid, monotonous stare at all the glory and splendour having something in it half miserable, and half ridiculous.

Upon the green carpet itself, and gathered round the altar, was a perfect army of cardinals and priests, in red, gold, purple, violet, white, and fine linen. Stragglers from these went to and fro among the crowd, conversing two and two, or giving and receiving introductions, and exchanging salutations; other functionaries in black gowns, and other functionaries in court dresses, were similarly engaged. In the midst of all these, and stealthy Jesuits creeping in and out, and the extreme restlessness of the Youth of England, who were perpetually wandering about, some few steady persons in black cassocks, who had knelt down with their faces to the wall, and were poring over their missals, became, unintentionally, a sort of human man-traps, and with their own devout legs tripped up other people's by the dozen.

There was a great pile of candles lying down on the floor near me, which a very old man in a rusty black gown with an open-work tippet, like a summer ornament for a fire-place in tissue paper, made himself very busy in dispensing to all the ecclesiastics: one apiece. They loitered about with these for some time, under their arms like walking-sticks, or in their hands like truncheons. At a certain period of the ceremony, however, each carried his candle up to the Pope, laid it across his two knees to be blessed, took it back again, and filed off. This was done in a very attenuated procession, as you may suppose, and occupied a long time. Not because it takes long to bless a candle through and through, but because there were so many candles to be blessed. At last they were all blessed, and then they were all lighted; and then the Pope was taken up, chair and all, and carried round the church. . . .

On Easter Sunday, as well as on the preceding Thursday, the Pope bestows his benediction on the people from the balcony in front of St. Peter's. This Easter Sunday was a day so bright and blue: so cloudless, balmy, wonderfully bright: that all the previous bad weather vanished from the recollection in a moment. I had seen the Thursday's benediction dropping damply on some hundreds of umbrellas, but there was not a sparkle then in all the hundred fountains of Rome — such fountains as they are! — and, on this Sunday morning, they were running diamonds. The miles of miserable streets through which we drove (compelled to a certain course by the Pope's dragoons: the Roman police on such occasions) were so full of colour, that nothing in them was capable of wearing a faded aspect. The common people came out in their gayest dresses; the richer people in their smartest vehicles; Cardinals rattled to the church of the Poor Fisherman in their state carriages; shabby magnificence flaunted its threadbare liveries and tarnished cocked-hats in the sun; and every coach in Rome was put in requisition for the Great Piazza of St. Peter's.

One hundred and fifty thousand people were there at least! Yet there was ample room. How many carriages were there I don't know; yet there was room for them too, and to spare. The great steps of the church were densely crowded. There were many of the Contadini, from Albano (who delight in red), in that part of the square, and the mingling of bright colours in the crowd was beautiful. Below the steps the troops were ranged. In the magnificent proportions of the place, they looked like a bed of flowers. Sulky Romans, lively peasants from the neighbouring country, groups of pilgrims from distant parts of Italy, sight-seeing foreigners of all nations, made a murmur in the clear air, like so many insects; and high above them all, plashing and bubbling, and making rainbow colours in the light, the two delicious fountains welled and tumbled bountifully.

A kind of bright carpet was hung over the front of the balcony; and the sides of the great window were bedecked with crimson drapery. An awning was stretched, too, over the top, to screen the old man from the hot rays of the sun. As noon approached, all eyes were turned up to this window. In due time the chair was seen approaching to the front, with the gigantic fans of peacock's feathers close behind. The doll within it (for the balcony is very high) then rose up, and stretched out its tiny arms, while all the male spectators in the square uncovered, and some, but not by any means the greater part, kneeled down The guns upon the ramparts of the Castle of St. Angelo proclaimed, next moment, that the benediction was given; drums beat; trumpets sounded; arms clashed; and the great mass below, suddenly breaking into smaller heaps, and scattering here and there in rills, was stirred like party-coloured sand. . . .

But, when the night came on, without a cloud to dim the full moon, what a sight it was to see the Great Square full once more, and the whole church, from the cross to the ground, lighted with innumerable lanterns, tracing out the architecture, and winking and shining all round the colonnade of the Piazza. And what a sense of exultation, joy, delight, it was, when the great bell struck half past seven — on the instant — to behold one bright red mass of fire soar gallantly from the top of the cupola to the extremest summit of the cross, and, the moment it leaped into its place, become the signal of a bursting out of countless lights, as great, and red, and blazing as itself, from every part of the gigantic church ; so that every cornice, capital, and smallest ornament of stone expressed itself in fire : and the black, solid groundwork of the enormous dome seemed to grow transparent as an egg-shell !

A train of gunpowder, an electric chain — nothing could be fired more suddenly and swiftly than this second illumination : and when we had got away, and gone upon a distant height, and looked toward it two hours afterward, there it still stood, shining and glittering in the calm night like a jewel ! Not a line of its proportions wanting ; not an angle blunted ; not an atom of its radiance lost.

Pictures from Italy (London, 1845).

THE CATHEDRAL OF STRASBURG.

VICTOR HUGO.

I ARRIVED in Nancy Sunday evening at seven o'clock; at eight the diligence started again. Was I more fatigued? Was the road better? The fact is I propped myself on the braces of the conveyance and slept. Thus I arrived in Phalsbourg.

I woke up about four o'clock in the morning. A cool breeze blew upon my face and the carriage was going down the incline at a gallop, for we were descending the famous Saverne.

It was one of the most beautiful impressions of my life. The rain had ceased, the mists had been blown to the four winds, and the crescent moon slipped rapidly through the clouds and sailed freely through the azure space like a barque on a little lake. A breeze which came from the Rhine made the trees, which bordered the road, tremble. From time to time they waved aside and permitted me to see an indistinct and frightful abyss: in the foreground, a forest beneath which the mountain disappeared; below, immense plains, meandering streams glittering like streaks of lightning; and in the background a dark, indistinct, and heavy line — the Black Forest — a magical panorama beheld by moonlight. Such incomplete visions have, perhaps, more distinction than any others. They are dreams which one can look upon and feel. I knew that my eyes rested upon France, Germany, and Switzerland, Strasburg with its spire, the Black Forest with its mountains, and the Rhine with its windings; I searched for everything and I saw nothing. I have never experienced a more extraordinary sensation. Add to that the hour, the journey, the horses dashing down the precipice, the violent noise of the wheels, the rattling of the windows, the frequent passage through dark woods, the breath of the morning upon the mountains, a gentle murmur heard through the valleys, and the beauty of the sky, and you will understand what I felt. Day is amazing in this valley; night is fascinating.

The descent took a quarter of an hour. Half an hour later came the twilight of morning; at my left the dawn quickened the lower sky, a group of white houses with black roofs became visible on the summit of a hill, the blue of day began to overflow the horizon, several peasants passed by going to their vines, a clear, cold, and violet light struggled with the ashy glimmer of the moon, the constellations paled, two of the Pleiades were lost to sight, the three horses in our chariot descended rapidly towards their stable with its blue doors, it was cold and I was frozen, for it had become necessary to open the windows. A moment afterwards the sun rose, and the first thing it showed to me was the village notary shaving at a broken mirror under a red calico curtain.

A league further on the peasants became more picturesque and the waggons magnificent; I counted in one thirteen mules harnessed far apart by long chains. You felt you were approaching Strasburg, the old German city.

Galloping furiously, we traversed Wasselonne, a long narrow trench of houses strangled in the last gorge of the Vosges by the side of Strasburg. There I caught a glimpse of one façade of the Cathedral, surmounted by three round and pointed towers in juxtaposition, which the movement of the diligence brought before my vision brusquely and then took it away, jolting it about as if it were a scene in the theatre.

Suddenly, at a turn in the road the mist lifted and I saw the Münster. It was six o'clock in the morning. The enormous Cathedral, which is the highest building that the hand of man has made since the great Pyramid, was clearly defined against a background of dark mountains whose forms were magnificent and whose valleys were flooded with sunshine. The work of God made for man and the work of man made for God, the mountain and the Cathedral contesting for grandeur. I have never seen anything more imposing.

Yesterday I visited the Cathedral. The Münster is truly a marvel. The doors of the church are beautiful, particularly the Roman porch, the façade contains some superb figures on horseback, the rose-window is beautifully cut, and the entire face of the Cathedral is a poem, wisely composed. But the real triumph of the Cathedral is the spire. It is a true tiara of stone with its crown and its cross. It is a prodigy of grandeur and delicacy. I have seen Chartres, and I have seen Antwerp, but Strasburg pleases me best.

THE CATHEDRAL OF STRASBURG.

The church has never been finished. The apse, miserably mutilated, has been restored according to that imbecile, the Cardinal de Rohan, of the necklace fame. It is hideous. The window they have selected is like a modern carpet. It is ignoble. The other windows, with the exception of some added panes, are beautiful, notably the great rose-window. All the church is shamefully whitewashed; some of the sculptures have been restored with some little taste. This Cathedral has been affected by all styles. The pulpit is a little construction of the Fifteenth Century, of florid Gothic of a design and style that are ravishing. Unfortunately they have gilded it in the most stupid manner. The baptismal font is of the same period and is restored in a superior manner. It is a vase surrounded by foliage in sculpture, the most marvellous in the world. In a dark chapel at the side there are two tombs. One, of a bishop of the time of Louis V., is of that formidable character which Gothic architecture always expresses. The sepulchre is in two floors. The bishop, in pontifical robes and with his mitre on his head, is lying in his bed under a canopy; he is sleeping. Above and on the foot of the bed in the shadow, you perceive an enormous stone in which two enormous iron rings are imbedded; that is the lid of the tomb. You see nothing more. The architects of the Sixteenth Century showed you the corpse (you remember the tombs of Brou?); those of the Fourteenth concealed it: that is even more terrifying. Nothing could be more sinister than these two rings. . . .

The tomb of which I have spoken is in the left arm of the cross. In the right arm there is a chapel, which scaffolding prevented me from seeing. At the side of this chapel runs a balustrade of the Fifteenth Century, leaning against a wall. A sculptured and painted figure leans against this balustrade and seems to be admiring a pillar surrounded by statues placed one over the other, which is directly opposite and which has a marvellous effect. Tradition says that this figure represents the first architect of the Münster — Erwyn von Steinbach. . . .

I did not see the famous astronomical clock, which is in the nave and which is a charming little building of the Sixteenth Century. They were restoring it and it was covered with a scaffolding of boards.

After having seen the church, I made the ascent of the steeple. You know my taste for perpendicular trips. I was very careful not to miss the highest spire in the world. The Münster of Strasburg is nearly five hundred feet high. It belongs to the family of spires which are open-worked stairways.

It is delightful to wind about in that monstrous mass of stone, filled with air and light hollowed out like a *joujou de Dieppe*, a lantern as well as a pyramid, which vibrates and palpitates with every breath of the wind. I mounted as far as the vertical stairs. As I went up I met a visitor who was descending, pale and trembling, and half-carried by the guide. There is, however, no danger. The danger begins where I stopped, where the spire, properly so-called, begins. Four open-worked spiral stairways, corresponding to the four vertical towers, unroll in an entanglement of delicate, slender, and beautifully-worked stone, supported by the spire, every angle of which it follows, winding until it reaches the crown at about thirty feet from the lantern surmounted by a cross which forms the summit of the bell-tower. The steps of these stairways are very steep and very narrow, and become narrower and narrower as you ascend, until there is barely ledge enough on which to place your foot.

In this way you have to climb a hundred feet which brings you four hundred feet above the street. There are no hand-rails, or such slight ones that they are not worth speaking about. The entrance to this stairway is closed by an iron grille. They will not open this grille without a special permission from the Mayor of Strasburg, and nobody is allowed to ascend it unless accompanied by two workmen of the roof, who tie a rope around your body, the end of which they fasten, in proportion as you ascend, to the various iron bars which bind the mullions. Only a week ago three German women, a mother and her two daughters, made this ascent. Nobody but the workmen of the roof, who repair the bell-tower, are allowed to go beyond the lantern. Here there is not even a stairway, but only a simple iron ladder.

From where I stopped the view was wonderful. Strasburg lies at your feet, — the old town with its dentellated gables, and its large roofs encumbered with chimneys, and its towers and churches — as picturesque as any town of Flanders. The Ill and the Rhine, two lovely rivers, enliven this dark mass with their plashing waters, so clear and green. Beyond the walls, as far as the eye can reach, stretches an immense country richly wooded and dotted with villages. The Rhine, which flows within a league of the town, winds through the landscape. In walking around this bell-tower you see three chains of mountains — the ridges of the Black Forest on the north, the Vosges on the west, and the Alps in the centre. . . .

The sun willingly makes a festival for those who are upon great heights. At the moment I reached the top of the Münster, it suddenly scattered the clouds, with which the sky had been covered all day, and turned the smoke of the city and all the mists of the valley to rosy flames, while it showered a golden rain on Saverne, whose magnificent slope I saw twelve leagues towards the horizon, through the most resplendent haze. Behind me a large cloud dropped rain upon the Rhine; the gentle hum of the town was brought to me by some puffs of wind; the bells echoed from a hundred villages; some little red and white fleas, which were really a herd of cattle, grazed in the meadow to the right; other little blue and red fleas, which were really gunners, performed field-exercise in the polygon to the left; a black beetle, which was the diligence, crawled along the road to Metz; and to the north on the brow of the hill the castle of the Grand Duke of Baden sparkled in a flash of light like a precious stone. I went from one tower to another, looking by turns upon France, Switzerland, and Germany, all illuminated by the same ray of sunlight.

Each tower looks upon a different country.

Descending, I stopped for a few moments at one of the high doors of the tower-stairway. On either side of this door are the stone effigies of the two architects of the Münster. These two great poets are represented as kneeling and looking behind them upward as if they were lost in astonishment at the height of their work. I put myself in the same posture and remained thus for several minutes. At the platform they made me write my name in a book; after which I went away.

Le Rhin (Paris, 1842).

THE SHWAY DAGOHN.

GWENDOLIN TRENCH GASCOIGNE.

THE "Shway Dagohn" at Rangoon, or Golden Pagoda, is one of the most ancient and venerated shrines which exists, and it certainly should hold a high place among the beautiful and artistic monuments of the world, for it is exquisite in design and form. Its proportions and height are simply magnificent; wide at the base, it shoots up 370 feet, tapering gradually away until crowned by its airy golden Htee, or umbrella-shaped roof. This delicate little structure is studded profusely with precious stones and hung round with scores of tiny gold and jewelled bells, which, when swung lightly by the soft breeze, give out the tenderest and most mystic of melodies. The Htee was the gift of King Mindohn-Min, and it is said to have cost the enormous sum of fifty thousand pounds.

The great pagoda is believed by the faithful to have been erected in 588 B. C.; but for many centuries previous to that date the spot where the pagoda now stands was held sacred, as the relics of three preceding Buddhas were discovered there when the two Talaing brothers (the founders of the Great Pagoda) brought the eight holy hairs of Buddha to the Thehngoothara Hill, the spot where the pagoda now stands. Shway Yoe (Mr. Scott) says that it also possesses

THE SHWAY DAGOHN.

in the Tapanahteik, or relic chamber, of the pagoda the drinking cup of Kaukkathan, the "thengan," or robe, of Gawnagohng, and the "toungway," or staff, of Kathapah. It is therefore so holy that pilgrims visit this shrine from far countries, such as Siam, and even the Corea. The height of the pagoda was originally only twenty-seven feet, but it has attained its present proportions by being constantly encased in bricks. It is a marvellously striking structure, raising up its delicate, glittering head from among a wondrous company of profusely carved shrines and small temples, whose colour and cunning workmanship make fit attendants to this stupendous monument.

It is always a delight to one's eyes to gaze upon its glittering spire, always a fairy study of artistic enchantment; but perhaps if it has a moment when it seems clothed with peculiar and almost ethereal, mystic attraction, it is in the early morning light, when the air has been bathed by dewdrops and is of crystal clearness, and when that scorching Eastern sun has only just begun to send forth his burning rays. I would say go and gaze on the pagoda at the awakening hour, standing there on the last spur of the Pegu Hills, and framed by a luxuriant tropical bower of foliage. The light scintillates and glistens like a myriad of diamonds upon its golden surface, and the dreamy beauty of its glorious personality seems to strike one dumb with deep, unspoken reverence and admiration.

Nestling on one side of it are a number of Pohn-gyee Kyoung (monasteries) and rest-houses for pilgrims. All these are quaint, carved, and gilded edifices from which you see endless yellow-robed monks issuing. The monasteries situated at the foot of the great pagoda seem peculiarly harmonious, as if they would seek protection and shelter beneath the wing of their great mother church.

The pagoda itself is approached on four sides by long flights of steps, but the southern is the principal entrance and that most frequented. At the base of this stand two gigantic lions made of brick and plastered over, and also decorated with coloured paint; their office is to guard the sacred place from nats (evil spirits) and demons, the fear of which seems ever to haunt the Burman's mind and be a perpetual and endless torment to him. From this entrance the steps of the pagoda rise up and are enclosed by a series of beautifully carved teak roofs, supported by wood and masonry pillars. There are several quaint frescoes of Buddha and saints depicted upon the ceiling of these roofs, but the steps which they cover are very rugged and irregular. It is, indeed, a pilgrimage to ascend them, although the foreigner is allowed to retain his shoes. The faithful, of course, leave theirs at the foot of the steps.

The entrance to the pagoda inspires one with a maze of conflicting emotions as one stands before it; joy, sorrow, pity, wonder, admiration follow so quickly upon each other that they mingle into an indescribable sense of bewilderment. The first sight of the entrance is gorgeous, full of Eastern colour and charm; and then sorrow and horror fill one's heart, as one's eyes fall suddenly upon the rows of lepers who line the way to the holy place. Each is a terrible, gruesome sight, a mass of ghastly corruption and disease, and each holds out with maimed, distorted hands a little tin vessel for your alms.

THE SHWAY DAGOHN.

Why should Providence allow so awful an affliction as leprosy to fall upon His creatures? Could any crime, however heinous, be foul enough for such a punishment? These are the thoughts that flit through your brain; and then, as you pass on, wonder takes their place at the quaint beauty of the edifice, and lastly intense and wild admiration takes entire possession of you, and all is forgotten in the glorious nearness of the great Golden Pagoda.

On either side of the rugged steps there are rows of most picturesque little stalls, at which are sold endless offerings to be made to Buddha — flowers of every shade and hue, fruit, glowing bunches of yellow plantains and pepia, candles, wondrous little paper devices and flags, and, lastly, the gold leaf, which the faithful delight to place upon the beloved pagoda. It is looked upon as a great act of merit to expend money in thus decorating the much loved and venerated shrine. . . .

As you mount slowly up the steep uneven steps of the pagoda, turn for a moment and glance back at the scene. It is a pagoda feast, and the place is crowded with the faithful from all parts, who have come from far and near to present offerings and perform their religious observances. It is an entrancing picture, a marvel of colour and picturesqueness — see, the stalls are laid out with their brightest wares, and the crowd is becoming greater every moment. Look at that group of laughing girls, they have donned their most brilliant tamehns, and dainty shawls, and the flowers in their hair are arranged with infinite coquettishness; behind them are coming a dazzling company of young men in pasohs of every indescribable shade; perchance they are the lovers of the girls whom they are following so eagerly, and they are bearing fruit and flowers to present to Buddha. Beyond them again are some yellow-robed Pohn-gyees; they are supposed to shade their eyes from looking upon women with their large lotus-shaped fans, but to-day they are gazing about them more than is permitted, and are casting covert glances of admiration on some of those dainty little maidens. Behind them again are a white-robed company, they are nuns, and their shroud-like garments flow around them in long graceful folds. Their hair is cut short, and they have not so joyous an expression upon their faces as the rest of the community, and they toil up the steep steps a trifle wearily. Behind them again are a little toddling group of children, with their little hands full of bright glowing flowers and fruits.

Shall we follow in the crowd and see where the steps lead? It is a wondrous study, the effects of light and shade; look at that sunbeam glinting in through the roof and laying golden fingers on the Pohn-gyees' yellow robes, and turning the soft-hued fluttering silks into brilliant luminous spots of light.

At last we have arrived at the summit! Let us pause and take breath morally and physically before walking round the great open-paved space in the centre of which rises the great and glorious pagoda. There it stands towering up and up, as though it would fain touch the blue heaven; it is surrounded by a galaxy of smaller pagodas, which seem to be clustering lovingly near their great high priest; around these again are large carved kneeling elephants, and deep urn-shaped vessels, which are placed there to receive the offerings of food brought to Buddha. The crows and the pariah dogs which haunt the place will soon demolish these devout offerings, and grow fat upon them as their appearance testifies; but this, curiously, does not seem in the least to annoy the giver. He has no objection to seeing a fat crow or a mangy dog gorging itself upon his offering, as the feeding of any animal is an act of merit, which is the one thing of importance to a Burman. The more acts of merit that he can accomplish in this life, the more rapid his incarnations will be in the next.

There are draped about the small golden pagodas and round the base of the large one endless quaint pieces of woven silk; these are offerings from women, and must be completed in one night without a break.

On the outer circle of this large paved space are a multitude of shrines, enclosing hundreds of images of Buddha. You behold Buddha standing, you behold him sitting, you behold him reclining; you see him large, you see him small, you see him medium size; you see him in brass, in wood, in stone, and in marble. Many of these statues are simply replicas of each other, but some differ slightly, though the cast of features is always the same, a placid, amiable, benign countenance, with very long lobes to the ears, which in Burmah are supposed to indicate the great truthfulness of the person who possesses them. Most of the images have suspended over them the royal white umbrella, which was one of the emblems of Burma, and only used in Thebaw's time to cover Buddha, the king, and the lord white elephant.

Among Pagodas and Fair Ladies (London, 1896).

THE CATHEDRAL OF SIENA.

JOHN ADDINGTON SYMONDS.

QUITTING the Palazzo, and threading narrow streets, paved with brick and overshadowed with huge empty palaces, we reach the highest of the three hills on which Siena stands, and see before us the Duomo. This church is the most purely Gothic of all Italian cathedrals designed by national architects. Together with that of Orvieto, it stands to show what the unassisted genius of the Italians could produce, when under the empire of mediæval Christianity and before the advent of the neopagan spirit. It is built wholly of marble, and overlaid, inside and out, with florid ornaments of exquisite beauty. There are no flying buttresses, no pinnacles, no deep and fretted doorways, such as form the charm of French and English architecture; but instead of this, the lines of party-coloured marbles, the scrolls and wreaths of foliage, the mosaics and the frescoes which meet the eye in every direction, satisfy our sense of variety, producing most agreeable combinations of blending hues and harmoniously connected forms. The chief fault which offends against our Northern taste is the predominance of horizontal lines, both in the construction of the façade, and also in the internal decoration. This single fact sufficiently proves

THE CATHEDRAL OF SIENA.

that the Italians had never seized the true idea of Gothic or aspiring architecture. But, allowing for this original defect, we feel that the Cathedral of Siena combines solemnity and splendour to a degree almost unrivalled. Its dome is another point in which the instinct of Italian architects has led them to adhere to the genius of their ancestral art rather than to follow the principles of Gothic design. The dome is Etruscan and Roman, native to the soil, and only by a kind of violence adapted to the character of pointed architecture. Yet the builders of Siena have shown what a glorious element of beauty might have been added to our Northern cathedrals, had the idea of infinity which our ancestors expressed by long continuous lines, by complexities of interwoven aisles, and by multitudinous aspiring pinnacles, been carried out into vast spaces of aërial cupolas, completing and embracing and covering the whole like heaven. The Duomo, as it now stands, forms only part of a vast original design. On entering we are amazed to hear that this church, which looks so large, from the beauty of its proportions, the intricacy of its ornaments, and the interlacing of its columns, is but the transept of the old building lengthened a little, and surmounted by a cupola and campanile. Yet such is the fact. Soon after its commencement a plague swept over Italy, nearly depopulated Siena, and reduced the town to penury for want of men. The Cathedral, which, had it been accomplished, would have surpassed all Gothic churches south of the Alps, remained a ruin. A fragment of the nave still stands, enabling us to judge of its extent. The eastern wall joins what was to have been the transept, measuring the mighty space which would have been enclosed by marble vaults and columns delicately wrought. The sculpture on the eastern door shows with what magnificence the Sienese designed to ornament this portion of their temple; while the southern façade rears itself aloft above the town, like those high arches which testify to the past splendour of Glastonbury Abbey; but the sun streams through the broken windows, and the walls are encumbered with hovels and stables and the refuse of surrounding streets. One most remarkable feature of the internal decoration is a line of heads of the Popes carried all round the church above the lower arches. Larger than life, white solemn faces, they lean, each from his separate niche, crowned with the triple tiara, and labelled with the name he bore. Their accumulated majesty brings the whole past history of the Church into the presence of its living members. A bishop walking up the nave of Siena must feel as a Roman felt among the waxen images of ancestors renowned in council or in war. Of course these portraits are imaginary for the most part; but the artists have contrived to vary their features and expression with great skill.

Not less peculiar to Siena is the pavement of the Cathedral. It is inlaid with a kind of *tarsia* work in stone, not unlike that which Baron Triqueti used in his "Marmor Homericum" — less elaborately decorative, but even more artistic and subordinate to architectural effect than the baron's mosaic. Some of these compositions are as old as the cathedral; others are the work of Beccafumi and his scholars. They represent, in the liberal spirit of mediæval Christianity, the history of the Church before the Incarnation. Hermes Trismegistus and the Sibyls meet us at the doorway: in the body of the church we find the mighty deeds of the old Jewish heroes — of Moses and Samson and Joshua and Judith. Independently of the artistic beauty of the designs, of the skill with which men and horses are drawn in the most difficult attitudes, of the dignity of some single figures, and of the vigour and simplicity of the larger compositions, a special interest attaches to this pavement in connection with the twelfth canto of the "Purgatorio." Did Dante ever tread these stones and meditate upon their sculptured histories? That is what we cannot say; but we read how he journeyed through the plain of Purgatory with eyes intent upon its storied floor, how "morti i morti, e i vivi parean vivi," how he saw "Nimrod at the foot of his great work, confounded, gazing at the people who were proud with him." The strong and simple outlines of the pavement correspond to the few words of the poet. Bending over these pictures and trying to learn their lesson, with the thought of Dante in our mind, the tones of an organ, singularly sweet and mellow, fall upon our ears, and we remember how he heard the *Te Deum* sung within the gateway of repentance.

Sketches in Italy and Greece (London, 1874).

THE TOWN HALL OF LOUVAIN.

GRANT ALLEN.

LOUVAIN is in a certain sense the mother city of Brussels. Standing on its own little navigable river, the Dyle, it was, till the end of the Fourteenth Century, the capital of the Counts and of the Duchy of Brabant. It had a large population of weavers, engaged in the cloth trade. Here, as elsewhere, the weavers formed the chief bulwark of freedom in the population. In 1378, however, after a popular rising, Duke Wenseslaus besieged and conquered the city; and the tyrannical sway of the nobles, whom he re-introduced, aided by the rise of Ghent, or later, of Antwerp, drove away trade from the city. Many of the weavers emigrated to Holland and England, where they helped to establish the woollen industry. . . .

As you emerge from the station, you come upon a small Place, adorned with a statue (by Geefs) of Sylvain van de Weyer, a revolutionary of 1830, and long Belgian minister to England. Take the long straight street up which the statue looks. This leads direct to the Grand' Place, the centre of the town, whence the chief streets radiate in every direction, the ground-plan recalling that of a Roman city.

THE TOWN HALL OF LOUVAIN.

The principal building in the Grand' Place is the Hôtel de Ville, standing out with three sides visible from the Place, and probably the finest civic building in Belgium. It is of very florid late-Gothic architecture, between 1448 and 1463. Begin first with the left façade, exhibiting three main storeys, with handsome Gothic windows. Above come a gallery, and then a gable-end, flanked by octagonal turrets, and bearing a similar turret on its summit. In this centre of the gable is a little projecting balcony of the kind so common on Belgic civic buildings. The architecture of the niches and turrets is of very fine florid Gothic, in better taste than that at Ghent of nearly the same period. The statues which fill the niches are modern. Those of the first storey represent personages of importance in the local history of the city; those of the second, the various mediæval guilds or trades; those of the third, the Counts of Louvain and Dukes of Brabant of all ages. The bosses or corbels which support the statues, are carved with scriptural scenes in high relief. I give the subjects of a few (beginning Left): the reader must decipher the remainder for himself. The Court of Heaven: The Fall of the Angels into the visible Jaws of Hell: Adam and Eve in the Garden: The Expulsion from Paradise: The Death of Abel, with quaint rabbits escaping: The Drunkenness of Noah: Abraham and Lot: etc.

The main façade has an entrance staircase, and two portals in the centre, above which are figures of St. Peter (Left) and Our Lady and Child (Right), the former in compliment to the patron of the church opposite. This façade has three storeys, decorated with Gothic windows, and capped by a gallery parapet, above which rises the high-pitched roof, broken by several quaint small windows. At either end are the turrets of the gable, with steps to ascend them. The rows of statues represent as before (in four tiers), persons of local distinction, mediæval guilds and the Princes who have ruled Brabant and Louvain. Here again the sculptures beneath the bosses should be closely inspected. Among the most conspicuous are the Golden Calf, the Institution of Sacrifices in the Tabernacle, Balaam's Ass, Susannah and the Elders, etc.

The gable-end to the Right, ill seen from the narrow street, resembles in its features the one opposite it, but this façade is even finer than the others.

The best general view is obtained from the door of St. Pierre, or near either corner of the Place directly opposite.

Cities of Belgium (London, 1897).

THE CATHEDRAL OF SEVILLE.

EDMONDO DE AMICIS.

THE Cathedral of Seville is isolated in the centre of a large square, yet its grandeur may be measured by a single glance. I immediately thought of the famous phrase in the decree uttered by the Chapter of the primitive church on July 8, 1401, regarding the building of the new Cathedral: " Let us build a monument which shall cause posterity to think we must have been mad." These reverend canons did not fail in their intention. But to fully appreciate this we must enter. The exterior of the Cathedral is imposing and magnificent; but less so than the interior. There is no façade: a high wall encloses the building like a fortress. It is useless to turn and gaze upon it, for you will never succeed in impressing a single outline upon your mind, which, like the introduction to a book, will give you a clear idea of the work; you admire and you exclaim more than once: " It is immense! " but you are not satisfied; and you hasten to enter the church, hoping that you may receive there a more complete sentiment of admiration.

On entering you are stunned, you feel as if you are lost in an abyss; and for several moments you can only let your glance wander over these immense curves in this immense space to assure yourself that your eyes and your imagination are not deceiving you. Then you approach a column, measure it, and contemplate the others from a distance: they are as large as towers and yet they seem so slender that you tremble to think they support the edifice. With a rapid glance you look at them from pavement to ceiling and it seems as if you could almost count the moments that it takes the eye to rise with them. There are five naves, each one of which might constitute a church. In the central one another cathedral could easily lift its high head surmounted by a cupola and bell-tower. Altogether there are sixty-eight vaults, so bold that it seems to you they expand and rise very slowly while you are looking at them. Everything in this Cathedral is enormous. The principal altar, placed in the centre of the great nave, is so high that it almost touches the vaulted ceiling, and seems to be an altar constructed for giant priests to whose knees only would ordinary altars reach; the paschal candle seems like the mast of a ship; and the bronze candlestick which holds it, is a museum of sculpture and carving which would in itself repay a day's visit. The chapels are worthy of the church, for in them are lavished the *chefs d'œuvre* of sixty-seven sculptors and thirty-eight painters. Montanes, Zurbaran, Murillo, Valdes, Herrera, Boldan, Roelas, and Campaña have left there a thousand immortal traces of their hands. St. Ferdinand's Chapel, containing the sepulchres of this king and of his wife Beatrice, of Alphonso the Wise, the celebrated minister Florida Blanca, and other illustrious personages, is one of the richest and most beautiful. The body of King Ferdinand, who delivered Seville from the dominion

THE CATHEDRAL OF SEVILLE.

of the Arabs, clothed in his military dress, with the crown and the royal mantle, reposes in a crystal casket covered with a veil. On one side is the sword which he carried on the day of his entrance into Seville; and on the other his staff, the symbol of command. In this same chapel a little ivory wand which the king carried to the wars, and other relics of great value are preserved. In the other chapels there are large marble altars, Gothic tombs and statues in stone, in wood and silver, enclosed in large caskets of silver with their bodies and hands covered with diamonds and rubies; and some marvellous pictures, which, unfortunately, the feeble light, falling from the high windows, does not illuminate sufficiently to let the admirer see their entire beauty.

But after a detailed examination of these chapels, paintings, and sculptures, you always return to admire the Cathedral's grand, and, if I may be allowed to say it, formidable aspect. After having glanced towards those giddy heights, the eye and mind are fatigued by the effort. And the abundant images correspond to the grandeur of the basilica; immense angels and monstrous heads of cherubim with wings as large as the sails of a ship and enormous floating mantles of blue. The impression that this Cathedral produces is entirely religious, but it is not sad; it creates a feeling which carries the mind into the infinite space and silence where Leopardi's thoughts were plunged; it creates a sentiment full of desire and boldness; it produces that shiver which is experienced at the brink of a precipice, — that distress and confusion of great thoughts, that divine terror of the infinite. . . .

It is needless to speak of the Feasts of Holy Week: they are famous throughout the world, and people from all parts of Europe still flock to them.

But the most curious privilege of the Cathedral of Seville is the dance *de los seises*, which is performed every evening at twilight for eight consecutive days after the Feast of Corpus Domini.

As I found myself in Seville at this time I went to see it. From what I had heard I expected a scandalous pasquinade, and I entered the church quite ready to be indignant at the profanation of a holy place. The church was dark; only the large altar was illuminated, and a crowd of women kneeled before it. Several priests were sitting to the right and left of the altar. At a signal given by one of the priests, sweet music from violins broke the profound silence of the church, and two rows of children moved forward in the steps of a *contre-danse*, and began to separate, interlace, break away, and again unite with a thousand graceful turnings; then everybody joined in a melodious and charming hymn which resounded in the vast Cathedral like a choir of angels' voices; and in the next moment they began to accompany their dance and song with castanets. No religious ceremony ever touched me like this. It is out of the question to describe the effect produced by these little voices under the immense vaults, these little creatures at the foot of this enormous altar, this modest and almost humble dance, this antique costume, this kneeling multitude, and the surrounding darkness. I went out of the church with as serene a soul as if I had been praying. . . .

THE CATHEDRAL OF SEVILLE.

The famous Giralda of the Cathedral of Seville is an ancient Arabian tower, constructed, according to tradition, in the year one thousand, on the plan of the architect Huevar, the inventor of algebra; it was modified in its upper part after the expulsion of the Moors and converted into a Christian bell-tower, yet it has always preserved its Arabian air and has always been prouder of the vanished standard of the conquered race than the Cross which the victors have placed upon it. This monument produces a novel sensation: it makes you smile: it is as enormous and imposing as an Egyptian pyramid and at the same time as gay and graceful as a garden kiosk. It is a square brick tower of a beautiful rose-colour, bare up to a certain height, and then ornamented all the way up by little Moorish twin-windows displayed here and there at haphazard and provided with little balconies which produce a very pretty effect. Upon the story, where formerly a roof of various colours rested, surmounted by an iron shaft which supported four enormous golden balls, the Christian bell-tower rises in three stories; the first containing the bells, the second enclosed by a balustrade, and the third forming a kind of cupola on which turns, like a weather-vane, a statue of gilt bronze representing Faith, holding a palm in one hand and in the other a standard visible at a long distance from Seville, and which, when touched by the sun, glitters like an enormous ruby imbedded in the crown of a Titan king who rules the entire valley of Andalusia with his glance.

La Spagna (Florence, 1873).

WINDSOR CASTLE.

WILLIAM HEPWORTH DIXON.

A STEEP chalk bluff, starting from a river margin with the heave and dominance of a tidal wave is Castle Hill, now crowned and mantled by the Norman keep, the royal house, the chapel of St. George, and the depending gardens, terraces, and slopes.

Trees beard the slope and tuft the ridge. Live waters curl and murmur at the base. In front, low-lying meadows curtsey to the royal hill. Outward, on the flanks, to east and west, run screens of elm and oak, of beech and poplar; here, sinking into clough and dell: there mounting up to smiling sward and wooded knoll. Far in the rear lie forest glades, with walks and chases, losing themselves in distant heath and holt. By the edges of dripping wells, which bear the names of queen and saint, stand aged oaks, hoary with time and rich in legend: patriarchs of the forest, wedded to the readers of all nations by immortal verse.

A gentle eminence, the Castle Hill springs from the bosom of a typical English scene.

Crowning a verdant ridge, the Norman keep looks northward on a wide and wooded level, stretching over

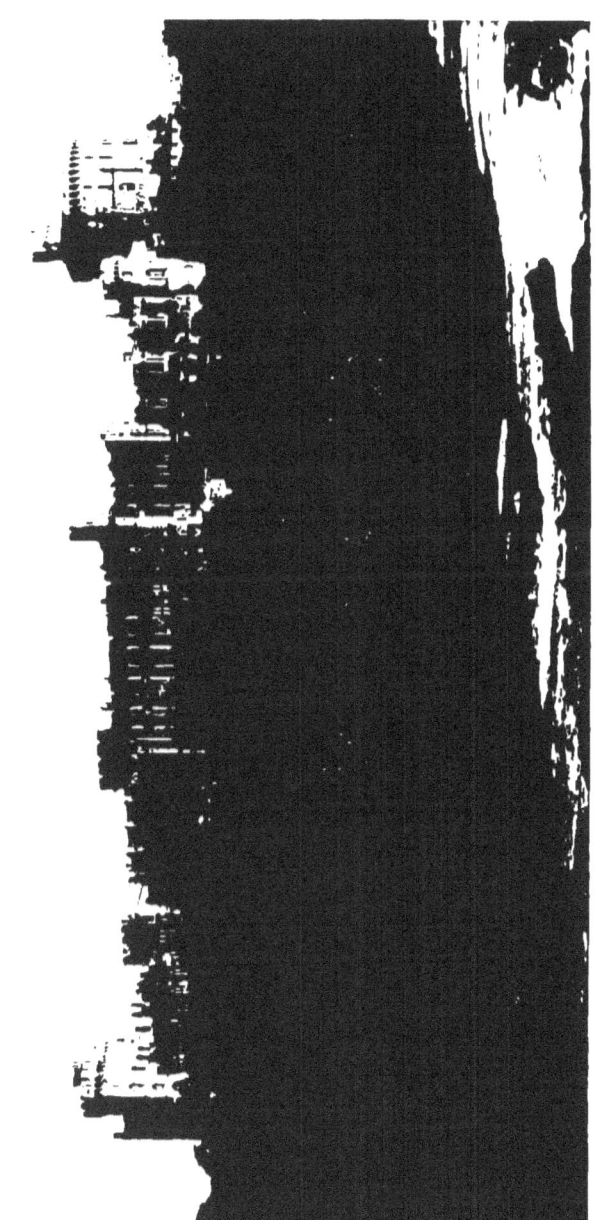

WINDSOR CASTLE.

many shires, tawny with corn and rye, bright with abundant pasture, and the red and white of kine and sheep, while here again the landscape is embrowned with groves and parks. The stream curves softly past your feet, unconscious of the capital, unruffled by the tide. Beyond the river bank lie open meadows, out of which start up the pinnacles of Eton College, the Plantagenet school and cloister, whence for twenty-one reigns the youth of England have been trained for court and camp, the staff, the mitre, and the marble chair. Free from these pinnacles, the eye is caught by darksome clump, and antique tower, and distant height; each darksome clump a haunted wood, each antique tower an elegy in stone, each distant height a storied and romantic hill. That darksome clump is Burnham wood; this antique tower is Stoke; yon distant heights are Hampstead Heath and Richmond Park. Nearer to the eye stand Farnham Royal, Upton park, and Langley Marsh; the homes of famous men, the sceneries of great events.

Swing round to east or south, and still the eye falls lovingly on household spots. There, beyond Datchet ferry, stood the lodge of Edward the Confessor, and around his dwelling spread the hunting-grounds of Alfred and other Saxon kings. Yon islet in the Thames is Magna Charta Island; while the open field, below the reach, is Runnymede.

The heights all round the Norman keep are capped with fame — one hallowed by a saint, another crowned with song. Here is St. Leonard's hill; and yonder, rising over Runnymede, is Cooper's hill. Saints, poets, kings and queens, divide the royalties in almost equal shares. St. George is hardly more a presence in the place than Chaucer and Shakespeare. Sanctity and poetry are everywhere about us; in the royal chapel, by the river-side, among the forest oaks, and even in the tavern yards. Chaucer and Shakespeare have a part in Windsor hardly less pronounced than that of Edward and Victoria, that of St. Leonard and St. George.

Windsor was river born and river named. The stream is winding, serpentine; the bank by which it rolls was called the "winding shore." The fact, common to all countries, gives a name which is common to all languages. Snakes, dragons, serpentines, are names of winding rivers in every latitude. There is a Snake river in Utah, another Snake river in Oregon; there is a Drach river in France, another Drach river in Switzerland. The straits between Paria and Trinidad is the Dragon's Mouth; the outfall of Lake Chiriqui is also the Dragon's Mouth. In the Morea, in Majorca, in Ionia, there are Dragons. There is a Serpent islet off the Danube, and a Serpentaria in Sardinia. We have a modern Serpentine in Hyde Park!

Windsor, born of that winding shore-line, found in after days her natural patron in St. George.

With one exception, all the Castle builders were men and women of English birth and English taste; Henry Beauclerc, Henry of Winchester, Edward of Windsor, Edward of York, Henry the Seventh, Queen Elizabeth, George the Fourth, and Queen Victoria; and these English builders stamped an English spirit on every portion of the pile — excepting on the Norman keep.

Ages before the Normans came to Windsor, a Saxon hunting-lodge had been erected in the forest; not on the bleak and isolated crest of hill, but by the river margin, on "the winding shore." This Saxon lodge lay hidden in the depths of ancient woods, away from any public road and bridge. The King's highway ran north, the Devil's Causeway to the south. The nearest ford was three miles up the stream, the nearest bridge was five miles down the stream. A bridle-path, such as may still be found in Spain or Sicily, led to that Saxon lodge; but here this path was lost among the ferns and underwoods. No track led on to other places. Free to the chase, yet severed from the world, that hunting-lodge was like a nest. Old oaks and elms grew round about as screens. Deep glades, with here and there a bubbling spring, extended league on league, as far as Chertsey bridge and Guildford down. This forest knew no tenants save the hart and boar, the chough and crow. An air of privacy, and poetry, and romance, hung about this ancient forest lodge.

Seeds of much legendary lore had been already sown. A builder of that Saxon lodge had been imagined in a mythical king — Arthur of the Round Table, Arthur of the blameless life — a legend which endures at Windsor to the present day. There, Godwin, sitting at the king's board, had met his death, choked with the lie in his wicked throat. There, Edward the Confessor had lisped his prayers, and cured the halt and blind. There, too, the Saxon princes, Tosti and Harold, were supposed to have fought in the king's presence, lugging out each other's locks, and hurling each other to the ground. Of later growth were other legends; ranging from the romance of the Fitz-Warines, through the Romaunt of the Rose, down to the rhyme of King Edward and the Shepherd, the mystery of Herne the Hunter, and the humours of the Merry Wives.

William the Conqueror preserved his Saxon hunting-lodge by the river-side, but built his Norman keep on the Castle Hill — perhaps on the ruins of a Celtic camp, certainly round the edges of a deep and copious well.

Henry Beauclerc removed his dwelling from the river margin to the crest of hill, building the First King's House. This pile extended from the Devil's tower to the Watch tower, now renamed Victoria tower. A part of Beauclerc's edifice remains in massive walls of the Devil's tower, and a cutting through the chalk, sustained by Norman masonry, leading from a shaft under the Queen's apartment to the southern ditch.

Henry of Winchester, a man of higher genius as an architect, built the Second King's House, sweeping into his lines the lower ground, which he covered by walls and towers, including Winchester tower, and the whole curtain by Curfew tower and Salisbury tower, round to the Lieutenant's lodgings, now called Henry the Third's tower. The Second King's House, long since ruined and removed, stood on the site of the present cloisters. Much of Henry of Winchester's work remains; in fact, the circuit of the lower ward is mainly his, both walls and towers, from the Devil's tower, touching the upper ward, round to Curfew tower in the north-west angle of the lower ward.

Edward of Windsor built the Third King's House,

fronting towards the north, and gave the upper ward its final shape. On introducing a new patron saint to Windsor, Edward removed his own lodging, and renounced the lower ward entirely to the service of St. George. First came the chapel of St. George; next came the College of St. George; then came the Canons of St. George; lastly, came the Poor Knights of St. George. The central ground was given up to the chapel, and the adjoining quarter to the college. From Curfew tower to the Lieutenant's lodgings, all the ground was consecrated to the saint. The first tower, reckoning from the south, became Garter House, the second Chancellor's tower, the third Garter tower, while the land within the walls was covered by residences for the military knights. An area equal to the upper baily was surrendered to his patron saint.

Edward of York rebuilt St. George's Chapel on a larger scale; for Edward of York had heavy sins to weigh him down, and pressing need for saintly help.

Henry of Richmond roofed that chapel, built a "new tower" in the King's House, and made a fair causeway from Windsor to London — the first road ever made between the castle and the capital.

Queen Elizabeth built the gallery which bears her name, and raised the great terraces above the Thames. Before her time the scarp was rough and steep: she built this solid wall, and laid this level road.

George the Fourth raised the Norman keep in height, flanked the park entrance with another tower, opened St. George's gate, buttressed the North-east tower, and called his new edifice Brunswick ·tower.

Like Queen Elizabeth, Queen Victoria has devoted her attention rather to the slopes and gardens than the structure; but the few additions of her reign have been effected with a proper reverence for the ancient pile. Her Majesty has cleared off slum and tenement from the slopes, and opened the southern terrace, just as Elizabeth opened the northern terrace. Work has been done in cloister and chapel. As Henry of Richmond made a road from Windsor to London, Queen Victoria has brought two railways to her castle gates.

Since the days of Edward of Windsor the Castle hill has kept the triple character — upper ward, middle ward, and lower ward — baily of the King, baily of the keep, and baily of St. George — the residence of our sovereign, the symbol of our power, the altar of our saint.

Royal Windsor (London, 1879).

THE CATHEDRAL OF COLOGNE.

ERNEST BRETON.

WE are now in the middle of the Tenth Century and in the city of Cologne; for several hours a man has been sitting upon the banks of a river, flowing majestically at the base of those ramparts which sixty years ago were erected by Philip von Heinsberg, and for several hours his thoughtful brow has not been lifted. This man was the first master-workman of his time; three centuries later he was called the prince of architects. The Archbishop of Cologne had said to him: "Master, we must build a cathedral here which will surpass all the buildings of the world in grandeur and magnificence." The artist replied: "I will do it;" and now he was pondering over ways of accomplishing his promise about which he was frightened. At this moment he was trying to think out a marvellous plan which would give lustre to his country and immortalize his name; but nothing came into his mind worthy of the prodigy he was trying to conceive and could not create.

An unknown old man now approached and sat beside him, regarding him with a mocking air, as if he rejoiced in his perplexity and despair; every now and then he gave a little, dry cough, and when he had attracted the attention of the artist, he rapidly traced on the sand with a ring some lines which he immediately effaced. These lines formed exactly that plan which always escaped the artist and whose fugitive image he could not seize.

"You would like to have this plan?" asked the old man.

"I would give all I possess for it."

"I exact nothing. The building that you construct will be the envy and the eternal despair of all your successors, the admiration of centuries to come, and your brilliant and celebrated name will be known to the most remote generations. Your life will be long; you will pass it in glory, wealth, and pleasure. For all that I only ask for your soul when your life draws to its close."

"*Vade retro Satanas!*" cried the agitated artist. "Better the nothingness of oblivion than eternal damnation."

"Patience," said Satan, "reflect: we shall see," and he vanished. The master-workman returned to his humble dwelling, sadder and more dreamful than when he left it; he could not close his eyes all night. Glory, wealth, and pleasure for many long years, and all that for one word! In vain he tried to shake himself free from the fatal temptation; at every moment, at every step he again saw the tempter showing him his transitory plan; he succumbed.

"To-morrow, at midnight," said Satan, "go to that spot and I will bring you the plan and the pact that you must sign."

The artist returned to the city, divided between remorse and dreams of pride and ambition. Remorse conquered, and before the appointed hour he had told everything to his confessor. "It will be a master-stroke," said the latter, "to deceive Satan himself and snatch the famous plan from him without paying the price of your soul," and he sketched out the line of conduct that he should follow.

At the appointed hour the two parties stood face to face. "Here," said Satan, "are the plan and pact; take it and sign it." Quick as lightning the master-workman snatched the plan with one hand and with the other he brandished a piece of the True Cross, which the wily confessor had given to him. "I am vanquished," cried Satan, "but you will reap little benefit through your treachery. Your name will be unknown and your work will never be completed."

Such is the legend of the Cathedral of Cologne. I have told it here so that the admiration of the Middle Ages for this plan, which could not be considered the work of any human genius, may be measured, and for six centuries the sinister prediction of Satan has held good.[1]

At the north-east end of the elevation occupied by the ancient *Colonia Agrippina*, in the spot where the choir of the Cathedral raises its magnificent pinnacles, there existed in very remote ages a Roman *Castellum*. At a later period this was replaced by a palace of the French kings, which Charlemagne gave to his chancellor and confessor Hildebold. . . .

The Cathedral of Cologne was one of the most ancient seats of Christianity in Germany; it contained in its jurisdiction the capital of Charlemagne's Empire, the city where the Emperors were crowned. In the Twelfth Century, Frederick Barbarossa enriched it with one of those sacred

---

[1] The spires of the Cathedral were finished in 1880, and the completion of the edifice was celebrated before the Emperor William I. on October 15th of that year. — E. S.

treasures which in a time of faith attracted entire populations and gave birth to the gigantic enterprises which seem so incredible in our positive and sceptical age. All eyes were turned to the Holy Land, and the pilgrims of Germany, as well as of other countries, before undertaking this perilous voyage came by the thousands to the tomb of the Magi, to pray to God that the same star which guided the Three Wise Men to Christ's cradle might lead them to his tomb. The celebrity and wealth of the Cologne Cathedral was greatly due to the custom of the Emperors visiting it after their coronation. Thus, from the moment it was in possession of the sacred relics, everything combined to augment its splendour; princes, emperors, and people of all classes were eager to add to its treasures. Therefore, it was only a natural consequence to erect on the site of the old Cathedral of St. Peter a building more vast and magnificent, and which would accord better with its important destiny. The Archbishop Angebert, Count of Altena and Berg, upon whom Frederick II. conferred the dignity of vicar of the empire, conceived the first idea; but at about the age of forty he was assassinated by his cousin, the Count of Ysembourg, in 1225, and the enterprise was abandoned. Finally, a great fire devoured the Cathedral in 1248 and its immediate reconstruction was indispensable. . . .

Everyone knows that almost all churches of the pointed arch which occupied several centuries in building show the special mark of the periods in which their various additions were constructed; this is not the case with the Cathedral of Cologne, which is peculiar in the fact that its foundations and its additions were all constructed on

THE CATHEDRAL OF COLOGNE.

one and the same plan, which preserves the original design, and therefore it presents a rare and admirable unity.

On the side of the Rhine, or rather on the Margreten, between the Trankgass and the Domhof, the choir of the basilica offers the most imposing effect. It is only from this side that the edifice seems to have an end. The end of the roof, edged in all its length by an open-worked ridge, is surmounted by an enormous cross, nine metres high, finished with a fleur-de-lis at each extremity. This cross, weighing 694 kil., was only placed there on August 3, 1825, but it was long in existence, having been, it is said, presented to the church by Marie de' Medici. In the centre of the transept there rose a bell-tower, 65 metres high, which was demolished in 1812. The plan carries a superb *flèche* of stone, open-worked like the spires of the façade, and about 100 metres high.

Fifteen flying-buttresses on each side proceed from the central window and sustain the choir, leaning against the buttresses and surmounted by elegant pyramids. Each of these pyramids carries twelve niches destined to hold angels two metres high, many of which have been restored lately by Wilhelm Imhoff. The upper part of the flying-buttresses, at the point where they meet the balustrade of the roof, is crowned by another and more simple pyramid. Finally, between these flying-buttresses in the upper part of the wall of the choir, magnificent mullioned windows are disclosed. The entire edifice is covered with gargoyles, each more bizarre than the other. . . .

Entering the cathedral by the door at the foot of the

northern tower, you find yourself in the double-lower northern nave. The first bays do not contain altars, but their windows reveal magnificent panes, of the beginning of the Sixteenth Century. The Archbishop Herman von Hesse, the Chapter, the City, and many noble families united to have them painted by the most distinguished artists of the period, which was the apogee of Art in Germany; and therefore here are many of the most admirable *chefs d'œuvre* of glass-painting. . . .

The Chapel of the Kings is almost entirely occupied by the building erected in 1688 and ornamented by Ionic pilasters of marble, and which, shut in by grilles and many locks, contains the marvellous reliquary in which are preserved the relics of the Three Magi. According to Buttler, these relics were found by Saint Helena, mother of Constantine, during her pilgrimage to the Holy Land; she carried them carefully to Constantinople. Soon afterwards the Archbishop Eustorge, to whom the Emperor had presented them, brought them to Milan, where they were deposited in the church subsequently consecrated to the same Eustorge, who was canonized. When Frederick Barbarossa invaded the town in 1163, Reinald von Dassile, Archbishop of Cologne, received them as a reward for the services which he had rendered to the Emperor during the siege. At the same time Reinald obtained several relics of the Maccabees, of the Saints Apollinaris, Felix, Nabor, Gregory di Spoletto, etc. He, himself, accompanied this treasure, which crossed Switzerland in triumph, descended the Rhine to Remagen, where he gave it to Philip of Heinsberg, then provost of the Chapter.

On July 23, 1164, the relics were deposited in the ancient cathedral, from which they were transferred to the new one; they were guarded there simply by an iron grille until the Archbishop Maximilian Heinrich constructed the building which encloses them to-day, upon whose pediment you see sculptured in marble, by Michael Van der Voorst of Antwerp, the Adoration of the Magi, Saint Felix, Saint Nabor, and two female figures guarding the arms of the Metropolitan Chapter, in the midst of which figure those of the Archbishop Maximilian Heinrich. On the frieze you read the inscription: "*Tribus ab oriente regibus devicto in agnitione veri numinis capitulum metropol. erexit.*" Above the grilled window, which is opened during grand ceremonies to permit the people to see the reliquary, is written:

"*Corpora sanctorum recubant hic terna magorum;
Ax his sublatum nihil est alibive locatum.*"

Finally, above the reliquary placed to the right and left between the columns one reads: "*Et apertis thesauris suis obtulerunt munera.*"

In 1794 the relics were carried to the treasury of Arnsberg, then to Prague, where the three crowns of diamonds were sold, and finally to Frankfort-on-the-Main. When they were brought back in 1804, the reliquary was repaired and put in its old place. This reliquary, a *chef d'œuvre* of Twelfth Century *orfèvrerie*, is of gilded copper with the exception of the front, which is of pure gold; its form is that of a tomb; its length 1 m. 85, its breadth 1 m. at the base, its height 1 m. 50; on the side turned to the west you see represented the Adoration of the Magi and the baptism of Jesus Christ. Above the sculpture is a kind of lid which may be raised, permitting you to see the skulls of the Three Kings ornamented with golden crowns garnished with Bohemian stones,—a kind of garnet; in the pediment is the image of the Divine Judge sitting between two angels who hold the attributes of the Passion; the two busts above represent Gabriel and Raphael; and, finally, an enormous topaz occupies the summit of the pediment. The right side of the reliquary is ornamented with images of the prophets, Moses, Jonah, David, Daniel, Amos, and Obadiah. The apostles Paul, Philip, Simon, Thomas, and Judas Thaddeus are placed in six niches above. In the left side you see the prophets Ezekiel, Jeremiah, Nahum, Solomon, Joel, and Aaron, and the apostles Bartholomew, Matthew, John the Lesser, Andrew, Peter, and John the Great. The back of the monument presents the flagellation of Jesus Christ, the Virgin Mary, Saint John, the Saviour on the Cross, Saint Felix, Saint Nabor, the Archbishop Reinald and eight busts of angels. The monument is surmounted by an open-work ridge of copper lace. This magnificent reliquary is covered with more than 1,500 precious stones and antique cameos representing subjects which are not exactly Christian such as the apotheosis of an Emperor, two heads of Medusa, a head of Hercules, one of Alexander, etc. Behind the reliquary is a bas-relief in marble 1 m. 33 in height and 1 m. 40 in length, representing the solemn removal of the relics. The bas-reliefs of richly-gilt bronze, placed below the windows which occupy the back of the chapel, represent the Adoration of the Magi: these were the gift of Jacques de Croy, Duke of Cambrai in 1516. This window is ornamented with beautiful panes of the Thirteenth Century, representing various subjects of sacred history.

Jules Gaillhabaud, *Monuments anciens et modernes* (Paris, 1865).

THE PALACE OF VERSAILLES.

AUGUSTUS J. C. HARE.

THE first palace of Versailles was a hunting-lodge built by Louis XIII. at the angle of the present Rue de la Pompe and Avenue de Saint-Cloud. This he afterwards found too small, and built, in 1627, a moated castle, on the site of a windmill in which he had once taken shelter for the night. The buildings of this *château* still exist, respected, as the home of his father, in all the alterations of Louis XIV., and they form the centre of the present place. In 1632 Louis XIII. became seigneur of Versailles by purchase from François de Gondi, Archbishop of Paris.

The immense works which Louis XIV. undertook here, and which were carried out by the architect Mansart, were begun in 1661, and in 1682 the residence of the Court was definitely fixed at Versailles, connected by new roads with the capital. Colbert made a last effort to keep the king at Paris, and to divert the immense sums which were being swallowed up in Versailles to the completion of the Louvre. The very dulness of the site of Versailles, leaving everything to be created, was an extra attraction in the eyes of Louis XIV. The great difficulty to be contended with in the creation of Versailles was the want of water,

THE PALACE OF VERSAILLES.

and this, after various other attempts had failed, it was hoped to overcome by a canal which was to bring the waters of the Eure to the royal residence. In 1681 22,000 soldiers and 6,000 horses were employed in this work, with such results of sickness that the troops encamped at Maintenon, where the chief part of the work was, became unfit for any service. On October 12, 1678, Mme. de Sévigné writes to Bussy-Rabutin: —

"The king wishes to go to Versailles; but it seems that God does not, to judge from the difficulty of getting the buildings ready for occupation and the dreadful mortality of the workmen who are carried away every night in waggons filled with the dead. This terrible occurrence is kept secret so as not to create alarm and not to decry the air of this *favori sans mérite.* You know this *bon mot* of Versailles."

Nine millions were expended in the Aqueduct or Maintenon, of which the ruins are still to be seen, then it was interrupted by the war of 1688, and the works were never continued. Instead, all the water of the pools and the snow falling on the plain between Rambouillet and Versailles was brought to the latter by a series of subterranean watercourses.

No difficulties, however — not even pestilence, or the ruin of the country by the enormous cost — were allowed to interfere with " *les plaisirs du roi.*" The palace rose, and its gigantic gardens were peopled with statues, its woods with villages.

Under Louis XV. Versailles was chiefly remarkable as being the scene of the extravagance of Mme. de Pompadour and the turpitude of Mme. du Barry. Mme. Campan has described for us the life, the very dull life, there of "Mesdames," daughters of the king. Yet, till the great Revolution, since which it has been only a shadow of its former self, the town of Versailles drew all its life from the *château*.

Approaching from the town on entering the grille of the palace from the *Place d'Armes* we find ourselves in the vast *Cour des Statues* — "*solennelle et morne*." In the centre is an equestrian statue of Louis XIV. by Petitot and Cartellier. Many of the surrounding statues were brought from the *Pont de la Concorde* at Paris. Two projecting wings shut in the *Cour Royale*, and separate it from the *Cour des Princes* on the left, and the *Cour de la Chapelle* on the right. Beyond the *Cour Royale*, deeply recessed amongst later buildings is the court called, from its pavement, the *Cour de Marbre*, surrounded by the little old red *château* of Louis XIII.

The *Cour de Marbre* was sometimes used as a theatre under Louis XIV., and the opera of *Alcestis* was given there. It has a peculiar interest, for no stranger can look up at the balcony of the first floor without recalling Marie Antoinette presenting herself there, alone, to the fury of the people, October 6, 1789.

The palace of Versailles has never been inhabited by royalty since the chain of carriages drove into this court on October 6, to convey Louis XVI. and his family to Paris.

From the *Grande Cour* the gardens may be reached by passages either from the *Cour des Princes* on the left, or from the *Cour de la Chapelle* on the right. This palace has had three chapels in turn. The first, built by Louis XIII., was close to the marble staircase. The second, built by Louis XIV., occupied the site of the existing *Salon d'Hercule*. The present chapel, built 1699–1710, is the last work of Mansart.

Here we may think of Bossuet, thundering before Louis XIV., "*les royaumes meurent, sire, comme les rois,*" and of the words of Massillon, "*Si Jésus-Christ paraissait dans ce temple, au milieu de cette assemblée, la plus auguste de l'univers, pour vous juger, pour faire le terrible discernement,*" etc. Here we may imagine Louis XIV. daily assisting at the Mass, and his courtiers, especially the ladies, attending also to flatter him, but gladly escaping, if they thought he would not be there. . . .

All the furniture of Versailles was sold during the Revolution (in 1793), and, though a few pieces have been recovered, the palace is for the most part unfurnished, and little more than a vast picture-gallery. From the ante-chamber of the chapel open two galleries on the ground floor of the north wing. One is the *Galerie des Sculptures;* the other, divided by different rooms looking on the garden, is the *Galerie de l'Histoire de France.* The first six rooms of the latter formed the apartments of the Duc de Maine, the much indulged son of Louis XIV. and Mme. de Maintenon.

At the end of the gallery (but only to be entered now from the Rue des Réservoirs) is the *Salle de l'Opéra*. In spite of the passion of Louis XIV. for dramatic representations, no theatre was built in the palace during his reign. Some of the plays of Molière and Racine were acted in improvised theatres in the park; others, in the halls of the palace, without scenery or costumes; the *Athalie* of Racine, before the King and Mme. de Maintenon, by the young ladies of Saint-Cyr. The present Opera House was begun by Jacques Ange-Gabriel under Louis XV. for Mme. de Pompadour and finished for Mme. du Barry.

The Opera House was inaugurated on the marriage of the Dauphin with Marie Antoinette, and nineteen years after was the scene of that banquet, the incidents of which were represented in a manner so fatal to the monarchy, given by the body-guard of the king to the officers of a regiment which had arrived from Flanders. . . .

The garden front of the palace has not yet experienced the soothing power of age: it looks almost new; two hundred years hence it will be magnificent. The long lines of the building, with its two vast wings, are only broken by the top of the chapel rising above the wing on the left.

The rich masses of green formed by the clipped yews at the sides of the gardens have the happiest effect, and contrast vividly with the dark background of chestnuts, of which the lower part is trimmed, but the upper falls in masses of heavy shade, above the brilliant gardens with their population of statues. These grounds are the masterpiece of Lenôtre, and of geometrical gardening, decorated with vases, fountains, and orange-trees. Lovers of the natural may find great fault with these artificial gardens, but there is much that is grandiose and noble in them; and, as Voltaire says: "*Il est plus facile de critiquer Versailles que de le refaire.*"

The gardens need the enlivenment of the figures, for which they were intended as a background, in the gay Courts of Louis XIV. and Louis XV. as represented in the pictures of Watteau; but the Memoirs of the time enable us to repeople them with a thousand forms which have long been dust, centring around the great king, "*Se promenant dans ses jardins de Versailles, dans son fauteuil à roues.*"

The sight of the magnificent terraces in front of the palace will recall the nocturnal promenades of the Court, so much misrepresented by the enemies of Marie Antoinette.

Very stately is the view down the main avenue — great fountains of many figures in the foreground; then the brilliant *Tapis Vert*, between masses of rich wood; then the *Bassin d'Apollon*, and the great canal extending to distant meadows and lines of natural poplars.

Days near Paris (London, 1887).

THE CATHEDRAL OF LINCOLN.

THOMAS FROGNALL DIBDIN.

WELCOME to Lincoln! Upwards of twenty summer suns have rolled their bright and genial courses since my first visit to this ancient city,— or rather, to this venerable Cathedral: for the former seems to be merged in the latter. There is no proportion between them. A population of only twelve thousand inhabitants and scarcely more than an ordinary sprinkling of low commonplace brick-houses, are but inharmonious accessories to an ecclesiastical edifice, built upon the summit of a steep and lofty hill — pointing upwards with its three beautiful and massive towers towards heaven, and stretching longways with its lofty nave, choir, ladye-chapel, side chapels, and double transepts. For *site*, there is no Cathedral to my knowledge which approaches it. . . .

Upon a comparative estimation with the Cathedral of York, Lincoln may be called a volume of more extensive instruction; and the antiquary clings to its pages with a more varied delight. The surface or exterior of Lincoln Cathedral presents at least four perfect specimens of the succeeding styles of the first four orders of Gothic architecture. The greater part of the front may be as old as

THE CATHEDRAL OF LINCOLN.

the time of its founder, Bishop Remigius,[1] at the end of the Eleventh Century: but even here may be traced invasions and intermixtures, up to the Fifteenth Century. The large indented windows are of this latter period, and exhibit a frightful heresy. The western towers carry you to the end of the Twelfth Century: then succeeds a wonderful extent of Early English, or the pointed arch. The transepts begin with the Thirteenth, and come down to the middle of the Fourteenth Century; and the interior, especially the choir and the side aisles, abounds with the most exquisitely varied specimens of that period. Fruits, flowers, vegetables, insects, *capriccios* of every description, encircle the arches or shafts, and sparkle upon the capitals of pillars. Even down to the reign of Henry VIII. there are two private chapels, to the left of the smaller south porch, on entrance, which are perfect gems of art.

Where a building is so diversified, as well as vast, it is difficult to be methodical; but the reader ought to know, as soon as possible, that there are here not only two sets of transepts, as at York, but that the larger transept is the longest in England, being not less than two hundred and fifty feet in length. The window of the south transept is circular, and so large as to be twenty-two feet in diameter; bestudded with ancient stained glass, now become somewhat darkened by time, and standing in immediate need of cleaning and repairing. I remember, on my first visit

[1] Remigius was a monk of Fescamp in Normandy, and brought over here by William the Conqueror. He was worthy of all promotion. Brompton tells us that he began to build the Cathedral in 1088, and finished it in 1092, when it was consecrated; but the founder died two days before its consecration.

to this Cathedral, threading the whole of the *clerestory* on the south side, and coming immediately under this magnificent window, which astonished me from its size and decorations. Still, for simplicity as well as beauty of effect, the delicately ornamented lancet windows of the north transept of York Cathedral have clearly a decided preference. One wonders how these windows, both at York and at this place, escaped destruction from Cromwell's soldiers. . . . The Galilee, to the left of the larger south transept, is a most genuine and delicious specimen of Early English architecture. In *this* feature, York, upon comparison, is both petty and repulsive.

Wherever the eye strays or the imagination catches a point upon which it may revel in building up an ingenious hypothesis, the exterior of Lincoln Cathedral (some five hundred feet in length) is a never failing source of gratification. . . .

Let us turn to the grand western front; and whatever be the adulterations of the component parts, let us admire its width and simplicity; — the rude carvings, or rather sculpture, commemorative of the life of the founder, St. Remigius: and although horrified by the indented windows, of the perpendicular style, let us pause again and again before we enter at the side-aisle door. All the three doors are too low; but see what a height and what a space this front occupies! It was standing on this spot, that Corio, my dear departed friend — some twenty years ago — assured me he remained almost from sunset to dawn of day, as the whole of the front was steeped in the soft silvery light of an autumnal full moon. He had seen nothing before so grand. He had felt nothing before so stirring. The planets and stars, as they rolled in their silent and glittering orbits, and in a subdued lustre, over the roof of the nave, gave peculiar zest to the grandeur of the whole scene: add to which, the awfully deepening sounds of Great Tom[1] made his very soul to vibrate! Here, as that bell struck the hour of two, seemed to sit the shrouded figures of Remigius, Bloet, and Geoffrey Plantagenet,[2] who, saluting each other in formal prostrations, quickly vanished at the sound "into thin air." The cock crew; the sun rose; and with it all enchantment was at an end. Life has few purer, yet more delirious enjoyments, than this. . . .

The reader may here, perhaps, expect something like the institution of a comparison between these two great rival Cathedrals of Lincoln and York; although he will have observed many points in common between them to have

[1] This must have been "Great Tom," the *First*, cast in 1610; preceded probably by one or more Great Toms, to the time of Geoffrey Plantagenet. "Great Tom," the *Second*, was cast by Mr. Mears of Whitechapel in 1834, and was hung in the central tower in 1835. Its weight is 5 tons, 8 cwt.; being one ton heavier than the great bell of St. Paul's Cathedral. . . . "Great Tom," the First, was hung in the north-west tower.

[2] Robert Bloet was a worthy successor of Remigius, the founder. Bloet was thirty years a bishop of this see — largely endowing it with prebendal stalls, and with rich gifts of palls, hoods, and silver crosses. He completed the western front — and, perhaps, finished the Norman portion of the nave, now replaced by the Early English. . . . Geoffrey Plantagenet was a natural son of Henry II., and was elected in 1173. . . . The latter years of his life seem to be involved in mystery, for he fled the kingdom five years before his death, which happened at Grosmont, near Rouen, in 1212.

been previously settled. The preference to Lincoln is given chiefly from its minute and varied *detail;* while its *position* impresses you at first sight, with such mingled awe and admiration, that you cannot divest yourself of this impression, on a more dispassionately critical survey of its component parts. The versed antiquary adheres to Lincoln, and would build his nest within one of the crocketted pinnacles of the western towers — that he might hence command a view of the great central tower; and, abroad of the straight Roman road running to Barton, and the glittering waters of the broad and distant Humber. But for one human being of this stamp, you would have one hundred collecting within and without the great rival at York. Its vastness, its space, its effulgence of light and breadth of effect : its imposing simplicity, by the comparative paucity of minute ornament — its lofty lantern, shining, as it were, at heaven's gate, on the summit of the central tower : and, above all, the soul-awakening devotion kindled by a survey of its vast and matchless choir leave not a shadow of doubt behind, respecting the decided superiority of this latter edifice.

A Bibliographical, Antiquarian, and Picturesque Tour in the Northern Counties of England and in Scotland (London, 1838).

THE TEMPLE OF KARNAK.

AMELIA B. EDWARDS.

WE now left the village behind, and rode out across a wide plain, barren and hillocky in some parts; overgrown in others with coarse halfeh grass; and dotted here and there with clumps of palms. The Nile lay low and out of sight, so that the valley seemed to stretch away uninterruptedly to the mountains on both sides. Now leaving to the left a Sheykh's tomb, topped by a little cupola and shaded by a group of tamarisks; now following the bed of a dry watercourse; now skirting shapeless mounds that indicated the site of ruins unexplored, the road, uneven but direct, led straight to Karnak. At every rise in the ground we saw the huge propylons towering higher above the palms. Once, but for only a few moments, there came into sight a confused and wide-spread mass of ruins, as extensive, apparently, as the ruins of a large town. Then our way dipped into a sandy groove bordered by mud-walls and plantations of dwarf-palms. All at once this groove widened, became a stately avenue guarded by a double file of shattered sphinxes, and led towards a lofty pylon standing up alone against the sky.

Close beside this grand gateway, as if growing there on purpose, rose a thicket of sycamores and palms; while beyond it were seen the twin pylons of a Temple. The sphinxes were colossal, and measured about ten feet in length. One or two were ram-headed. Of the rest — some forty or fifty in number — all were headless, some split asunder, some overturned, others so mutilated that they looked like torrent-worn boulders. This avenue once reached from Luxor to Karnak. Taking into account the distance (which is just two miles from Temple to Temple) and the short intervals at which the sphinxes are placed, there cannot originally have been fewer than five hundred of them; that is to say, two hundred and fifty on each side of the road.

Dismounting for a few minutes, we went into the Temple; glanced round the open courtyard with its colonnade of pillars; peeped hurriedly into some ruinous side-chambers; and then rode on. Our books told us that we had seen the small Temple of Rameses the Third. It would have been called large anywhere but at Karnak.

I seem to remember the rest as if it had all happened in a dream. Leaving the small Temple, we turned towards the river, skirted the mud-walls of the native village, and approached the Great Temple by way of its main entrance. Here we entered upon what had once been another great avenue of sphinxes, ram-headed, couchant on plinths deep cut with hieroglyphic legends, and leading up from some grand landing-place beside the Nile.

And now the towers that we had first seen as we sailed by in the morning rose straight before us, magnificent in ruin, glittering to the sun, and relieved in creamy light against blue depths of sky. One was nearly perfect; the

THE TEMPLE OF KARNAK.

other, shattered as if by the shock of an earthquake, was still so lofty that an Arab clambering from block to block midway of its vast height looked no bigger than a squirrel.

On the threshold of this tremendous portal we again dismounted. Shapeless crude-brick mounds, marking the limits of the ancient wall of circuit, reached far away on either side. An immense perspective of pillars and pylons leading up to a very great obelisk opened out before us. We went in, the great walls towering up like cliffs above our heads, and entered the First Court. Here, in the midst of a large quadrangle open to the sky stands a solitary column, the last of a central avenue of twelve, some of which, disjointed by the shock, lie just as they fell, like skeletons of vertebrate monsters left stranded by the Flood.

Crossing this Court in the glowing sunlight, we came to a mighty doorway between two more propylons — the doorway splendid with coloured bas-reliefs; the propylons mere cataracts of fallen blocks piled up to right and left in grand confusion. The cornice of the doorway is gone. Only a jutting fragment of the lintel stone remains. That stone, when perfect, measured forty feet and ten inches across. The doorway must have been full a hundred feet in height.

We went on. Leaving to the right a mutilated colossus engraven on arm and breast with the cartouche of Rameses II., we crossed the shade upon the threshold, and passed into the famous Hypostyle Hall of Seti the First.

It is a place that has been much written about and often painted; but of which no writing and no art can convey more than a dwarfed and pallid impression. To describe it, in the sense of building up a recognisable image by means of words, is impossible. The scale is too vast; the effect too tremendous; the sense of one's own dumbness, and littleness, and incapacity, too complete and crushing. It is a place that strikes you into silence; that empties you, as it were, not only of words but of ideas. Nor is this a first effect only. Later in the year, when we came back down the river and moored close by, and spent long days among the ruins, I found I never had a word to say in the Great Hall. Others might measure the girth of those tremendous columns; others might climb hither and thither, and find out points of view, and test the accuracy of Wilkinson and Mariette; but I could only look, and be silent.

Yet to look is something, if one can but succeed in remembering; and the Great Hall of Karnak is photographed in some dark corner of my brain for as long as I have memory. I shut my eyes, and see it as if I were there — not all at once, as in a picture; but bit by bit, as the eye takes note of large objects and travels over an extended field of vision. I stand once more among those mighty columns, which radiate into avenues from whatever point one takes them. I see them swathed in coiled shadows and broad bands of light. I see them sculptured and painted with shapes of Gods and Kings, with blazonings of royal names, with sacrificial altars, and forms of sacred beasts, and emblems of wisdom and truth. The shafts of these columns are enormous. I stand at the foot of one — or of what seems to be the foot; for the original pavement lies buried seven feet below. Six men standing with extended arms, finger-tip to finger-tip, could barely span it round. It casts a shadow twelve feet in breadth — such a shadow as might be cast by a tower. The capital that juts out so high above my head looks as if it might have been placed there to support the heavens. It is carved in the semblance of a full-blown lotus, and glows with undying colours — colours that are still fresh, though laid on by hands that have been dust these three thousand years and more. It would take not six men, but a dozen to measure round the curved lip of that stupendous lily.

Such are the twelve central columns. The rest (one hundred and twenty-two in number) are gigantic too; but smaller. Of the roof they once supported, only the beams remain. Those beams are stone — huge monoliths carved and painted, bridging the space from pillar to pillar, and patterning the trodden soil with bands of shadow.

Looking up and down the central avenue, we see at the one end a flame-like obelisk; at the other, a solitary palm against a background of glowing mountain. To right, to left, showing transversely through long files of columns, we catch glimpses of colossal bas-reliefs lining the roofless walls in every direction. The King, as usual, figures in every group, and performs the customary acts of worship. The Gods receive and approve him. Half in light, half in shadow, these slender, fantastic forms stand out sharp, and clear, and colourless; each figure some eighteen or twenty feet in height. They could scarcely have looked more weird when the great roof was in its place and perpetual twilight reigned. But it is difficult to imagine the roof on, and the sky shut out. It all looks right as it is; and one feels, somehow, that such columns should have nothing between them and the infinite blue depths of heaven. . . .

It may be that the traveller who finds himself for the first time in the midst of a grove of *Wellingtonia gigantea* feels something of the same overwhelming sense of awe and wonder; but the great trees, though they have taken three thousand years to grow, lack the pathos and the mystery that comes of human labour. They do not strike their roots through six thousand years of history. They have not been watered with the blood and tears of millions.[1] Their leaves know no sounds less musical than the singing of the birds, or the moaning of the night-wind as it sweeps over the highlands of Calaveros. But every breath that wanders down the painted aisles of Karnak seems to echo back the sighs of those who perished in the quarry, at the oar, and under the chariot-wheels of the conqueror.

A Thousand Miles up the Nile (London, 2d ed., 1889).

[1] It has been estimated that every stone of these huge Pharaonic temples cost, at least, one human life.

SANTA MARIA DEL FIORE.

CHARLES YRIARTE.

THE document by which the council of the municipality of Florence decided the erection of her Cathedral, in 1294, is an historic monument in which is reflected the generous spirit of the Florentines.

"Considering that all the acts and works of a people who boast of an illustrious origin should bear the character of grandeur and wisdom, we order Arnolfo, director of the works of our commune, to make the model, or a design of the building, which shall replace the church of Santa Reparata. It shall display such magnificence that no industry nor human power shall surpass it. . . . A government should undertake nothing unless in response to the desire of a heart more than generous, which expresses in its beatings the heart of all its citizens united in one common wish: it is from this point of view that the architect charged with the building of our cathedral must be regarded."

It must be admitted that it would be difficult to express a more noble idea and a more elevated sentiment than this.

The name of the Cathedral is evidently an allusion to the lily, the heraldic emblem of Florence. The ceremony of laying the first stone took place on September 8th, 1298;

Pope Boniface VIII. was represented by his legate, Cardinal Pietro Valeriano. Arnolfo's plan was a Latin cross with three naves, each nave divided into four arcades with sharp pointed arches. In the centre of the cross, under the vault of the dome, was reserved a space enclosed by a *ringhiera*, having open sides, with an altar in its axis, and in each of its little arms five rectangular chapels were placed. The walls were naked, and the architecture alone served for decoration; the effect, however, was altogether imposing.

Arnolfo did not finish his work; he died about 1230, leaving the church completed only as far as the capitals destined to support the arches. In 1332 Giotto was nominated to succeed him, and for about two hundred years the work was continued without interruption, under the direction of the most worthy men.

It is to Giotto that we owe that extraordinary annex to the Duomo, so celebrated throughout the world under the name of Campanile; its foundation was laid in 1334, after the little church of San Zanobio was razed. It is 85 metres high; Giotto, however, had calculated 94 metres in his plan and intended to finish the square column with a pyramid, like the Campanile of Saint Mark's in Venice; but he was unable to complete his work, and his successor, Taddeo Gaddi, suppressed this appendix. The Campanile has six divisions; the first and the second, which are easily examined, are ornamented with sculpture executed by Andrea Pisano, after Giotto's designs. . . .

Even at the risk of banality, the saying attributed to Charles V. when he entered Florence after the siege should

SANTA MARIA DEL FIORE.

be mentioned here; he paused before the Campanile, contemplated it for a long while, and then exclaimed: "They should make a case for the Campanile and exhibit it as a jewel."

Mounting to the top of the tower, we can count, one by one, the domes, the towers, and the monuments, and gaze upon the beautiful landscape which surrounds the city of flowers. There are in this tower seven bells, the largest of which, cast in 1705 to replace the one that had been broken, does not weigh less than 15,860 pounds.

Among the architects who succeeded Giotto, we must count the master of masters, who was, perhaps, the most incontestably illustrious of the Fifteenth Century architects — Filippo Brunelleschi. It was in 1421 that he began the superb dome which crowns the Cathedral. This was his masterpiece, surpassing in audacity and harmony all the monuments of modern art. Everyone knows that this dome is double: the interior casing is spherical, and between it and the exterior dome are placed the stairways, chains, counter-weights, and all the accessories of construction which render it enduring. It was only fifteen years after the death of the great Philippo that this dome was finished (1461). It inspired Michael Angelo for Saint Peter's in Rome, and Leon Battista Alberti took it for his model in building the famous temple of Rimini which he left unfinished. Andrea del Verocchio, the beautiful sculptor of the *Enfant au dauphin* and the Tomb of the Medicis in the old sacristy, designed and executed the ball, and Giovanni di Bartolo completed the node on which the Cross stands.

The church contains several tombs, among others those of Giotto, commissioned to Benedetto da Maiano by Lorenzo the Magnificent, and that of the famous organist, Antonio Squarcialupi, a favourite of Lorenzo to whom " The Magnificent " wrote an epitaph. It is thought that the Poggio rests in Santa Maria del Fiore. The sarcophagus of Aldobrandino Ottobuoni is near the door of the Servi.

I have said that the walls are naked, that is to say that architecture does not play a great part on them, but the building contains a number of works of the highest order by Donatello, Michelozzo, Ghiberti, della Robbia, Sansovino, Bandinelli, and Andrea del Castagno. It was by the door of the Servi that Dominico di Michelino on January 30, 1465, painted Dante, a tribute paid tardily to the memory of the prince of poets by the society of Florentines, who were none other than the workmen employed in the construction of the Cathedral. Under these arches where Boccaccio made his passionate words resound to the memory of the author of the *Divina Comedia*, Michelino painted Dante clothed in a red toga and crowned with laurel, holding in one hand a poem and with the other pointing to the symbolical circles. The inscription states that the execution of this fresco is due to one of Dante's commentators, Maestro Antonio, of the order of the Franciscans.

Florence: l'histoire — Les Medicis — Les humanistes — Les lettres — Les arts (Paris, 1881).

GIOTTO'S CAMPANILE.

GIOTTO'S CAMPANILE.

MRS. OLIPHANT.

OF all the beautiful things with which Giotto adorned his city, not one speaks so powerfully to the foreign visitor — the *forestiere* whom he and his fellows never took into account, though we occupy so large a space among the admirers of his genius nowadays — as the lovely Campanile which stands by the great Cathedral like the white royal lily beside the Mary of the Annunciation, slender and strong and everlasting in its delicate grace. It is not often that a man takes up a new trade when he is approaching sixty, or even goes into a new path out of his familiar routine. But Giotto seems to have turned without a moment's hesitation from his paints and panels to the less easily-wrought materials of the builder and sculptor, without either faltering from the great enterprise or doubting his own power to do it. His frescoes and altar-pieces and crucifixes, the work he had been so long accustomed to, and which he could execute pleasantly in his own workshop, or on the cool new walls of church or convent, with his trained school of younger artists round to aid him, were as different as possible from the elaborate calculations and measurements by which alone the lofty tower, straight and lightsome as a lily, could have sprung so high and stood so lightly against that Italian sky. No longer mere pencil or brush, but compasses and quaint mathematical tools, figures not of art by arithmetic, elaborate weighing of proportions and calculations of quantity and balance, must have changed the character of those preliminary studies in which every artist must engage before he begins a great work. Like the poet or the romancist when he turns from the flowery ways of fiction and invention, where he is unincumbered by any restrictions save those of artistic keeping and personal will, to the grave and beaten path of history — the painter must have felt when he too turned from the freedom and poetry of art to this first scientific undertaking. The Cathedral was so far finished by this time, its front not scarred and bare as at present, but adorned with statues according to old Arnolfo's plan, who was dead more than thirty years before; but there was no belfry, no companion peal of peace and sweetness to balance the hoarse old *vacca* with its voice of iron. Giotto seems to have thrown himself into the work not only without reluctance but with enthusiasm. The foundation-stone of the building was laid in July of that year, with all the greatness of Florence looking on; and the painter entered upon his work at once, working out the most poetic effort of his life in marble and stone, among masons' chippings and the dust and blaze of the public street. At the same time he designed, though it does not seem sure whether he lived long enough to execute, a new façade for the Cathedral, replacing Arnolfo's old statues by something better, and raising over the doorway the delicate tabernacle work which we see in Pocetti's picture of St. Antonino's consecration as bishop of St. Mark's. It would be pleasant to believe that while the foundations of the Campanile were being laid and the ruder mason-work progressing, the painter began immediately upon the more congenial labour, and made the face of the Duomo fair with carvings, with soft shades of those toned marbles which fit so tenderly into each other, and elaborate canopies as delicate as foam; but of this there seems no certainty. Of the Campanile itself it is difficult to speak in ordinary words. The enrichments of the surface, which is covered by beautiful groups set in a graceful framework of marble, with scarcely a flat or unadorned spot from top to bottom, has been ever since the admiration of artists and of the world. But we confess, for our own part, that it is the structure itself that affords us that soft ecstasy of contemplation, sense of a perfection before which the mind stops short, silenced and filled with the completeness of beauty unbroken, which Art so seldom gives, though Nature often attains it by the simplest means, through the exquisite perfection of a flower or a stretch of summer sky. Just as we have looked at a sunset, we look at Giotto's tower, poised far above in the blue air, in all the wonderful dawns and moonlights of Italy, swift darkness shadowing its white glory at the tinkle of the Ave Mary, and a golden glow of sunbeams accompanying the midday Angelus. Between the solemn antiquity of the old Baptistery and the historical gloom of the great Cathedral, it stands like the lily — if not, rather, like the great Angel himself hailing her who was blessed among women, and keeping up that lovely salutation, musical and sweet as its own beauty, for century after century, day after day.

The Makers of Florence (London, 1876).

GIOTTO'S CAMPANILE.

JOHN RUSKIN.

IN its first appeal to the stranger's eye there is something unpleasing; a mingling, as it seems to him, of over severity with over minuteness. But let him give it time, as he should to all other consummate art. I remember well how, when a boy, I used to despise that Campanile, and think it meanly smooth and finished. But I have since lived beside it many a day, and looked out upon it from my windows by sunlight and moonlight, and I shall not soon forget how profound and gloomy appeared to me the savageness of the Northern Gothic, when I afterwards stood, for the first time, beneath the front of Salisbury. The contrast is indeed strange, if it could be quickly felt, between the rising of those grey walls out of their quiet swarded space, like dark and barren rocks out of a green lake, with their rude, mouldering, rough-grained shafts, and triple lights, without tracery or other ornament than the martins' nests in the height of them, and that bright, smooth, sunny surface of glowing jasper, those spiral shafts and fairy traceries, so white, so faint, so crystalline, that their slight shapes are hardly traced in darkness on the pallor of the Eastern sky, that serene height of mountain alabaster, coloured like a morning cloud, and chased like a sea shell. And if this be, as I believe it, the model and mirror of perfect architecture, is there not something to be learned by looking back to the early life of him who raised it? I said that the Power of human mind had its growth in the Wilderness; much more must the love and the conception of that beauty, whose every line and hue we have seen to be, at the best, a faded image of God's daily work, and an arrested ray of some star of creation, be given chiefly in the places which He has gladdened by planting there the fir-tree and the pine. Not within the walls of Florence, but among the far away fields of her lilies, was the child trained who was to raise that head-stone of Beauty above the towers of watch and war. Remember all that he became; count the sacred thoughts with which he filled Italy; ask those who followed him what they learned at his feet; and when you have numbered his labours, and received their testimony, if it seem to you that God had verily poured out upon this His servant no common nor restrained portion of His Spirit, and that he was indeed a king among the children of men, remember also that the legend upon his crown was that of David's : — "I took thee from the sheepcote, and from following the sheep."

The Seven Lamps of Architecture (London, 1849).

THE HOUSE OF JACQUES CŒUR IN BOURGES.

AD. BERTY.

CERTAINLY Jacques Cœur, that citizen of humble birth, who, by his merit reached the highest dignity of state at an epoch when aristocracy reigned supreme, this man of genius, who, while creating a maritime commerce for France, amassed so great a fortune for himself that he was able to help towards the deliverance of his own country in supporting at his own expense four armies at the same time, was not one of the least important figures of the Fifteenth Century. Posterity has not always been just to this illustrious upstart: he should be ranked immediately after Jeanne d'Arc, for the sword of the Maid of Domrémy would, perhaps, have been powerless to chase the enemy from the soil (which a cowardly king did not think of repulsing), without the wise economy and the generous sacrifices of him, who, at a later period, was abandoned by the king to the rapacity of his courtiers with that same ignoble ingratitude which he had shown to the *sainte libertrice* of the great nation over which he was so unworthy to rule.

Jacques Cœur was the son of a furrier, or according to some authorities, a goldsmith of Bourges. He was probably following his father's business when his intelligence and talents brought him into the notice of Charles VII., who had been forced to take refuge in the capital of Berry on account of the English conquests. The king appointed him to the mint, then made him master of this branch of administration, and, finally, *argentier*, a title equivalent to superintendent of finance. Cœur, in his new and brilliant position, did not abandon commerce to which he owed his fortune; his ships continued to furrow the seas, and three hundred clerks aided him in bartering European products for the silks and spices of the East and in realizing a fortune. Always fortunate in his enterprises, ennobled [1] by the king in 1440, and charged by him with many important political missions, he probably did not know how to resist the vertigo which always seizes those of mean origin who attain great eminence. He exhibited an extraordinary luxury, whose splendours humiliated the pride of the noble courtiers, excited their hatred and envy, and contributed to his ruin. With little regard for the great services which he had rendered to the country, such as, for example, the gift of 200,000 crowns in gold at the time of the expedition of Normandy, the nobles only saw in the magnificent *argentier* an unworthy gambler, who should be deprived of his immense wealth [2] for their profit. For this purpose they organized a cabal. Cœur was charged with a multitude of crimes: he was accused of having poisoned Agnès Sorel, who had made

---

[1] The arms of Cœur were what are called *parlantes*: azure, fess *or*, charged with three shells *or* (recalling those of St. James his patron), accompanied by three hearts, *gules*, in allusion to his name.

[2] The fortune of Jacques Cœur became proverbial: they said: "Riche comme Jacques Cœur."

him her testamentary executor, of having altered money, and of various other peculations; he was also reproached for having extorted money for various purposes in the name of the king. . . .

The sentence of Jacques Cœur was not entirely executed; he was not banished, but, on the contrary, was imprisoned in the Convent des Cordeliers de Beaucaire. Aided by one of his clerks, Jean de Village, who had married his niece, he made his escape and went to Rome, where Pope Calixtus III., at that moment preparing an expedition against the Turks, gave him command of a flotilla. Cœur then departed, but, falling ill on the way, he disembarked at Chio, where he died in 1461. His body was buried in the church of the Cordeliers in that island.

Of the different houses which Jacques Cœur possessed, the one considered among the most beautiful in all France, exists almost intact, and is still known under the name of the *Maison de Jacques Cœur*, although it now serves for a hall of justice and mayoralty. This house, or rather this *hôtel*, was built between the years 1443 and 1453, and cost a sum equal to 215,000 francs of our money. For its construction, Cœur, having bought one of the towers of the ramparts of Bourges, commonly called *Tour de la chaussée*, from the fief of this name, built on a level with it another and more beautiful tower, and these two towers served as a beginning for the *manoir*, which was called, in consequence, the *Hôtel de la chaussée*. In building it they used stones taken from the old Roman walls of the town, which were on the site of the new *hôtel*, and which had already been pulled down by virtue of a charter given by Louis VIII.

THE HOUSE OF JACQUES CŒUR.

in 1224, by which, permission had been granted for building upon the ramparts and fortifications. At the time of the revision of the law-suit of Jacques Cœur under Louis XI. the *hôtel* was given back to his heirs, who in 1552 sold it to Claude de l'Aubespine, secretary of state. By a descendant of the latter it was ceded to Colbert in 1679; Colbert sold it again to the town of Bourges on January 30, 1682, for the sum of 33,000 livres. Jacques Cœur's house was therefore destined to become a *hôtel-de-ville*, and, as we have said, still exists to-day.

The plan of the building is an irregular pentagon, composed of different bodies of buildings joined without any symmetry, according to the general disposition of almost all mediæval civil and military buildings. The large towers are Jacques Cœur's original ones. One was entirely reconstructed by him with the exception of the first story, which is of Roman work, as the layers of brick and masonry indicate; the other, on the contrary, received only its crown and a new interior construction, and, like the first, was flanked by a tower destined to serve as a cage for the stairway. The court of honour is vast, and arranged so that it was easy to communicate with the different parts of the *hôtel*.

The façade is composed of a pavilion flanked by two wings. Following an arrangement borrowed from military architecture, two doors were contrived, the little one for the foot-passengers and the large one, which was the door of honour, through which the Cavaliers entered. Both had pointed arches and were ornamented with an archivolt with crockets. One of them still possessed, until about a dozen years ago, its ancient sculptured panels and ornamental iron-work. Above these doors is a large niche with very rich ornamentation, which originally sheltered the equestrian statue of Charles VII. On its right and left is a false window, in which you see the statue of a man-servant in the one and that of a maid-servant in the other, both in the costume of the period. Above this niche the wall is pierced by a large window with four panes, whose tracery reproduces hearts, *armes parlantes* of the proprietor, and a *fleur-de-lis*, a sign of his recognition by King Charles. A cornice of foliage forms the top of the wall of the pavilion, which is crowned by a very high roof with four sloping and concave sides. Upon the front and back faces of this roof is a large skylight-window and on its lateral faces, a stock of chimneys. On the summit of the roof is an imposing ridge which ends with two long spikes.

The back of the pavilion is exactly like the front, with the exception of a statue of Cœur corresponding to that of the king. To the right of the pavilion there rises an octagonal campanile of great elegance; at its base is a balustrade in whose open-work runs a phylactery, carrying the motto, which is frequently repeated in the building and which characterizes perfectly him who adopted it:

À vaillans cœurs[1] *rien d'impossible.*

Notwithstanding the mutilations to which the house of Jacques Cœur has been condemned by its fate, it is certainly one of the most interesting and best preserved of all the civil

---

[1] The word *cœurs* is indicated by hearts.

buildings of the Middle Ages. A vast amount of information regarding the intimate life of the people, which has so great an attraction for the archæologist, is to be found here. If the fact that the study of buildings should be the inseparable companion to that of history was less evident, the house of Jacques Cœur would afford us an opportunity to demonstrate the truth; in reality, when we have studied this building we certainly gain a much clearer idea of the manners of Charles VII.'s reign than could be obtained from a host of lecturers upon history.

Jules Gailhabaud, *Monuments anciens et modernes* (Paris, 1865).

WAT PHRA KAO.

CARL BOCK.

THE first glimpse of Siam which the traveller obtains at Paknam is a fair sample of what is to be seen pretty well throughout the country. As Constantinople is called the City of Mosques, so Bangkok may, with even more reason, be termed the City of Temples. And not in Bangkok only and its immediate neighbourhood, but in the remotest parts of the country, wherever a few people live now, or ever have lived, a Wat with its image, or collection of images, of Buddha, is to be found, surrounded by numberless phrachedees, those curious structures which every devout Buddhist — and all Buddhists are in one sense or another devout — erects at every turn as a means of gaining favour with the deity, or of making atonement for his sins. On the rich plains, in the recesses of the forests, on the tops of high mountains, in all directions, these monuments of universal allegiance to a faith which, more perhaps than any other, claims a devotee in almost every individual inhabitant of the lands over which it has once obtained sway, are to be found. The labour, the time, and the wealth lavished upon these structures are beyond calculation. . . .

WAT PHRA KAO.

WAT PHRA KAO.

The work which, in popular estimation at least, will make his Majesty's reign most memorable in Siam, is the completion and dedication of the great royal temple, Phra Sri Ratana Satsadaram, or, as it is usually called, Wat Phra Kao. The erection of this magnificent pile of buildings was commenced by Phra Puttha Yot Fa Chulalok, " as a temple for the Emerald Buddha, the palladium of the capital, for the glory of the king, and as an especial work of royal piety." This temple was inaugurated with a grand religious festival in the year Maseng, 7th of the cycle, 1147 (A. D. 1785), but, having been very hastily got ready for the celebration of the third anniversary of the foundation of the capital, it was incomplete, only the church and library being finished. Various additions were made from time to time, but the Wat remained in an unfinished state until the present king came to the throne. The vow to complete the works was made on Tuesday, the 23rd of December, 1879. The works were commenced during the next month and completed on Monday, the 17th of April, 1882, a period of two years, three months, and twenty days. Thus it was reserved for King Chulalonkorn, at an enormous outlay, entirely defrayed out of his private purse, and by dint of great exertions on the part of those to whom the work was immediately entrusted, to complete this structure, and, on the hundredth anniversary of the capital of Siam, to give the city its crowning glory.

The work was placed under the direct superintendence of the king's brothers, each of whom had a particular part of the work allotted to him. One, for instance, relaid the marble pavement, and decorated the Obosot with pictures of the sacred elephant; while a second renewed the stone inscriptions inside the Obosot; a third laid down a brass pavement in the Obosot; a fourth undertook to restore all the inlaid pearl work; another undertook the work of repairing the ceiling, paving, and wall-decoration, and made three stands for the seals of the kingdom; another changed the decayed roof-beams; another covered the great phrachedee with gold tiles — the effect of which in the brilliant sunlight is marvellously beautiful — and repaired and gilded all the small phrachedees; another renewed and repaired and redecorated all the stone ornaments and flower-pots in the temple-grounds, and made the copper-plated and gilt figures of demons, and purchased many marble statues; two princes divided between them the repairs of the cloisters, renewing the roof where required, painting, gilding, paving with stone, and completing the capitals of columns, and so on. Thus, by division of labour, under the stimulus of devotion to the religion of the country, and of brotherly loyalty to the king, the great work was at length completed, after having been exactly one hundred years in course of construction. On the 21st of April, 1882, the ceremony of final dedication was performed, with the greatest pomp, and amid general rejoicings.

Under the name " Wat Phra Kao " are included various buildings covering a large area of ground, which is surrounded by walls decorated with elaborate frescoes. In the centre is a temple, called the Phra Marodop, built in the form of a cross, where on festive occasions the

WAT PHRA KAO.

king goes to hear a sermon from the prince-high-priest. The walls of this building are richly decorated with inlaid work, and the ceiling painted with a chaste design in blue and gold. The most striking feature, however, is the beautiful work in the ebony doors, which are elaborately inlaid with mother-of-pearl figures representing Thewedas, bordered by a rich scroll. Behind this chapel-royal is the great phrachedee, called the Sri Ratana Phrachedee, entirely covered with gilt tiles, which are specially made for the purpose in Germany to the order of H. R. H. Krom Mun Aditson Udom Det.

There are several other large buildings in the temple-grounds, but the structure in which the interest of the place centres is the Obosot, which shelters the famous "Emerald Buddha," a green jade figure of matchless beauty, which was found at Kiang Hai in A. D. 1436, and, after various vicissitudes of fortune, was at last placed in safety in the royal temple at Bangkok. This image is, according to the season of the year, differently attired in gold ornaments and robes. The Emerald Buddha is raised so high up, at the very summit of a high altar, that it is somewhat difficult to see it, especially as light is not over plentiful, the windows being generally kept closely shuttered. For the convenience of visitors, however, the attendants will for a small fee open one or two of the heavy shutters, which are decorated on the outside with gilt figures of Thewedas in contorted attitudes. When at last the sun's rays are admitted through the "dim religious light," and the beam of brightness shines on the resplendent figure — enthroned above a gorgeous array of coloured vases, with real flowers and their waxen imitations, of gold, silver, and bronze representations of Buddha, of Bohemian glassware, lamps, and candlesticks, with here and there a flickering taper still burning, and surrounded with a profusion of many-storied umbrellas, emblems of the esteem in which the gem is held — the scene is remarkably beautiful, and well calculated to have a lasting effect on the minds of those who are brought up to see in the calm, solemn, and dignified form of Buddha the representation of all that is good here, and the symbol of all happiness hereafter. The floor of the Obosot is of tessellated brass, and the walls are decorated with the usual perspectiveless frescoes, representing scenes in Siamese or Buddhist history.

It is in this Obosot that the semi-annual ceremony of *Tunam*, or drinking the water of allegiance, takes place, when the subjects of Siam, through their representatives, and the princes and high officers of state, renew or confirm their oath of allegiance. The ceremony consists of drinking water sanctified by the priests, and occurs twice a year — on the third day of the waxing of the Siamese fifth month (i. e., the 1st of April), and on the thirteenth day of the waning of the Siamese tenth month (i. e., the 21st of September).

The foregoing description gives but a faint idea of this sacred and historic edifice, which will henceforth be regarded as a symbol of the rule of the present Siamese dynasty, and the completion of which will mark an epoch in Siamese history.

Temples and Elephants (London, 1884).

THE CATHEDRAL OF TOLEDO.

THÉOPHILE GAUTIER.

THE exterior of the Cathedral of Toledo is far less ornate than that of the Cathedral of Burgos: it has no efflorescence of ornaments, no arabesques, and no collarette of statues enlivening the porches; it has solid buttresses, bold and sharp angles, a thick facing of stone, a stolid tower, with no delicacies of the Gothic jewel-work, and it is covered entirely with a reddish tint, like that of a piece of toast, or the sunburnt skin of a pilgrim from Palestine; as if to make up the loss, the interior is hollowed and sculptured like a grotto of stalactites.

The door by which we entered is of bronze, and bears the following inscription: *Antonio Zurreno del arte de oro y plata, faciebat esta media puerta.* The first impression is most vivid and imposing; five naves divide the church: the middle one is of an immeasurable height, and the others beside it seem to bow their heads and kneel in token of admiration and respect; eighty-eight pillars, each as large as a tower and each composed of sixteen spindle-shaped columns bound together, sustain the enormous mass of the building; a transept cuts the large nave between the choir and the high altar, and forms the arms of the cross. The architecture of the entire building is homogeneous and perfect, a very rare virtue in Gothic cathedrals, which have generally been built at different periods; the original plan has been adhered to from one end to the other, with the exception of a few arrangements of the chapels, which, however, do not interfere with the harmony of the general effect. The windows, glittering with hues of emerald, sapphire, and ruby set in the ribs of stone, worked like rings, sift in a soft and mysterious light which inspires religious ecstasy; and, when the sun is too strong, blinds of spartium are let down over the windows, and through the building is then diffused that cool half-twilight which makes the churches of Spain so favourable for meditation and prayer.

The high altar, or *retablo*, alone might pass for a church; it is an enormous accumulation of small columns, niches, statues, foliage, and arabesques, of which the most minute description would give but a faint idea; all this sculpture, which extends up to the vaulted roof and all around the sanctuary, is painted and gilded with unimaginable wealth. The warm and tawny tones of the antique gold, illumined by the rays and patches of light interrupted in their passage by the tracery and projections of the ornaments, stand out superbly and produce the most admirable effects of grandeur and richness. The paintings, with their backgrounds of gold which adorn the panels of this altar, equal in richness of colour the most brilliant Venetian canvases; this union of colour with the severe and almost hieratic forms of mediæval art is rarely found; some of these paintings might be taken for Giorgione's first manner.

Opposite to the high altar is placed the choir, or *silleria*, according to the Spanish custom; it is composed of three

THE CATHEDRAL OF TOLEDO.

rows of stalls in sculptured wood, hollowed and carved in a marvellous manner with historical, allegorical, and sacred bas-reliefs. Gothic Art, on the borderland of the Renaissance, has never produced anything more pure, more perfect, or better drawn. This work, the details of which are appalling, has been attributed to the patient chisels of Philippe de Bourgogne and Berruguete. The archbishop's stall, which is higher than the rest, is shaped like a throne and marks the centre of the choir; this prodigious carpentry is crowned by gleaming columns of brown jasper, and on the entablature stand alabaster figures, also by Philippe de Bourgogne and Berruguete, but in a freer and more supple style, elegant and admirable in effect. Enormous bronze reading-desks supporting gigantic missals, large spartium mats, and two colossal organs placed opposite to each other, one to the right and one to the left, complete the decorations. . . .

The Mozarabic Chapel, which is still in existence, is adorned with Gothic frescoes of the highest interest: the subjects are the combats between the Toledans and the Moors; they are in a state of perfect preservation, their colours are as bright as if they had been laid on yesterday, and by means of them an archæologist would gain a vast amount of information regarding arms, costumes, accoutrements, and architecture, for the principal fresco represents a view of old Toledo, which is, doubtless, very accurate. In the lateral frescoes the ships which brought the Arabs to Spain are painted in detail; a seaman might gather much useful information from them regarding the obscure history of the mediæval navy. The arms of Toledo — five stars, *sable* on a field, *argent* — are repeated in several places in this low-vaulted chapel, which, according to the Spanish fashion, is enclosed by a grille of beautiful workmanship.

The Chapel of the Virgin, which is entirely faced with beautifully polished porphyry, jasper, and yellow and violet *breccia*, is of a richness surpassing the splendours of the *Thousand and One Nights;* many relics are preserved here, among them a reliquary presented by Saint Louis, which contains a piece of the True Cross.

To recover our breath, let us make, if you please, the tour of the cloisters, whose severe yet elegant arcades surround beautiful masses of verdure, kept green, notwithstanding the devouring heat of this season, by the shadow of the Cathedral; the walls of this cloister are covered with frescoes in the style of Vanloo, by a painter named Bayeu. These compositions are simple and pleasing in colour, but they do not harmonize with the style of the building, and probably supplant ancient works damaged by centuries, or found too Gothic for the people of good taste in that time. It is very fitting to place a cloister near a church; it affords a happy transition from the tranquillity of the sanctuary to the turmoil of the city. You can go to it to walk about, to dream, or to reflect, without being forced to join in the prayers and ceremonies of a cult; Catholics go to the temple, Christians remain more frequently in the cloisters. This attitude of mind has been perfectly understood by that marvellous psychologist the Catholic Church. In religious countries the Cathedral is always the most ornamented, richest, most gilded, and most florid of all buildings in the town; it is there that one finds the coolest shade and the deepest peace; the music there is better than in the theatre; and it has no rival in pomp of display. It is the central point, the magnetic spot, like the Opéra in Paris. We Catholics of the North, with our Vottairean temples, have no idea of the luxury, elegance, and comfort of the Spanish cathedrals; these churches are furnished and animated, and have nothing of that glacial, desert-like appearance of ours; the faithful can live in them on familiar terms with their God.

The sacristies and rooms of the Chapter in the Cathedral of Toledo have a more than royal magnificence; nothing could be more noble and picturesque than these vast halls decorated with that solid and severe luxury of which the Church alone has the secret. Here are rare carpentry-work in carved walnut or black oak, *portières* of tapestry or Indian damask, curtains of *brocatelle*, with sumptuous folds, figured brocades, Persian carpets, and paintings of fresco. We will not try to describe them in detail; we will only speak of one room ornamented with admirable frescoes depicting religious subjects in the German style of which the Spaniards have made such successful imitations, and which have been attributed to Berruguete's nephew, if not to Berruguete himself, for these prodigious geniuses followed simultaneously three branches of art. We will also mention an enormous ceiling by Luca Giordano, where is collected a whole world of angels and allegorical figures in the most rapidly executed foreshortening which produce a singular optical illusion. From the middle of the roof springs a ray of light so wonderfully painted on the flat surface that it seems to fall perpendicularly on your head, no matter from which side you view it.

It is here that they keep the treasure, that is to say the beautiful copes of brocade, cloth of gold and silver damask, the marvellous laces, the silver-gilt reliquaries, the monstrances of diamonds, the gigantic silver candlesticks, the embroidered banners, — all the material and accessories for the representation of that sublime Catholic drama which we called the Mass.

In the cupboards in one of the rooms is preserved the wardrobe of the Holy Virgin, for cold, naked statues of marble or alabaster do not suffice for the passionate piety of the Southern race; in their devout transport they load the object of their worship with ornaments of extravagant richness; nothing is good enough, brilliant enough, or costly enough for them; under this shower of precious stones, the form and material of the figure disappear: nobody cares about that. The main thing is that it should be an impossibility to hang another pearl in the ears of the marble idol, to insert another diamond in its golden crown, or to trace another leaf of gems in the brocade of its dress.

Never did an ancient queen, — not even Cleopatra who drank pearls, — never did an empress of the Lower Empire, never did a Venetian courtesan in the time of Titian, possess more brilliant jewels nor a richer wardrobe than Our Lady of Toledo. They showed us some of her robes: one of them left you no idea as to the material of which it was made, so entirely was it covered with flowers and arabesques of seed-pearls, among which there were

THE CATHEDRAL OF TOLEDO. 169

others of a size beyond all price and several rows of black pearls, which are of almost unheard-of rarity; suns and stars of jewels also constellate this precious gown, which is so brilliant that the eye can scarcely bear its splendour, and which is worth many millions of francs.

We ended our visit by ascending the bell-tower, the summit of which is reached by a succession of ladders, sufficiently steep and not very reassuring. About half way up, in a kind of store-room, through which you pass, we saw a row of gigantic *marionettes*, coloured and dressed in the fashion of the last century, and used in I don't know what kind of a procession similar to that of Tarascon.

The magnificent view which is seen from the tall spire amply repays you for all the fatigue of the ascent. The whole town is presented before you with all the sharpness and precision of M. Pelet's cork-models, so much admired at the last *Exposition de l'industrie*. This comparison is doubtless very prosaic and unpicturesque; but really I cannot find a better, nor a more accurate one. The dwarfed and misshapen rocks of blue granite, which encase the Tagus and encircle the horizon of Toledo on one side, add still more to the singularity of the landscape, inundated and dominated by crude, pitiless, blinding light, which no reflections temper and which is increased by the cloudless and vapourless sky quivering with white heat like iron in a furnace.

Voyage en Espagne (Paris, new ed. 1865).

THE CHÂTEAU DE CHAMBORD.

JULES LOISELEUR.

CHAMBORD is the Versailles of the feudal monarchy; it was to the Château de Blois, that central residence of the Valois, what Versailles was to the Tuileries; it was the country-seat of Royalty. Tapestries from Arras, Venetian mirrors, curiously sculptured chests, crystal chandeliers, massive silver furniture, and miracles of all the arts, amassed in this palace during eight reigns and dispersed in a single day by the breath of the Revolution, can never be collected again save under one condition : that there should be a sovereign sufficiently powerful and sufficiently artistic, sufficiently concerned about the glory and the memories of the ancient monarchy to make of Chambord what has been made out of the Louvre and Versailles — a museum consecrated to all the intimate marvels, to all the curiosities of the Arts of the Renaissance, at least to all those with which the sovereigns were surrounded, something like the way the Hôtel de Cluny exhibits royal life.

It has often been asked why François I., to whom the banks of the Loire presented many marvellous sites, selected a wild and forsaken spot in the midst of arid plains for the erection of the strange building which he planned. This peculiar choice has been attributed to that prince's passion for the chase and in memory of his *amours* with the beautiful Comtesse de Thoury, *châtelaine* in that neighbourhood, before he ascended the throne.

Independently of these motives, which doubtless counted greatly in his selection, perhaps the very wildness of this place, this distance from the Loire, which reminded him too much of the cares of Royalty, was a determining reason. Kings, like private individuals, and even more than they, experience the need at times of burying themselves, and therefore make a hidden and far-away nest where they may be their own masters and live to please themselves. Moreover, Chambord, with its countless rooms, its secret stairways, and its subterranean passages, seems to have been built for a love which seeks shadow and mystery. At the same time that he hid Chambord in the heart of the uncultivated plains of the Sologne, François I. built in the midst of the Bois de Boulogne a *château*, where, from time to time, he shut himself up with learned men and artists, and to which the courtiers, who were positively forbidden there, gave the name of Madrid, in memory of the prison in which their master had suffered. Chambord, like Madrid, was not a prison : it was a retreat.

That sentiment of peculiar charm which is attached to the situation of Chambord will be felt by every artist who visits this strange realization of an Oriental dream. At the end of a long avenue of poplars breaking through thin underbrush which bears an illustrious name, like all the roads to this residence, you see, little by little, peeping and mounting upward from the earth, a fairy building, which, rising in the midst of arid sand and heath, produces the most striking and unexpected effect. A genie of the Orient, a poet has said, must have stolen it from the country of sunshine to hide it in the country of fog for the *amours* of a handsome prince. At the summit of an imposing mass of battlements, of which the first glance discerns neither the style nor the order, above terraces with ornamental balustrades, springs up, as if from a fertile and inexhaustible soil, an incredible vegetation of sculptured stone, worked in a thousand different ways. It is a forest of campaniles, chimneys, sky-lights, domes, and towers, in lace-work and open-work, twisted according to a caprice which excludes neither harmony nor unity, and which ornaments with the Gothic F the salamanders and also the mosaics of slate imitating marble, — a singular poverty in the midst of so much wealth. The beautiful open-worked tower of the large staircase dominates the entire mass of pinnacles and steeples, and bathes in the blue sky its colossal fleur-de-lis, the last point of the highest pinnacle among pinnacles, the highest crown among all crowns. . . .

We must take Chambord for what it is, an ancient Gothic *château* dressed out in great measure according to the fashion of the Renaissance.

In no other place is the transition from one style to another revealed in a way so impressive and naïve; nowhere else does the brilliant butterfly of the Renaissance show itself more deeply imprisoned in the heavy Gothic chrysalis. If Chambord, by its plan which is essentially French and feudal, by its enclosure flanked with towers, and by the breadth of its heavy mass, slavishly recalls the mediæval *manoirs*, by its lavish profusion of ornamentation it suggests

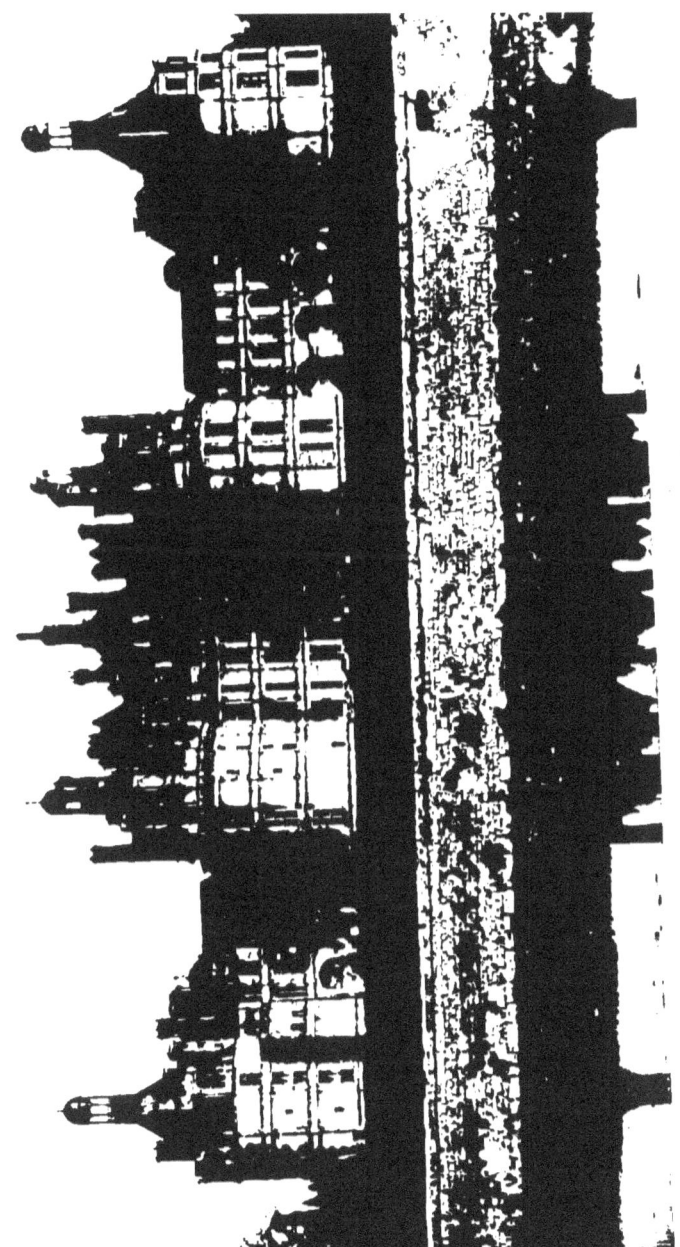

THE CHÂTEAU DE CHAMBORD.

the creations of the Sixteenth Century as far as the beginning of the roofs; it is Gothic as far as the platform; and it belongs to the Renaissance when it comes to the roof itself. It may be compared to a rude French knight of the Fourteenth Century, who is wearing on his cuirass some fine Italian embroideries, and on his head the plumed felt of François I.,—assuredly an incongruous costume, but not without character. . . .

The *château* should be entered by one of the four doors which open in the centre of the donjon. Nothing is more fantastic, and, at the same time, magnificent than the spectacle which greets the eye. It seems more like one of those fairy palaces which we see at the Opera, than a real building. Neglect and nakedness give it an additional value and double its immensity. On entering this vast solitude of stone, we are seized with that respectful silence which involuntarily strikes us under high and solitary vaults. In the centre of the vast Salle des Gardes, which occupies the entire ground-floor, and to which the four towers of the donjon give the form of the Greek cross, rises a monumental stairway which divides this hall into four equal parts, each being fifty feet long and thirty feet broad. This bold conception justifies its celebrity: the stairway at Chambord is in itself a monument. The staircase, completely isolated and open-worked, is composed of posts which follow the winding. Two flights of stairs, one above the other, unfold in helices and pass alternately one over the other without meeting. This will explain how two persons could ascend at the same time without meeting, yet perceiving each other at intervals.

Even while looking at this, it is difficult to conceive this arrangement. These two helices, which are placed above each other and which turn over and over each other without ever uniting, have exactly the curve of a double corkscrew. I believe that no other comparison can give a more exact idea of this celebrated work which has exhausted the admiration and the eulogy of all the *connaisseurs*. "What merits the greatest praise," writes Blondel in his *Leçons d'architecture*, "is the ingenious disposition of that staircase of double flights, crossing each other and both common to the same newel. One cannot admire too greatly the lightness of its arrangement, the boldness of its execution, and the delicacy of its ornaments, — perfection which astonishes and makes it difficult to conceive how any one could imagine a design so picturesque and how it could be put into execution." The author of *Cinq Mars* taking up this same idea says: "It is difficult to conceive how the plan was drawn and how the orders were given to the workmen: it seems a fugitive thought, a brilliant idea which must have taken material form suddenly — a realized dream." . . .

In going through the high halls and long corridors which lead from one chapel to the other, one likes to restore in imagination the rich furniture, the tapestries, the glazed tiles of faïence, and the ceilings incrusted with tin fleur-de-lis, which formed its decoration. Each gallery was filled with frescoes by Jean Cousin and the principal works of Leonardo da Vinci. . . . The breath of the Revolution has scattered and destroyed all these rarities. For fifteen days the frippers ran from all points of the province to divide the paintings, the precious enamels, the chests of oak and ebony, the sculptured pulpits, and the high-posted beds covered with armorial hangings. They sold at auction all the souvenirs of the glory of the monarchy. What they could not sell, they burned. . . .

When we descend the noble staircase which François I. ordered, which an unknown artist executed, and which deserves to be credited to Primaticcio, it is impossible not to look back upon the Past. What illustrious feet have trod, what eyes have beheld these marvels! What hands, now cold, charming hands of queens, or courtesans more powerful than those queens, and rude hands of warriors, or statesmen, have traced on these white stones names celebrated in that day, but now effaced from the walls, as they are each day more and more effaced from the memory of men! The wheel of Time, which broke in its revolution, has only left enough in this *château* for us to observe and reconstruct in imagination personages great enough to harmonize with such grandeur, and to excite in us that pious respect which must always be attached to everything about to end. Another turn of the wheel and ruin will begin. " *Ce château*," a poet has said, "*est frappé de malédiction.*"[1] . . .

To-day, and during two Revolutions, the chief of the eldest branch of the Bourbons has remained the master of Chambord. Between this exiled master and this deserted castle there is an intimate and sad relation which will touch the most unsympathetic heart. Each stone that falls in the grass-grown court without a human ear to take

[1] Chateaubriand, *La Vie de Rancé*.

note of the noise, — is it not the parallel of an obliterated memory, a hope that is ever weakening? In the absence of this master, who, doubtless, will never return, the old *château* falls into the shadow and silence which belong to fallen majesty. It awaits in this grave and slightly morose sorrow those great vicissitudes, which are imposed on stones, as on men, that the Future has in store.

Les Résidences royales de la Loire (Paris, 1863).

THE TEMPLES OF NIKKO.

PIERRE LOTI.

> He who has not beheld Nikko, has no right to make use of the word *splendour*.   *Japanese Proverb.*

IN the heart of the large island of Niphon and in a mountainous and wooded region, fifty leagues from Yokohama, is hidden that marvel of marvels—the necropolis of the Japanese Emperors.

There, on the declivity of the Holy Mountain of Nikko, under cover of a dense forest and in the midst of cascades whose roar among the shadows of the cedars never ceases, is a series of enchanting temples, made of bronze and lacquer with roofs of gold, which look as if a magic ring must have called them into existence among the ferns and mosses and the green dampness, over-arched by dark branches and surrounded by the wildness and grandeur of Nature.

Within these temples there is an inconceivable magnificence, a fairy-like splendour. Nobody is about, except a few guardian bonzes who chant hymns, and several white-robed priestesses who perform the sacred dances whilst waving their fans. Every now and then the slow vibrations of an enormous bronze gong, or the dull, heavy blows on a monstrous prayer-drum are heard in the deep and echoing forest. At other times there are certain sounds which really seem to be a part of the silence and solitude, the chirp of the grasshoppers, the cry of the falcons in the air, the chatter of the monkeys in the branches, and the monotonous fall of the cascades.

All this dazzling gold in the mystery of the forest makes these sepulchres unique. This is the Mecca of Japan; this is the heart, as yet inviolate, of this country which is now gradually sinking in the great Occidental current, but which has had a magnificent Past. Those were strange mystics and very rare artists who, three or four hundred years ago, realized all this magnificence in the depths of the woods and for their dead. . . .

We stop before the first temple. It stands a little off to itself in a kind of glade. You approach it by a garden with raised terraces; a garden with grottos, fountains, and dwarf-trees with violet, yellow, or reddish foliage.

The vast temple is entirely red, and blood-red; an enormous black and gold roof, turned up at the corners, seems to crush it with its weight. From it comes a kind of religious music, soft and slow, interrupted from time to time by a heavy and horrible blow.

It is wide open, open so that its entire façade with columns is visible; but the interior is hidden by an immense white *velum*. The *velum* is of silk, only ornamented in its entire white length by three or four large, black, heraldic roses, which are very simple, but I cannot describe their exquisite distinction, and behind this first and half-lifted hanging, the light bamboo blinds are let down to the ground.

We walk up several granite steps, and, to permit my

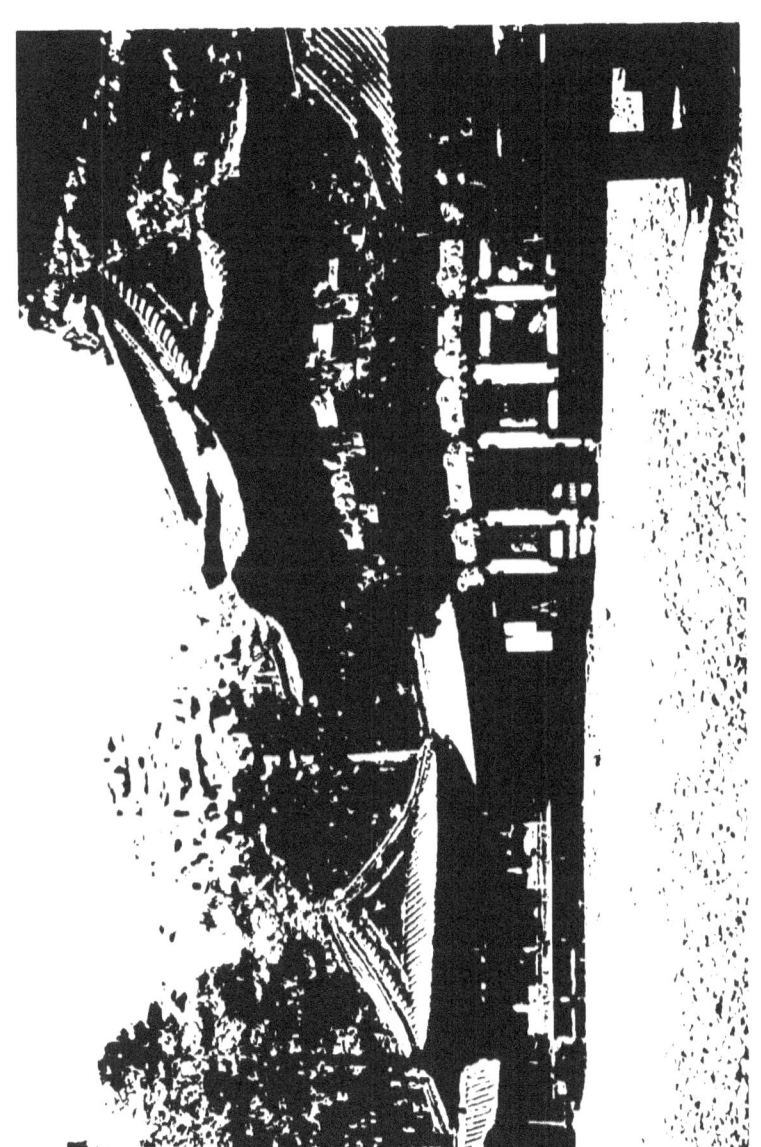

THE TEMPLES OF NIKKO.

entrance, my guide pushes aside a corner of the Veil: the sanctuary appears.

Within everything is in black lacquer and gold lacquer, with the gold predominating. Above the complicated cornice and golden frieze there springs a ceiling in compartments, in worked lacquer of black and gold. Behind the colonnade at the back, the remote part, where, doubtless, the gods are kept, is hidden by long curtains of black and gold brocade, hanging in stiff folds from the ceiling to the floor. Upon white mats on the floor large golden vases are standing, filled with great bunches of golden lotuses as tall as trees. And finally from the ceiling, like the bodies of large dead serpents or monstrous boas, hang a quantity of astonishing caterpillars of silk, as large as a human arm, blue, yellow, orange, brownish-red, and black, or strangely variegated like the throats of certain birds of those islands.

Some bonzes are singing in one corner, seated in a circle around a prayer-drum, large enough to hold them all. . . .

We go out by the back door, which leads into the most curious garden in the world: it is a square filled with shadows shut in by the forest cedars and high walls, which are red like the sanctuary; in the centre rises a very large bronze obelisk flanked with four little ones, and crowned with a pyramid of golden leaves and golden bells; — you would say that in this country bronze and gold cost nothing; they are used in such profusion, everywhere, just as we use the mean materials of stone and plaster. — All along this blood-red wall which forms the back of the temple, in order to animate this melancholy garden, at about the height of a man there is a level row of little wooden gods, of all forms and colours, which are gazing at the obelisk; some blue, others yellow, others green; some have the shape of a man, others of an elephant: a company of dwarfs, extraordinarily comical, but which express no merriment.

In order to reach the other temples, we again walk through the damp and shadowy woods along the avenues of cedars, which ascend and descend and intersect in various ways, and really constitute the streets of this city of the dead.

We walk on pathways of fine sand, strewn with these little brown needles which drop from the cedars. Always in terraces, they are bordered with balustrades and pillars of granite covered with the most delicious moss; you would say all the hand-rails have been garnished with a beautiful green velvet, and at each side of the sanded pathway invariably flow little fresh and limpid brooks, which join their crystal notes to those of the distant torrents and cascades.

At a height of one hundred, or two hundred metres, we arrive at the entrance of something which seems to indicate magnificence: above us on the mountain in the medley of branches, walls taper upward, while roofs of lacquer and bronze, with their population of monsters, are perched everywhere, shining with gold.

Before this entrance there is a kind of open square, a narrow glade, where a little sunlight falls. And here in its luminous rays two bonzes in ceremonial costume pass across the dark background: one, in a long robe of violet silk with a surplice of orange silk; the other, in a robe of pearl-grey with a sky-blue surplice; each wears a high and rigid head-dress of black lacquer, which is seldom worn now.

THE TEMPLES OF NIKKO. 181

(These were the only human beings whom we met on the way, during our pilgrimage.) They are probably going to perform some religious office, and, passing before the sumptuous entrance, they make profound bows.

This temple before which we are now standing is that of the deified soul of the Emperor Yeyaz (Sixteenth Century), and, perhaps, the most marvellous of all the buildings of Nikko.

You ascend by a series of doors and enclosures, which become more and more beautiful as you get higher and nearer the sanctuary, where the soul of this dead Emperor dwells. . . .

At the door of the Palace of the Splendour of the Orient we stop to take off our shoes according to custom. Gold is everywhere, resplendent gold.

An indescribable ornamentation has been chosen for this threshold; on the enormous posts are a kind of wavy clouds, or ocean-billows, in the centre of which here and there appear the tentacles of medusæ, the ends of paws, the claws of crabs, the ends of long caterpillars, flat and scaly, — all kinds of horrible fragments, imitated in colossal size with a striking fidelity, and making you think that the beasts to which they belong must be hidden there within the walls ready to enfold you and tear your flesh. This splendour has mysteriously hostile undercurrents; we feel that it has many a surprise and menace. Above our heads the lintels are, however, ornamented with large, exquisite flowers in bronze, or gold: roses, peonies, wistaria, and spring branches of full-blown cherry-blossoms; but, still higher, horrible faces with fixed death's-head grimaces lean toward us;

terrible things of all shapes hang by their golden wings from the golden beams of the roof; we perceive in the air rows of mouths split open with atrocious laughter, and rows of eyes half-closed in an unquiet sleep.

An old priest, aroused by the noise of our footsteps on the gravel in the silence of the court, appears before us on the bronze threshold. In order to examine the permit which I present to him, he puts a pair of round spectacles on his nose, which make him look like an owl.

My papers are in order. A bow, and he steps aside to let me enter.

It is gloomy inside this palace, with that mysterious semi-twilight which the Spirits delight in. The impressions felt on entering are grandeur and repose.

The walls are of gold and the ceiling is of gold, supported on columns of gold. A vague, trembling light, illuminating as if from beneath, enters through the very much grated and very low windows; the dark, undetermined depths are full of the gleamings of precious things.

Yellow gold, red gold, green gold; gold that is vital, or tarnished; gold that is brilliant, or lustreless; here and there on the friezes and on the exquisite capitals of the columns, a little vermilion, and a little emerald green; very little, nothing but a thin thread of colour, just enough to relieve the wing of a bird and the petal of a lotus, a peony, or a rose. Despite so much richness nothing is overcharged; such taste has been displayed in the arrangement of the thousands of diverse forms and such harmony in the extremely complicated designs, that the effect of the whole is simple and reposeful.

THE TEMPLES OF NIKKO. 183

Neither human figures nor idols have a part in this sanctuary of Shintoism. Nothing stands upon the altars but large vases of gold filled with natural flowers in sheaves, or gigantic flowers of gold.

No idols, but a multitude of beasts, flying or crawling, familiar or chimerical, pursue each other upon the walls, and fly away from the friezes and ceiling in all attitudes of fury and struggle, of terror and flight. Here, a flock of swans hurry away in swift flight the whole length of the golden cornice; in other places are butterflies with tortoises; large and hideous insects among the flowers, or many death-combats between fantastic beasts of the sea, medusæ with big eyes, and imaginary fishes. On the ceiling innumerable dragons bristle and coil. The windows, cut out in multiple trefoils, in a form never before seen and which give little light, seem only a pretext for displaying all kinds of marvellous piercings: trellises of gold entwined with golden leaves, among which golden birds are sporting; all of this seems accumulated at pleasure and permits the least possible light to enter into the deep golden shadows of the temple. The only really simple objects are the columns of a fine golden lacquer ending with capitals of a very sober design, forming a slight calix of the lotus, like those of certain ancient Egyptian palaces.

We could spend days in admiring separately each panel, each pillar, each minute detail; the least little piece of the ceiling, or the walls would be a treasure for a museum. And so many rare and extravagant objects have succeeded in making the whole a composition of large quiet lines; many living forms, many distorted bodies, many ruffled wings, stiff claws, open mouths, and squinting eyes have succeeded in producing a calm, an absolute calm, by force of an inexplicable harmony, twilight, and silence.

I believe, moreover, that here is the quintessence of Japanese Art, of which the specimens brought to our collections of Europe cannot give the true impression. And we are struck by feeling that this Art, so foreign to us, proceeds from an origin so different; nothing here is derived, ever so remotely, from what we call antiquities — Greek, Latin, or Arabian — which always influence, even if we are not aware of it, our native ideas regarding ornamental form. Here the least design, the smallest line, — everything — is as profoundly strange as if it had come from a neighbouring planet which had never held communication with our side of the world.

The entire back of the temple, where it is almost night, is occupied by great doors of black lacquer and gold lacquer, with bolts of carved gold, shutting in a very sacred place which they refuse to show me. They tell me, moreover, that there is nothing in these closets; but that they are the places where the deified souls of the heroes love to dwell; the priests only open them on certain occasions to place in them poems in their honour, or prayers wisely written on rice-paper.

The two lateral wings on each side of the large golden sanctuary are entirely of *marqueterie*, in prodigious mosaics composed of the most precious woods left in their natural colour. The representations are animals and plants: on the walls are light leaves in relief, bamboo, grasses of extreme delicacy, gold convolvulus falling in clusters of flowers, birds of resplendent plumage, peacocks and pheasants with spread tails. There is no painting here, no gold-work; the whole effect is sombre, the general tone that of dead wood; but each leaf of each branch is composed of a different piece; and also each feather of each bird is shaded in such a way as to almost produce the effect of changing colours on the throats and wings.

And at last, at last, behind all this magnificence, the most sacred place which they show me last, the most strange of all strange places, is the little mortuary court which surrounds the tomb. It is hollowed out of a mountain between whose rocky walls water is dripping: the lichens and moss have made a damp carpet here and the tall, surrounding cedars throw their dark shadows over it. There is an enclosure of bronze, shut by a bronze door which is inscribed across its centre with an inscription in gold,— not in the Japanese language, but in Sanscrit to give more mystery; a massive, lugubrious, inexorable door, extraordinary beyond all expression, and which is the ideal door for a sepulchre. In the centre of this enclosure is a kind of round turret also in bronze having the form of a pagoda-bell, of a kneeling beast, of I don't know what unknown and disturbing thing, and surmounted by a great astonishing heraldic flower: here, under this singular object, rests the body of the little yellow *bonhomme*, once the Emperor Yeyaz, for whom all this pomp has been displayed. . . .

A little breeze agitates the branches of the cedars this morning and there falls a shower of these little dry, brown needles, a little brown rain on the greyish lichens, on the green velvet moss, and upon the sinister bronze objects. The voice of the cascades is heard in the distance like perpetual sacred music. An impression of nothingness and supreme peace reigns in this final court, to which so much splendour leads.

In another quarter of the forest the temple of the deified soul of Yemidzou is of an almost equal magnificence. It is approached by a similar series of steps, little carved and gilded light-towers, doors of bronze and enclosures of lacquer; but the plan of the whole is a little less regular, because the mountain is more broken. . . .

A solemn hour on the Holy Mountain is at night-fall, when they close the temples. It is even more lugubrious at this autumnal season, when the twilight brings sad thoughts. With heavy, rumbling sounds which linger long in the sonorous forest, the great panels of lacquer and bronze are rolled on their grooves to shut in the magnificent buildings which have been open all day, although visited by nobody. A cold and damp shiver passes through the black forest. For fear of fire, which might consume these marvels, not a single light is allowed in this village of Spirits, where certainly darkness falls sooner and remains longer than anywhere else; no lamp has ever shone upon these treasures, which have thus slept in darkness in the very heart of Japan for many centuries; and the cascades increase their music while the silence of night enshrouds the forest so rich in enchantment.

Japoneries d'automne (15th ed., Paris, 1889).

THE PALACE OF HOLYROOD.

THE PALACE OF HOLYROOD.

DAVID MASSON.

JUST after the middle of August, 1561, as we learn from contemporary records, there was a *haar* of unusual intensity and continuance over Edinburgh and all the vicinity. It began on Sunday the 17th, and it lasted with slight intermissions, till Thursday the 21st. "Besides the surfett weat and corruptioun of the air," writes Knox, then living in Edinburgh, "the myst was so thick and dark that skairse mycht any man espy ane other the length of two pair of butts." It was the more unfortunate because it was precisely in those days of miserable fog and drizzle that Mary, Queen of Scots, on her return to Scotland after her thirteen years of residence and education in France, had to form her first real acquaintance with her native shores and the capital of her realm.

She had left Calais for the homeward voyage on Thursday the 14th of August, with a retinue of about one hundred and twenty persons, French and Scottish, embarked in two French state galleys, attended by several transports. They were a goodly company, with rich and splendid baggage. The Queen's two most important uncles, indeed, — the great Francis de Lorraine, Duke of Guise, and his brother, Charles de Lorraine, the Cardinal, — were not on board. They, with the Duchess of Guise and other senior lords and ladies of the French Court, had bidden Mary farewell at Calais, after having accompanied her thither from Paris, and after the Cardinal had in vain tried to persuade her not to take her costly collection of pearls and other jewels with her, but to leave them in his keeping till it should be seen how she might fare among her Scottish subjects. But on board the Queen's own galley were three others of her Guise or Lorraine uncles, — the Duc d'Aumale, the Grand Prior, and the Marquis d'Elbeuf, — with M. Damville, son of the Constable of France, and a number of French gentlemen of lower rank, among whom one notes especially young Pierre de Bourdeilles, better known afterwards in literary history as Sieur de Brantôme, and a sprightly and poetic youth from Dauphiné, named Chastelard, one of the attendants of M. Damville. With these were mixed the Scottish contingent of the Queen's train, her four famous "Marys" included, — Mary Fleming, Mary Livingstone, Mary Seton, and Mary Beaton. They had been her playfellows and little maids of honour long ago in her Scottish childhood; they had accompanied her when she went abroad, and had lived with her ever since in France; and they were now returning with her, Scoto-Frenchwomen like herself, and all of about her own age, to share her new fortunes.

It is to Brantôme that we owe what account we have of the voyage from Calais. He tells us how the Queen could hardly tear herself away from her beloved France, but kept gazing at the French coast hour after hour so long as it was in sight, shedding tears with every look, and exclaiming again and again, " Adieu, ma chère France! Je ne vous verray jamais plus!" . . .

THE PALACE OF HOLYROOD. 189

It was in the afternoon of Wednesday, the 20th of August, that there was a procession on horseback of the Queen, her French retinue, and the gathered Scottish lords and councillors, through the two miles of road which led from Leith to Holyrood. On the way the Queen was met by a deputation of the Edinburgh craftsmen and their apprentices, craving her royal pardon for the ringleaders in a recent riot, in which the Tolbooth had been broken open and the Magistrates insulted and defied. This act of grace accorded as a matter of course, the Queen was that evening in her hall of Holyrood, the most popular of sovereigns for the moment, her uncles and other chiefs of her escort with her, and the rest dispersed throughout the apartments, while outside, in spite of the fog, there were bonfires of joy in the streets and up the slopes of Arthur's Seat, and a crowd of cheering loiterers moved about in the space between the palace-gate and the foot of the Canongate. Imparting some regulation to the proceedings of this crowd, for a while at least, was a special company of the most " honest " of the townsmen, " with instruments of musick and with musicians," admitted within the gate, and tendering the Queen their salutations, instrumental and vocal, under her chamber window. " The melody, as she alledged, lyked her weill, and she willed the same to be continewed some nightis after." This is Knox's account; but Brantôme tells a different story. After noting the wretchedness of the hackneys provided for the procession from Leith to Holyrood, and the poorness of their harnessings and trappings, the sight of which, he says, made the Queen weep, he goes on to mention the evening serenade under the windows of Holyrood, as the very completion of the day's disagreeables. The Abbey itself, he admits, was a fine enough building; but, just as the Queen had supped and wanted to go to sleep, "there came under her window five or six hundred rascals of the town to serenade her with vile fiddles and rebecks, such as they do not lack in that country, setting themselves to sing psalms, and singing so ill and in such bad accord that there could be nothing worse. Ah! what music, and what a lullaby for the night!" Whether Knox's account of the Queen's impressions of the serenade or Brantôme's is to be accepted, there can be no doubt that the matter and intention of the performance were religious. Our authentic picture, therefore, of Queen Mary's first night in Holyrood after her return from France is that of the Palace lit up from within, the dreary fog still persistent outside, the bonfires on Arthur's Seat and other vantage-grounds flickering through the fog, and the portion of the wet crowd nearest the Palace singing Protestant psalms for the Queen's delectation to an accompaniment of violins.

Next day, Thursday the 21st, this memorable Edinburgh *haar* of August 1561 came to an end. Arthur's Seat and the other heights and ranges of the park round Holyrood wore, we may suppose, their freshest verdure; and Edinburgh, dripping no longer, shone forth, we may hope, in her sunniest beauty. The Queen could then become more particularly acquainted with the Palace in which she had come to reside, and with the nearer aspects of the town to which the Palace was attached, and into which she had yet to make her formal entry.

Then, as now, the buildings that went by the general

name of Holyrood were distinguishable into two portions. There was the Abbey, now represented only by the beautiful and spacious fragment of ruin, called the Royal Chapel, but then, despite the spoliations to which it had been subjected by recent English invasions, still tolerably preserved in its integrity as the famous edifice, in Early Norman style, which had been founded in the Twelfth Century by David I., and had been enlarged in the Fifteenth by additions in the later and more florid Gothic. Close by this was Holyrood House, or the Palace proper, built in the earlier part of the Sixteenth Century, and chiefly by James IV., to form a distinct royal dwelling, and so supersede that occasional accommodation in the Abbey itself which had sufficed for Scottish sovereigns before Edinburgh was their habitual or capital residence. One block of this original Holyrood House still remains in the two-turreted projection of the present Holyrood which adjoins the ruined relic of the Abbey, and which contains the rooms now specially shown as " Queen Mary's Apartments." But the present Holyrood, as a whole, is a construction of the reign of Charles II., and gives little idea of the Palace in which Mary took up her abode in 1561. The two-turreted projection on the left was not balanced then, as now, by a similar two-turreted projection on the right, with a façade of less height between, but was flanked on the right by a continued château-like frontage, of about the same height as the turreted projection, and at a uniform depth of recess from it, but independently garnished with towers and pinnacles. The main entrance into the Palace from the great outer courtyard was through this château-like flank, just about the spot where there is the entrance through the present middle façade; and this entrance led, like the present, into an inner court or quadrangle, built round on all the four sides. That quadrangle of château, touching the Abbey to the back from its north-eastern corner, and with the two-turreted projection to its front from its north-western corner, constituted, indeed, the main bulk of the Palace. There were, however, extensive appurtenances of other buildings at the back or at the side farthest from the Abbey, forming minor inner courts, while part of that side of the great outer courtyard which faced the entrance was occupied by offices belonging to the Palace, and separating the courtyard from the adjacent purlieus of the town. For the grounds of both Palace and Abbey were encompassed by a wall, having gates at various points of its circuit, the principal and most strongly guarded of which was the Gothic porch admitting from the foot of the Canongate into the front courtyard. The grounds so enclosed were ample enough to contain gardens and spaces of plantation, besides the buildings and their courts. Altogether, what with the buildings themselves, what with the courts and gardens, and what with the natural grandeur of the site,—a level of deep and wooded park, between the Calton heights and crags on the one hand and the towering shoulders of Arthur Seat and precipitous escarpment of Salisbury Crags on the other,—Holyrood in 1561 must have seemed, even to an eye the most satiated with palatial splendours abroad, a sufficiently impressive dwelling-place to be the metropolitan home of Scottish royalty.

Edinburgh Sketches and Memories (London and Edinburgh, 1892).

SAINT-GUDULE.

SAINT-GUDULE.

VICTOR HUGO.

THE windows of Saint-Gudule are of a kind almost unknown in France, real paintings, real pictures on glass of a marvellous style, with figures like Titian and architecture like Paul Veronese.

The pulpit of this church is carved in wood by Henry Verbruggen and bears the date of 1699. The whole of creation, the whole of philosophy, the whole of poetry are expressed here by an enormous tree which supports the pulpit in its boughs and shelters a world of birds and animals among its leaves, while at its base Adam and Eve are pursued by a sorrowful angel, followed by Death who seems triumphant, and separated by the tail of the serpent. At its summit, the cross — Truth — and the infant Jesus, whose foot rests upon the head of the bruised serpent. This poem is sculptured and carved out of oak alone, in the strongest, the most tender, and the most *spirituelle* manner. The effect is prodigiously rococo and prodigiously beautiful. No matter what the fanatics of the severe school would say, it is true. This pulpit is one of those rare instances in art where the beautiful and the rococo meet. Watteau and Coypel have also occasionally discovered such points of intersection. . . .

It was three o'clock when I entered Saint-Gudule. They were celebrating the Office of the Virgin. A

Madonna, covered with jewels and clothed in a robe of English lace, glittered on a dais of gold in the centre of the nave through a luminous cloud of incense which was dispersed around her. Many people were praying in the shadow motionless, and a strong ray of sunlight from above dispelled the gloom and shone full upon the large statues of proud mien arranged against the columns. The worshippers seemed of stone, the statues seemed alive.

And then a beautiful chant of mingled deep and ringing voices fell mysteriously with the tones of the organ from the highest rails hidden by the mists of incense. I, during this time, had my eye fixed dreamily upon Verbruggen's pulpit, teeming with life, — that magic pulpit which is always suggestive. — Frame this with windows, ogives, and Renaissance tombs of white marble and black, and you will understand why a sublime sensation was produced by this scene. . . .

I climbed the towers of Saint-Gudule. It was beautiful. The entire city lay beneath me, the toothed and voluted roofs of Brussels half-hidden by the smoke, the sky (a stormy sky), full of clouds, golden and curled above, solid as marble below; in the distance a large cloud from which rain was falling like fine sand from a bag which has burst; the sun shone above everything; the magnificent openwork, lantern-like belfry stood out sombre against the white mists; then the confused noise of the town reached me, then the verdure of the lovely hills on the horizon: it was truly beautiful. I admired everything like a provincial from Paris, which I am, — everything, even the mason who was hammering on a stone and whistling near me.

En Voyage: France et Belgique (Paris, 1892).

THE ESCURIAL.

THE ESCURIAL.

EDMONDO DE AMICIS.

BEFORE my departure for Andalusia, I went to see the famous Convent of the Escurial, the leviathan of architecture, the eighth wonder of the world, the largest mass of granite upon the earth, and, if you desire other imposing epithets, then you must imagine them, for you will not find one that has not been used to describe it. I left Madrid in the early morning. The village of the Escurial, from which the Convent received its name, is eight leagues from the city, not far from the Guadarrama; you pass through an arid and uninhabited country whose horizon is bounded by snow-covered mountains. A light, fine, and cold rain was falling when I reached the station of the Escurial. From it to the village there is a rise of half a mile. I clambered into an omnibus, and at the end of a few minutes, I was deposited in a solitary street bordered on the left by the Convent and on the right by the houses of the village, and shut in by the mountains. At the first glance you understand nothing; you expect to see a building and you find a city; you do not know if you are already in the Convent, or if you are outside; you are hemmed in by walls. You advance, and find yourself in a square; you look about you and see streets;

you have not yet entered, and already the Convent surrounds you: you are at your wit's end, and no longer know which way to turn. The first feeling is one of depression: the entire edifice is of mud-coloured stone, and all the layers are marked by a white stripe; the roofs are covered with lead. You might call it a building made of earth. The very high walls are naked and pierced by a great number of windows which resemble barbicans. You might call it a prison rather than a convent. You find this gloomy colour everywhere: there is not a living soul here, and the silence is that of a deserted fortress; and beyond the black roofs, the black mountain, which seems to be suspended over the building, gives it mysterious solitude. It seems as if the founder must have chosen the spot, the plan, and the colours, everything, in fact, with the intention of producing a sad and solemn spectacle. You lose your gaiety before entering; you can smile no longer, you are thinking. You pause at the door of the Escurial with a kind of quaking, as if at the entrance of a dead city; it seems to you that if the terrible Inquisition is reigning in any corner of the world, it must be between these walls; for it is here that you can see its last traces and hear its last echo.

Everybody knows that the Basilica and the Convent of the Escurial were founded by Philip II. after the battle of San Quintino to fulfil his vow made during the war to Saint Laurence when he was forced to cannonade a church consecrated to this saint. Don Juan Batista of Toledo commenced the building and Herrera finished it, and the work upon it lasted for twenty-one years. Philip II. wished the building to have the form of a gridiron in memory of Saint Laurence's martyrdom; and, in reality, this is its form. The plan is a rectangular parallelogram. Four large square towers with pointed roofs rise at the four corners, and represent the four feet of a gridiron; the church and the royal palace, which extend on one side, represent the handle; and the interior buildings, which are placed across the two long sides, represent the parallel bars. Other smaller buildings rise outside of the parallelogram, not far from the Convent, along one of the long sides and one of the courts, forming two large squares; the other two sides are occupied by gardens. Façades, doors, and entrance-halls, are all in harmony with the grandeur and character of the edifice: it is useless to multiply descriptions. The royal Palace is magnificent, and in order to keep a clear impression of each individual building, it is better to see it before you enter the Convent and Church. This palace is in the north-east corner of the building. Several halls are filled with pictures, others are hung from the ceiling to the floor with tapestries, representing bull-fights, dances, games, *fêtes*, and Spanish costumes, after Goya; others are decorated and furnished in princely style; the floor, the doors, and the windows are covered with marvellous mosaics and dazzling gold-work. But among all the rooms, that of Philip II. is especially remarkable. It is a dark and bare cell, whose alcove communicates with the royal oratory of the church in such a way that, when the doors were open, from his bed he could see the priest celebrating Mass. Philip II. slept in this room, had his last illness there, and died there. You can still see some of the chairs he used, two little benches on which he rested his gouty leg, and a writing-desk. The walls are white, the ceiling is unornamented, and the floor is of stone.

When you have seen the royal Palace, you go out of the building, cross the square, and re-enter the great door. A guide joins you and you pass through the large entrance to find yourself in the Kings' court-yard. Here you gain an idea of the enormous structure of the building. This court is entirely shut in by walls; opposite the door is the façade of the Church. Above a wide stairway stand six enormous Doric columns; each of these supports a large pedestal, and each pedestal upholds a statue. These six colossal statues are by Batista Monegro, representing Jehoshaphat, Ezekiel, David, Solomon, Joshua, and Manasseh. The court-yard is paved and bunches of damp grass grow here and there; the walls look like rocks cut in points; everything is rigid, massive, and heavy, and presents the indescribable aspect of a fantastic edifice hewn by Titans from a mountain and capable of defying earthquakes and lightnings. At this point you really begin to understand the Escurial. . . .

After seeing the Church and the Sacristy, you visit the Picture-Gallery, which contains a large number of paintings by artists of all countries, not the best examples, however, for these have been taken to the Madrid gallery, but of sufficient value to merit a thoughtful visit of half a day. From the Picture-Gallery you go to the Library by means of the large stairway, over which is rounded an enormous vaulted ceiling, painted all over with frescoes by Luca Giordano. The Library is an immense hall adorned with large allegorical paintings, and contains more than fifty thousand rare volumes, four thousand of which were given by Philip II., and beyond this is another hall, which contains a very valuable collection of manuscripts. From the Library you go to the Convent. Here human imagination is completely lost. If my reader knows Espronceda's *Estudiante de Salamanca*, he will remember that the persistent young man, when following the mysterious lady whom he met at night at the foot of a tabernacle, runs from street to street, from square to square, and from alley to alley, turning and returning, until he arrives at a spot where he can no longer see the houses of Salamanca and where he discovers that he is in an unknown city; and in proportion as he advances the town seems to grow larger, the streets longer and the intertwining alleys more tortuous; but he goes on and on without stopping, not knowing if he is awake or dreaming, if he is intoxicated or mad; terror begins to enter his brave heart and the most peculiar phantoms crowd into his distracted mind: this is what happens to the stranger in the Convent of the Escurial. You pass through a long subterranean corridor, so narrow that you can touch the wall with your elbows, so low that your head almost hits the ceiling, and as damp as a grotto under the sea; on reaching its end, you turn, and you are in another corridor. You go on, pass through doors, and look around: other corridors extend as far as your eye can see. At the end of some of them you notice a feeble light, at the end of others an open door which reveals a suite of rooms. Every now and then you hear a footstep: you stop; all is silent; then you hear it again; you do not know if it is above your head, or to the right, or the left, or before you, or behind you.

You are about to enter a door; you recoil in terror: at the end of a long corridor you see a man, motionless as a spectre, who is staring at you. You continue your journey and arrive in a strange court, surrounded by high walls and overgrown with grass, full of echoes, and illuminated by a wan light which seems to come from some strange sun; it reminds you of the haunts of witches described to you in your childhood. You go out of the court, walk up a stairway, arrive in a gallery, and look down: there beneath you is another, and deserted, court. You walk down another corridor, you descend another stairway, and you find yourself in a third court; then again more corridors, stairways, suites of empty rooms, and narrow courts, and everywhere granite, a wan light, and the stillness of death. For a short time you think you could retrace your steps; then your memory forsakes you, and you recall nothing: it seems as if you had walked ten leagues, that you have been in this labyrinth for a month, and that you will never get out of it. You come to a court, and exclaim: "I have seen this before!" No you are mistaken: it is another one. You think you are on one side of the building and you are on the opposite one. You ask your guide for the cloister, and he replies: "It is here," and you continue walking for half an hour. You fancy you are dreaming: you have glimpses of long walls, frescoed, and adorned with pictures, the crucifix, and with inscriptions; you see and you forget; you ask yourself "Where am I?" You see a light as if from another world: you have never conceived of such a peculiar light. Is it the reflection of the granite? Is it moonlight? No, it is daylight; but a daylight sadder than darkness; it is a false, sinister, fantastic daylight. Let us go on! From corridor to corridor, from court to court, you look before you with mistrust; you expect to see suddenly at the turn of a corner a row of skeleton monks with hoods drawn over their eyes and their arms folded; you think of Philip II.; you fancy you hear his step growing ever fainter down the distant passages; you remember all you have read of him, of his terrors, of the Inquisition; and everything becomes suddenly plain; you understand it all for the first time: the Escurial is Philip II., you see him at every step, and you hear him breathe; for he is here, living and fearful, and the image of his terrible God is with him. Then you want to revolt, to raise your thought to the God of your heart and hope, and to conquer the mysterious terror which this place inspires; but you cannot; the Escurial envelops you, possesses you, crushes you; the cold of its stones penetrates into your very bones, the sadness of its sepulchral labyrinths takes possession of your soul. If you were with a friend, you would say: "Let us go!"; if you were with your loved one, you would tremblingly clasp her to your heart; if you were alone, you would take flight. Finally you ascend the stairway, and, entering a room, go to the window to salute rapturously the mountains, the sunshine, liberty, and the great and generous God who loves and pardons.

How one breathes again at this window!

From it you see the gardens, which occupy a restricted space and which are very simple, but elegant and beautiful, and in perfect harmony with the building. You see in them twelve charming fountains, each surrounded by four squares of box-wood, representing the royal escutcheons, designed with such skill and trimmed with such precision that in looking at them from the windows they seem to be made of plush and velvet, and they stand out from the white sand of the walks in a very striking manner. There are no trees, nor flowers, nor pavilions here; in all the gardens nothing is to be seen but fountains and squares of box-wood and these two colours — white and green — and such is the beauty of this noble simplicity that the eye is enchanted with it, and when it has passed out of sight, the thought returns and rests there with pleasure mingled with a gentle melancholy. . . .

An illustrious traveller has said that after having spent a day in the Convent of the Escurial, one should feel happy for the remainder of his life in thinking that he might be still between those walls, but that he has escaped. That is very nearly true. Even now, after so long a time, on rainy days when I am sad I think about the Escurial, then I look around the walls of my room and I become gay; during nights of insomnia, I see the courts of the Escurial; when I am ill and drop into a feverish and heavy sleep, I dream that all night I am wandering in these corridors, alone and followed by the phantom of a monk, screaming and knocking at all the doors without finding a way out, until I decide to go to the Pantheon, where the door bangs behind me and shuts me in among the tombs.

With what delight I saw the myriad lights of the *Puerta del Sol*, the crowded *cafés* and the great and noisy street of the Alcala! When I went into the house I made such a noise, that the servant, who was a good and simple Gallician, ran excitedly to her mistress and said: "*Me parece el italiano se ha vuelto loco.*" (I think the Italian has lost his senses).

La Spagna (Florence, 1873).

THE TEMPLE OF MADURA.

JAMES FERGUSSON.

THERE does not seem to be any essential difference either in plan or form between the Saiva and Vaishnava temples in the south of India. It is only by observing the images or emblems worshipped, or by reading the stories represented in the numerous sculptures with which a temple is adorned, that we find out the god to whom it is dedicated. Whoever he may be, the temples consist almost invariably of the four following parts, arranged in various manners, as afterwards to be explained, but differing in themselves only according to the age in which they were executed: —

1. The principal part, the actual temple itself, is called the *Vimana*. It is always square in plan, and surmounted by a pyramidal roof of one or more storeys; it contains the cell in which the image of the god or his emblem is placed.

2. The porches or *Mantapas*, which always cover and precede the door leading to the cell.

3. Gate pyramids, *Gopuras*, which are the principal features in the quadrangular enclosures which always surround the *Vimanas*.

4. Pillared halls or *Choultries*, used for various purposes, and which are the invariable accompaniments of these temples.

THE TEMPLE OF MADURA.

Besides these, a temple always contains tanks or wells for water — to be used either for sacred purposes or the convenience of the priests, — dwellings for all the various grades of the priesthood attached to it, and numerous other buildings designed for state or convenience. . . .

The population of southern India in the Seventeenth and Eighteenth Century was probably hardly less than it is now — some thirty millions — and if one-third or one-fourth of such a population were to seek employment in building, the results, if persevered in through centuries, would be something astonishing. A similar state of affairs prevailed apparently in Egypt in the time of the Pharaohs, but with very different results. The Egyptians had great and lofty ideas, and a hankering after immortality, that impressed itself on all their works. The southern Indians had no such aspirations. Their intellectual status is, and always was, mediocre; they had no literature of their own — no history to which they could look back with pride, and their religion was, and is, an impure and degrading fetishism. It is impossible that anything grand and imposing should come out of such a state of things. What they had to offer to their gods was a tribute of labour, and that was bestowed without stint. To cut a chain of fifty links out of a block of granite and suspend it between two pillars, was with them a triumph of art. To hollow deep cornices out of the hardest basalt, and to leave all the framings, as if of the most delicate woodwork, standing free, was with them a worthy object of ambition, and their sculptures are still inexplicable mysteries, from our ignorance of how it was possible to execute them. All that millions of hands working through centuries could do, has been done, but with hardly any higher motive than to employ labour and to conquer difficulties, so as to astonish by the amount of the first and the cleverness with which the second was overcome — and astonished we are; but without some higher motive true architecture cannot exist. The Dravidians had not even the constructive difficulties to overcome which enabled the Mediæval architects to produce such noble fabrics as our cathedrals. The aim of architects in the Middle Ages was to design halls which should at the same time be vast, but stable, and suited for the accommodation of great multitudes to witness a lofty ritual. In their struggles to accomplish this they developed intellectual powers which impress us still through their works. No such lofty aims exercised the intellectual faculties of the Hindu. His altar and the statue of his god were placed in a dark cubical cell wholly without ornament, and the porch that preceded that was not necessarily either lofty or spacious. What the Hindu architect craved for, was a place to display his powers of ornamentation, and he thought he had accomplished all his art demanded when he covered every part of his building with the most elaborate and most difficult designs he could invent. Much of this ornamentation, it is true, is very elegant, and evidences of power and labour do impress the human imagination, often even in defiance of our better judgment, and nowhere is this more apparent than in these Dravidian temples. It is in vain, however, we look among them for any manifestation of those lofty aims and noble results which constitute the merit and the greatness of true architectural art, and which generally characterise the best works in the true styles of the western world. . . .

Immediately in front of his choultrie, Tirumulla Nayak commenced a gopura, which, had he lived to complete it, would probably have been the finest edifice of its class in southern India. It measures 174 ft. from north to south, and 107 ft. in depth. The entrance through it is 21 ft. 9 in. wide; and if it be true that its gateposts are 60 ft. (Tripe says 57 ft.) in height, that would have been the height of the opening. It will thus be seen that it was designed on even a larger scale than that at Seringham, and it certainly far surpasses that celebrated edifice in the beauty of its details. Its doorposts alone, whether 57 ft. or 60 ft. in height, are single blocks of granite, carved with the most exquisite scroll patterns of elaborate foliage, and all the other carvings are equally beautiful. Being unfinished, and consequently never consecrated, it has escaped whitewash, and alone, of all the buildings of Madura, its beauties can still be admired in their original perfection.

The great temple at Madura is a larger and far more important building than the choultrie; but, somehow or other, it has not attracted the attention of travellers to the same extent that the latter has. No one has ever attempted to make a plan of it, or to describe it in such detail as would enable others to understand its peculiarities. It possesses, however, all the characteristics of a first-class Dravidian temple, and, as its date is perfectly well known, it forms a landmark of the utmost value in enabling us to fix the relative date of other temples.

THE TEMPLE OF MADURA.

The sanctuary is said to have been built by Viswanath, the first king of the Nayak dynasty, A. D. 1520, which may possibly be the case; but the temple itself certainly owes all its magnificence to Tirumulla Nayak, A. D. 1622–1657, or to his elder brother, Muttu Virappa, who preceded him, and who built a mantapa, said to be the oldest thing now existing here. The Kalyana mantapa is said to have been built A. D. 1707, and the Tatta Suddhi in 1770. These, however, are insignificant parts compared with those which certainly owe their origin to Tirumulla Nayak.

The temple itself is a nearly regular rectangle, two of its sides measuring 720 ft. and 729 ft., the other two 834 ft. and 852 ft. It possessed four gopuras of the first class, and five smaller ones; a very beautiful tank, surrounded by arcades; and a hall of 1000 columns, whose sculptures surpass those of any other hall of its class I am acquainted with. There is a small shrine, dedicated to the goddess Minakshi, the tutelary deity of the place, which occupies the space of fifteen columns, so the real number is only 985; but it is not their number, but their marvellous elaboration that makes it the wonder of the place, and renders it, in some respects, more remarkable than the choultrie about which so much has been said and written. I do not feel sure that this hall alone is not a greater work than the choultrie; taken in conjunction with the other buildings of the temple, it certainly forms a far more imposing group.

History of Indian and Eastern Architecture (New York, 1891).

THE CATHEDRAL OF MILAN.

THÉOPHILE GAUTIER.

THE Cathedral absorbs the attention of every traveller who visits Milan. It dominates the town, standing in the centre as its chief attraction and marvel. To it one hastens immediately on arriving, even on a night when there is no moon, to grasp at least a few of its outlines.

The *piazza del Duomo*, irregular enough in its form, is bordered with houses of which it is customary to speak ill; the guide never omits telling the traveller that these should be razed to make this a symmetrical square in the Rivoli taste. I am not of this opinion. These houses with their massive pillars and their saffron-coloured awnings standing opposite to some irregular buildings of unequal height, make a very good setting for the Cathedral. Edifices often lose more than they gain by not being obstructed: I have been convinced of this by several Gothic monuments, the effect of which was not spoiled by the stalls and the ruins which had gathered around them, as might have been believed; this is not, however, the case with the Cathedral, which is perfectly isolated; but I think that nothing is more favourable to a palace, a church, or any regularly constructed building than to be surrounded by heterogeneous buildings which bring out the proportions of the noble order.

When we look at the Cathedral from the square, the effect is ravishing: the whiteness of the marble, standing out from the blue of the sky, strikes you first; one would say that an immense piece of silver lace had been placed against a background of *lapis lazuli*. This is the first impression, and it will also be the last memory. Whenever I think of the Duomo of Milan, it always appears like this. The Cathedral is one of those rare Gothic churches of Italy, yet this Gothic resembles ours but little. We do not find here that sombre faith, that disquieting mystery, those dark depths, those severe forms, that darting up from earth towards the sky, that character of austerity which repudiates beauty as too sensual and only selects from a subject what is necessary to bring you a step nearer to God; this is a Gothic full of elegance, grace, and brilliancy, which one dreams of for fairy palaces and with which one could build alcazars and mosques as well as a Catholic temple. The delicacy in its enormous proportions and its whiteness make it look like a glacier with its thousand needles, or a gigantic concretion of stalactites; it is difficult to believe it the work of man.

The design of the façade is of the simplest: it is an angle sharp as the gable-end of an ordinary house and bordered with marble lace, resting upon a wall without any fore-part, of no distinct order of architecture, pierced by five doors and eight windows and striped with six groups of columns with fillets, or rather mouldings which end in hollowed out points surmounted by statues and filled in their interstices with brackets and niches supporting and sheltering figures of angels, saints, and patriarchs. Back of these spring out from innumerable fillets, like the pipes of a basaltic grotto, forests of little steeples, pinnacles, minarets, and needles of white marble, while the central spire which resembles frost-work, crystallized in the air, rises in the azure to a terrific height and places the Virgin, who is standing upon its tip with her foot on a crescent, within two steps of Heaven. In the middle of the façade these words are inscribed: *Mariae nascenti*, the dedication of the Cathedral.

Begun by Jean Galéas Visconti, continued by Ludovico le More, the basilica of Milan was finished by Napoleon. It is the largest church known after Saint Peter's in Rome. The interior is of a majestic and noble simplicity: rows of columns in pairs form five naves. Notwithstanding their actual mass, these groups of columns have a lightness of effect on account of the grace of their shafts. Above the capitals of the pillars there is a kind of gallery, perforated and carved, where statues of saints are placed; then the mouldings continue until they unite at the summit of the vault, which is ornamented with trefoils and Gothic knots made with such perfection that they would deceive the eye, if the plaster, which has fallen in places, did not reveal the naked stone.

In the centre of the cross an opening, surrounded by a balustrade, allows you to look down into the crypt, where the remains of Saint Charles Borromeo rest in a crystal coffin covered with plates of silver. Saint Charles Borromeo is the most revered saint of the district. His virtues and his conduct during the plague in Milan made him popular, and his memory is always kept alive.

At the entrance of the choir upon a grille which supports a crucifix, surrounded by angels in adoration, we read the following inscription framed in wood : *Attendite ad petram unde excisi estis.* On each side there are two magnificent pulpits of wood, supported by superb bronze figures and ornamented with silver bas-reliefs, the subjects of which are their least value. The organs, placed not far from the pulpits, have fine paintings by Procacini, if my memory does not deceive me, for shutters; above the choir there is a *Road to the Cross*, sculptured by Andrea Biffi and several other Milanese sculptors. The weeping angels, which mark the stations, have a great variety of attitudes and are charming, although their grace is somewhat effeminate.

The general impression is simple and religious; a soft light invites you to reflection; the large pillars spring to the vault with a movement full of vitality and faith; not a single detail is here to destroy the majesty of the whole. There is no overcharging and no surfeit of luxury: the lines follow each other from one end to the other, and the design of the edifice is understood in a single glance. The superb elegance of the exterior seems but a veil for mystery and humility within; the blatant hymn of marble makes you lower your voice and speak in a hushed tone: the exterior, by reason of its lightness and whiteness, is, perhaps, Pagan ; the interior is, most assuredly, Christian.

In the corner of a nave, just before ascending the dome, we glance at a tomb filled with allegorical figures cast in bronze by the Cavalier Aretin after Michael Angelo in a bold and superb style. You arrive straightway on the roof of the church after climbing a stairway decorated at every

THE CATHEDRAL OF MILAN.

angle with prohibitive, or threatening inscriptions, which do not speak well in favour of the Italians' piety or sense of propriety.

This roof all bristling with steeples and ribbed with flying-buttresses at the sides, which form corridors in perspective, is made of great slabs of marble, like the rest of the edifice. Even at this point it is higher than the highest monuments of the city. A bas-relief of the finest execution is sunk in each buttress; each steeple is peopled with twenty-five statues. I do not believe there is another place in the world that holds in the same amount of space so large a number of sculptured figures. One could make an important city with the marble population of the Cathedral statues. Six thousand, seven hundred and sixteen have been counted. I have heard of a church in the Morea painted in the Byzantine style by the monks of Mount Athos, which did not contain less than three thousand figures. This is as nothing in comparison to the Cathedral of Milan. With regard to persons painted and sculptured, I have often had this dream — that if ever I were invested with magical power I would animate all the figures created by art in granite, in stone, in wood, and on canvas and people with them a country which would be a realization of the landscapes in the pictures. The sculptured multitude of this Cathedral bring back this fantasy. Among these statues there is one by Canova, a Saint Sebastian, lodged in an *aiguille*, and an Eve by Cristoforo Gobi, of such a charming and sensual grace that it is a little astonishing to see her in such a place. However, she is very beautiful, and the birds of the sky do not appear to be scandalized by her Edenesque costume.

From this platform there unfolds an immense panorama: you see the Alps and the Apennines, the vast plains of Lombardy, and with a glass you can regulate your watch from the dial of the church of Monza, whose stripes of black and white stones may be distinguished. . . .

The ascent of the spire, which is perforated and open to the light, is not at all dangerous, although it may affect people who are subject to vertigo. Frail stairways wind through the towers and lead you to a balcony, above which there is nothing but the cap of the spire and the statue which crowns the edifice.

I will not try to describe this gigantic basilica in detail. A volume would be needed for its monograph. As a mere artist I must be content with a general view and a personal impression. After one has descended into the street and has made the tour of the church one finds on the lateral façades and apses the same crowd of statues, the same multitude of bas-reliefs: it is a terrifying debauch of sculpture, an incredible heap of wonders.

Around the Cathedral all kinds of little industries prosper, stalls of second-hand booksellers, opticians selling their wares in the open air, and even a theatre of marionnettes, whose performances I promise myself not to miss. Human life with its trivialities swarms and stirs at the foot of this majestic edifice, which, like petrified fireworks, is bursting its white rockets in the sky; here, as everywhere, we find the same contrast of sublimity of idea and vulgarity of fact. The temple of the Saviour throws its shadow across the hut of Punchinello.

Voyage en Italie (Paris, new ed., 1884).

THE MOSQUE OF HASSAN.

AMELIA B. EDWARDS.

THE mosque of Sultan Hassan, confessedly the most beautiful in Cairo, is also perhaps the most beautiful in the Moslem world. It was built at just that happy moment when Arabian art in Egypt, having ceased merely to appropriate or imitate, had at length evolved an original architectural style out of the heterogeneous elements of Roman and early Christian edifices. The mosques of a few centuries earlier (as, for instance, that of Tulûn, which marks the first departure from the old Byzantine model) consisted of little more than a courtyard with colonnades leading to a hall supported on a forest of pillars. A little more than a century later, and the national style had already experienced the beginnings of that prolonged eclipse which finally resulted in the bastard Neo-Byzantine Renaissance represented by the mosque of Mehemet Ali. But the mosque of Sultan Hassan, built ninety-seven years before the taking of Constantinople, may justly be regarded as the highest point reached by Saracenic art in Egypt after it had used up the Greek and Roman material of Memphis, and before its new-born originality became modified by influence from beyond the Bosphorus. Its pre-eminence is due neither to the greatness of its dimensions, nor to the splendour of its materials. It is neither so large as the great mosque at Damascus, nor so rich in costly marbles as Saint Sophia in Constantinople; but in design, proportion, and a certain lofty grace impossible to describe, it surpasses these, and every other mosque, whether original or adapted, with which the writer is acquainted.

The whole structure is purely national. Every line and curve in it, and every inch of detail, is in the best style of the best period of the Arabian school. And above all, it was designed expressly for its present purpose. The two famous mosques of Damascus and Constantinople having, on the contrary, been Christian churches, betray evidences of adaptation. In Saint Sophia, the space once occupied by the figure of the Redeemer may be distinctly traced in the mosaic-work of the apse, filled in with gold tesseræ of later date; while the magnificent gates of the great mosque at Damascus are decorated, among other Christian emblems, with the sacramental chalice. But the mosque of Sultan Hassan built by En Nasîr Hassan in the high and palmy days of the Memlook rule, is marred by no discrepancies. For a mosque it was designed, and a mosque it remains. Too soon it will be only a beautiful ruin.

A number of small streets having lately been demolished in this quarter, the approach to the mosque lies across a desolate open space littered with débris, but destined to be laid out as a public square. With this desirable end in view, some half dozen workmen were lazily loading as many camels with rubble, which is the Arab way of carting rubbish. If they persevere, and the Minister of Public Works continues to pay their wages with due punctuality,

THE MOSQUE OF HASSAN.

the ground will perhaps get cleared in eight or ten years' time.

Driving up with some difficulty to the foot of the great steps, which were crowded with idlers smoking and sleeping, we observed a long and apparently fast-widening fissure reaching nearly from top to bottom of the main wall of the building, close against the minaret. It looked like just such a rent as might be caused by a shock of earthquake, and, being still new to the East, we wondered the Government had not set to work to mend it. We had yet to learn that nothing is ever mended in Cairo. Here, as in Constantinople, new buildings spring up apace, but the old, no matter how venerable, are allowed to moulder away, inch by inch, till nothing remains but a heap of ruins.

Going up the steps and through a lofty hall, up some more steps and along a gloomy corridor, we came to the great court, before entering which, however, we had to take off our boots and put on slippers brought for the purpose. The first sight of this court is an architectural surprise. It is like nothing that one has seen before, and its beauty equals its novelty. Imagine an immense marble quadrangle, open to the sky and enclosed within lofty walls, with, at each side, a vast recess framed in by a single arch. The quadrangle is more than 100 feet square, and the walls are more than 100 feet high. Each recess forms a spacious hall for rest and prayer, and all are matted; but that at the eastern end is wider and considerably deeper than the other three, and the noble arch that encloses it like the proscenium of a splendid stage, measures, according to Fergusson, 69 feet 5 inches in the span. It looks much larger. This principal hall, the floor of which is raised one step at the upper end, measures 90 feet in depth and 90 in height. The dais is covered with prayer-rugs, and contains the holy niche and the pulpit of the preacher. We observed that those who came up here came only to pray. Having prayed, they either went away or turned aside into one of the other recesses to rest. There was a charming fountain in the court, with a dome-roof as light and fragile-looking as a big bubble, at which each worshipper performed his ablutions on coming in. This done, he left his slippers on the matting and trod the carpeted dais barefoot. . . .

While we were admiring the spring of the roof and the intricate Arabesque decorations of the pulpit, a custode came up with a big key and invited us to visit the tomb of the founder. So we followed him into an enormous vaulted hall a hundred feet square, in the centre of which stood a plain, railed-off tomb, with an empty iron-bound coffer at the foot. We afterwards learned that for five hundred years — that is to say, ever since the death and burial of Sultan Hassan — this coffer had contained a fine copy of the Koran, traditionally said to have been written by Sultan Hassan's own hand; but that the Khedive, who is collecting choice and antique Arabic MSS., had only the other day sent an order for its removal.

Nothing can be bolder or more elegant than the proportions of this noble sepulchral hall, the walls of which are covered with tracery in low relief incrusted with discs and tesseræ of turquoise-coloured porcelain; while high up, in order to lead off the vaulting of the roof, the corners are rounded by means of recessed clusters of exquisite Arabesque woodwork, like pendant stalactites. But the tesseræ are fast falling out, and most of their places are vacant; and the beautiful woodwork hangs in fragments, tattered and cobwebbed, like time-worn banners which the first touch of a brush would bring down.

Going back again from the tomb to the courtyard, we everywhere observed traces of the same dilapidation. The fountain, once a miracle of Sarascenic ornament, was fast going to destruction. The rich marbles of its basement were cracked and discoloured, its stuccoed cupola was flaking off piecemeal, its enamels were dropping out, its lace-like wood tracery shredding away by inches.

Presently a tiny brown and golden bird perched with pretty confidence on the brink of the basin, and having splashed, and drunk, and preened its feathers like a true believer at his ablutions, flew up to the top of the cupola and sang deliciously. All else was profoundly still. Large spaces of light and shadow divided the quadrangle. The sky showed overhead as a square opening of burning solid blue; while here and there, reclining, praying, or quietly occupied, a number of turbaned figures were picturesquely scattered over the matted floors of the open halls around. Yonder sat a tailor cross-legged, making a waistcoat; near him, stretched on his face at full length, sprawled a basket-maker with his half-woven basket and bundle of rushes beside him; and here, close against the main entrance, lay a blind man and his dog; the master asleep, the dog keeping watch. It was, as I have said, our first mosque, and I well remember the surprise with which we saw that tailor sewing on his buttons, and the sleepers lying about in the shade.

We did not then know that a Mohammedan mosque is as much a place of rest and refuge as of prayer; or that the houseless Arab may take shelter there by night or day as freely as the birds may build their nests in the cornice, or as the blind man's dog may share the cool shade with the sleeping master.

A Thousand Miles up the Nile (London, 2d ed., 1889).

THE CATHEDRAL OF TRÈVES.

THE CATHEDRAL OF TRÈVES.

EDWARD AUGUSTUS FREEMAN.

THE ancient capital of the Treveri has the privilege of being known by two modern names, native and foreign, each of which preserves a letter of the ancient name which is lost in its rival. *Treveris* is by its own people contracted into *Trier*, while by its neighbours it is cut short into *Trèves*. But one who looks out from the amphitheatre beyond its walls on the city which boasts itself to have stood for thirteen hundred years longer than Rome, will be inclined to hold that the beauty of its position and the interest of its long history cannot lose their charm under any name. It was not without reason that the mythical Trebetas, son of Ninus, after wandering through all lands, pitched on the spot by the Mosel as the loveliest and richest site that he could find for the foundation of the first city which arose on European soil. . . .

Trier holds, north of the Alps, a position which is in some respects analogous to the position of Ravenna south of the Alps. The points both of likeness and unlikeness between the two cities may be instructively compared. In physical position no two cities can well be more opposite. No two spots can be more unlike than Trier, with its hills, its river, and its bridge, and Ravenna, forsaken by the sea, left in its marshy flat, with its streets, which were once canals like those of Venice, now canals no longer. In their history the two cities have thus much in common, that each was a seat of the Imperial power of Rome in the days of its decline. Each too is remarkable for its rich store of buildings handed on from the days of its greatness, buildings which stamp upon each city an unique character of its own. But, when we more minutely compare either the history or the surviving antiquities of the two cities, when we compare the circumstances under which each city rose to greatness, we shall find on the whole less of likeness than of unlikeness. The difference may be summed up when we say that Trier is the city of Constantine, that Ravenna is the city of Honorius. . . .

Ravenna has nothing of any consequence belonging either to heathen Roman or to mediæval times; its monuments belong to the days of Honorius and Placidia, to the days of the Gothic kingdom, to the very first days of the restored Imperial rule. To these, except one or two of the churches of Rome, there is nothing in the West to answer. The monuments of Trier are spread over a far wider space of time. They stretch from the first days of Roman occupation to an advanced stage of the Middle Ages. The mighty pile of the Black Gate, the *Porta Nigra* or *Porta Martis*, a pile to which Ravenna, and Rome herself, can supply no rival, is a work which it is hard to believe can belong to any days but those when the city was the dwelling-place of Emperors. Yet scholars are not lacking who argue that it really dates from the early days of the Roman only, from a date earlier than that which some other scholars assign to the first foundations of the colony, from the days of Claudius. The amphitheatre is said to date from the reign of Trajan. The basilica, so strangely changed into a Protestant church by the late King of Prussia, can hardly fail to be the work of Constantine. But, after all, the building at Trier which will most reward careful study is the metropolitan church. At the first glimpse it seems less unique than the Porta Nigra; its distinct outline is massive and picturesque, but it is an outline with which every one who has seen many of the great churches of Germany must be thoroughly familiar. Or, if it has a special character of its own, it seems to come from the blending of the four towers of the main buildings with a fifth, the massive tower of the *Liebfrauenkirche*, which, in the general view, none would fancy to be one of the most perfect and graceful specimens of the early German Gothic of the Thirteenth Century. It is only gradually that the unique character of the building dawns on the inquirer. What at first sight seemed to be a church of the type of Mainz, Worms, and Speyer, and inferior to them in lacking the central tower or cupola, turns out to be something which has no parallel north of the Alps, nor, we may add, south of them either. It is a Roman building of the Sixth Century — none the less Roman for being built under a Frankish king — preserving large portions of a yet earlier building of the Fourth. The capitals of its mighty columns peep out from amid the later work, and fragments of the pillars lie about in the cloister and before the western door, as the like fragments do in the Forum of Trajan. Repaired and enlarged in the Eleventh Century in remarkably close imitation of the original design, the church has gone through a series of additions and recastings, in order to change it into the likeness of an ordinary mediæval German church. Had St. Vital at Ravenna, had St. Sophia itself, stood where the *Dom* of Trier stands, the same misapplied labour would most likely have been bestowed upon them. But, well pleased as we should have been to have had such a building as this kept to us in its original form, there is no denying that those who enjoy spelling out the changes which a great building has gone through, comparing the statements of the local chroniclers with the evidence of the building itself — a process which, like every other process of discovery, is not without its charm — will find no more attractive problem of the kind than is supplied by the venerable minster of Trier.

Historical and Architectural Sketches (London, 1876).

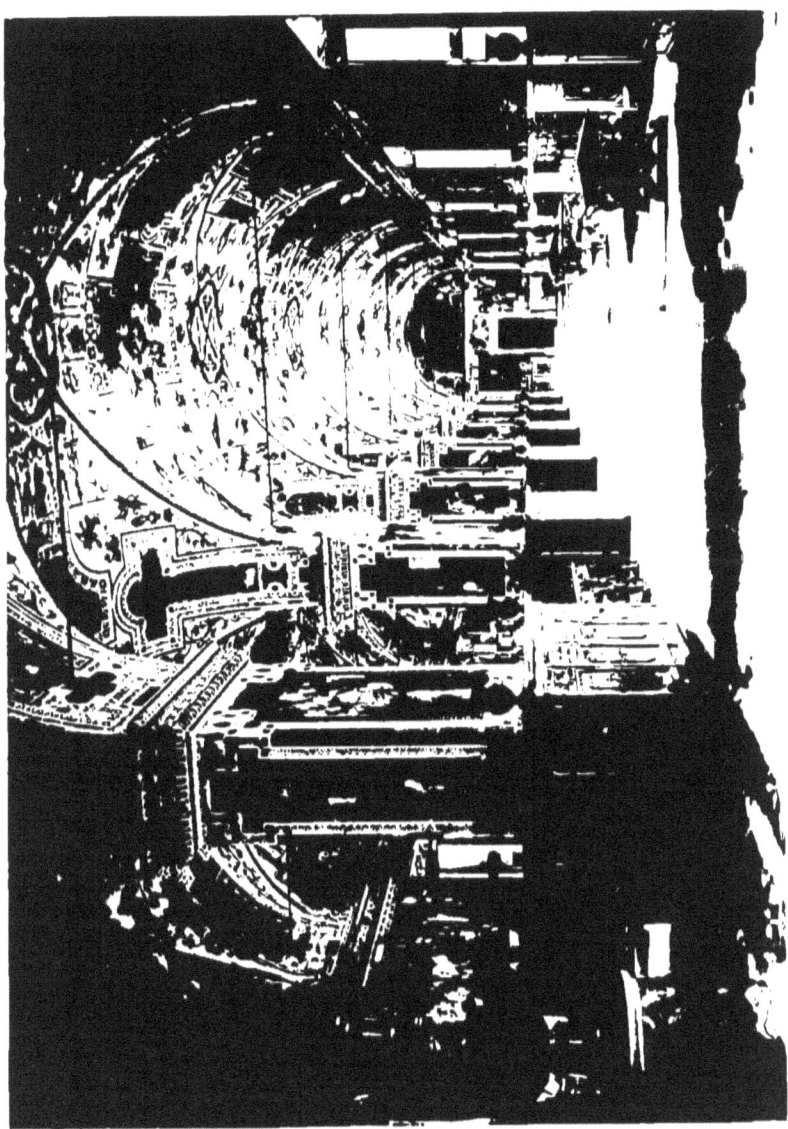

THE VATICAN.

AUGUSTUS J. C. HARE.

THE hollow of the Janiculum between S. Onofrio and the Monte Mario is believed to have been the site of Etruscan divination.

> " Fauni vatesque canebant."
> *Ennius.*

Hence the name, which is now only used in regard to the Papal palace and the Basilica of S. Peter, but which was once applied to the whole district between the foot of the hill and the Tiber near S. Angelo.

> ". . . Ut paterni
> Fluminis ripae, simul et jocosa
> Redderet laudes tibi Vaticani
> Montis imago."
> *Horace,* Od. i. 20.

Tacitus speaks of the unwholesome air of this quarter. In this district was the Circus of Caligula, adjoining the gardens of his mother Agrippina, decorated by the obelisk which now stands in the front of S. Peter's, near which many believe that S. Peter suffered martyrdom.[1]

Here Seneca describes that while Caligula was walking

---
[1] Pliny xxxv. 15.

by torchlight he amused himself by the slaughter of a number of distinguished persons — senators and Roman ladies. Afterwards it became the Circus of Nero, who from his adjoining gardens used to watch the martyrdom of the Christians[1] — mentioned by Suetonius as "a race given up to a new and evil superstition" — and who used their living bodies, covered with pitch and set on fire, as torches for his nocturnal promenades.

The first residence of the Popes at the Vatican was erected by S. Symmachus (A. D. 498–514) near the forecourt of the old S. Peter's, and here Charlemagne is believed to have resided on the occasion of his several visits to Rome during the reigns of Adrian I. (772–795) and Leo III. (795–816). During the Twelfth Century this ancient palace having fallen into decay, it was rebuilt in the Thirteenth by Innocent III. It was greatly enlarged by Nicholas III. (1277–81); but the Lateran continued to be the Papal residence, and the Vatican palace was only used on state occasions, and for the reception of any foreign sovereigns visiting Rome. After the return of the Popes from Avignon, the Lateran palace had fallen into decay, and, for the sake of the greater security afforded by the vicinity of S. Angelo, it was determined to make the Pontifical residence at the Vatican, and the first Conclave was held there in 1378. In order to increase its security, John XXIII. constructed the covered passage to S. Angelo in 1410. Nicholas V. (1447–55) had the idea of making it the most magnificent palace in the world, and of uniting in it all the government offices and dwellings of the

[1] Tac. Ann. xv. 44.

cardinals. He wished to make it for Christendom that which the Milliarium Aureum in the Forum was to the Roman Empire, the centre whence all the messengers of the spiritual empire should go forth, bearing words of life, truth, and peace.[1] Unfortunately Nicholas died before he could carry out his designs. The building which he commenced was finished by Alexander VI., and still exists under the name of Tor di Borgia. In the reign of this Pope, his son Cesare murdered Alphonso, Duke of Bisceglia, husband of his sister Lucrezia, in the Vatican (August 18, 1500). To Paul II. was due the Court of S. Damasus. In 1473 Sixtus IV. built the Sixtine Chapel, and in 1490 "the Belvedere" was erected as a separate garden-house by Innocent VIII. from designs of Antonio da Pollajuolo. Julius II., with the aid of Bramante, united this villa to the palace by means of one vast courtyard, and erected the Loggie around the court of S. Damasus; he also laid the foundation of the Vatican Museum in the gardens of the Belvedere. The Loggie were completed by Leo X.; the Sala Regia and the Paoline Chapel were built by Paul III. Sixtus V. divided the great court of Bramante into two by the erection of the library, and began the present residence of the Popes, which was finished by Clement VIII. (1592–1605). Urban VIII. built the Scala Regia; Clement XIV. and Pius VI., the Museo Pio-Clementino (for which the latter pulled down the chapel of Innocent VIII., full of precious frescoes by Mantegna); Pius VII., the Braccio Nuovo; Leo XII., the picture-gallery; Gregory XVI., the Etruscan Museum,

[1] See Rio.

and Pius IX., the handsome staircase leading to the court of Bramante.

The length of the Vatican Palace is 1151 English feet; its breadth, 767. It has eight grand staircases, twenty courts, and is said to contain 11,000 chambers of different sizes.

The principal entrance to the Vatican is at the end of the right colonnade of S. Peter's. Hence a door on the right opens upon the staircase leading to the Cortile di S. Damaso, and is the nearest way to all the collections, and the one by which visitors were admitted until the fall of the Papal government. The fountain of the Cortile, designed by Algardi in 1649, is fed by the Acqua Damasiana, due to Pope Damasus in the Fourth Century.

Following the great corridor, and passing on the left the entrance to the portico of S. Peter's, we reach the Scala Regia, a magnificent work of Bernini, watched by the picturesque Swiss guard of the Pope. Hence we enter the Sala Regia, built in the reign of Paul III. by Antonio di Sangallo, and used as a hall of audience for ambassadors. It is decorated with frescoes illustrative of the history of the Popes.

On the right is the entrance of the Paoline Chapel (Cappella Paolina), also built (1540) by Antonio di Sangallo for Paul III. Its decorations are chiefly the work of Sabbatini and F. Zucchero, but it contains two frescoes by Michelangelo.

On the left of the approach from the Scala Regia is the Sixtine Chapel (Cappella Sistina), built by Baccio Pintelli in 1473 for Sixtus IV.

The lower part of the walls of this wonderful chapel was formerly hung on festivals with the tapestries executed from the cartoons of Raffaelle; the upper portion is decorated in fresco by the great Florentine masters of the Fifteenth Century. . . .

On the pillars between the windows are the figures of twenty-eight Popes, by Sandro Botticelli. . . .

The avenue of pictures is a preparation for the surpassing grandeur of the ceiling.

The pictures from the Old Testament, beginning from the altar, are : — 1. The Separation of Light and Darkness ; 2. The Creation of the Sun and Moon ; 3. The Creation of Trees and Plants ; 4. The Creation of Adam ; 5. The Creation of Eve; 6. The Fall and the Expulsion from Paradise ; 7. The Sacrifice of Noah ; 8. The Deluge ; 9. The Intoxication of Noah.

The lower portion of the ceiling is divided into triangles occupied by the Prophets and Sibyls in solemn contemplation, accompanied by angels and genii. Beginning from the left of the entrance, their order is — 1. Joel; 2. Sibylla Erythraea ; 3. Ezekiel ; 4. Sibylla Persica ; 5. Jonah ; 6. Sibylla Libyca ; 7. Daniel ; 8. Sibylla Cumaea ; 9. Isaiah ; 10. Sibylla Delphica.

In the recesses between the Prophets and Sibyls are a series of lovely family groups representing the Genealogy of the Virgin, and expressive of calm expectation of the future. The four corners of the ceiling contain groups illustrative of the power of the Lord displayed in the especial deliverance of His chosen people.

Only 3000 ducats were paid to Michelangelo for all his

great work on the ceiling of the Sixtine; less than a common decorator obtains in the Nineteenth Century.

It was when Michelangelo was already in his sixtieth year that Clement VII. formed the idea of effacing the three pictures of Perugino at the end of the chapel, and employing him to paint the vast fresco of *The Last Judgment* in their place. It occupied the artist for seven years, and was finished in 1541, when Paul III. was on the throne. During this time Michelangelo frequently read and re-read the wonderful sermons of Savonarola, to refresh his mind, and that he might drink in the inspiration of their own religious awe and Dantesque imagination. . . .

The small portion of the Vatican inhabited by the Pope is never seen except by those who are admitted to a special audience. The three rooms occupied by the pontiff are furnished with a simplicity which would be inconceivable in the abode of any other sovereign prince. The furniture is confined to the merest necessaries of life; strange contrast to Lambeth and Fulham! The apartment consists of the bare Green Saloon; the Red Saloon, containing a throne flanked by benches; and the bedroom, with yellow draperies, a large writing table, and a few pictures by old masters. The Papal life is a lonely one, as the dread of an accusation of nepotism has prevented any of the later Popes from having any of their family with them, and etiquette always obliges them to dine, etc., alone. Pius IX. seldom saw his family, but Leo XIII. is often visited twice a day by his relations — " La Sainte Famille," as they are generally called.

No one, whatever the difference of creed, can look upon

this building, inhabited by the venerable men who have borne so important a part in the history of Christianity and of Europe, without the deepest interest. . . .

The windows of the Egyptian Museum look upon the inner *Garden of the Vatican*, which may be reached by a door at the end of the long gallery of the Museo Chiaramonti, before ascending to the Torso. The garden which is thus entered, called *Giardino della Pigna*, is in fact merely the second great quadrangle of the Vatican, planted, under Pius IX., with shrubs and flowers, now a desolate wilderness — its lovely garden having been destroyed by the present Vatican authorities to make way for a monumental column to the Council of 1870. Several interesting relics are preserved here. In the centre is the *Pedestal of the Column of Antoninus Pius*, found in 1709 on the Monte Citorio. The column was a simple memorial pillar of granite, erected by the two adopted sons of the Emperor, Marcus Aurelius and Lucius Verus. It was broken up to mend the obelisk of Psammeticus I. at the Monte Citorio. Among the reliefs of the pedestal is one of a winged genius guiding Antoninus and Faustina to Olympus. The modern pillar and statue are erections of Leo XIII. In front of the great semicircular niche of Bramante, at the end of the court-garden, is the famous *Pigna*, a gigantic fir-cone, which is said once to have crowned the summit of the Mausoleum of Hadrian. Thence it was first removed to the front of the old basilica of S. Peter's, where it was used for a fountain. In the fresco of the old S. Peter's at S. Martino al Monte the pigna is introduced, but it is there placed in the centre of the nave, a position it never occupied. It bears the name of the bronze-founder who cast it — " P. Cincivs. P. L. Calvivs. fecit." Dante saw it at S. Peter's, and compares it to a giant's head (it is eleven feet high) which he saw through the mist in the last circle of hell.

> " La faccia mi parea longa e grossa
> Come la pina di S. Pietro in Roma."
> *Inf.* xxxi. 58.

On either side of the pigna are two lovely bronze peacocks, which are said to have stood on either side of the entrance of Hadrian's Mausoleum.

A flight of steps leads from this court to the narrow *Terrace of the Navicella*, in front of the palace, so called from a bronze ship with which its fountain is decorated. The visitor should beware of the tricksome waterworks upon this terrace.

Beyond the courtyard is the entrance to the larger garden, which may be reached in a carriage by the courts at the back of S. Peter's. Admittance is difficult to obtain, as the garden is constantly used by the Pope. Pius IX. used to ride here upon his white mule. It is a most delightful retreat for the hot days of May and June, and before that time its woods are carpeted with wild violets and anemones. No one who has not visited them can form any idea of the beauty of these ancient groves, interspersed with fountains and statues, but otherwise left to nature, and forming a fragment of sylvan scenery quite unassociated with the English idea of a garden. . . .

The Sixteenth Century was the golden age for the

Vatican. Then the splendid court of Leo X. was the centre of artistic and literary life, and the witty and pleasure-loving Pope made these gardens the scene of his banquets and concerts; and, in a circle to which ladies were admitted, as in a secular court, listened to the recitations of the poets who sprang up under his protection, beneath the shadow of their woods.

Walks in Rome (13th ed., London, 1896).

THE CATHEDRAL OF AMIENS.

JOHN RUSKIN.

IT is the admitted privilege of a custode who loves his cathedral to depreciate, in its comparison, all the other cathedrals of his country that resemble, and all the edifices on the globe that differ from it. But I love too many cathedrals — though I have never had the happiness of becoming the custode of even one — to permit myself the easy and faithful exercise of the privilege in question; and I must vindicate my candour and my judgment in the outset, by confessing that the Cathedral of AMIENS has nothing to boast of in the way of towers, — that its central *flèche* is merely the pretty caprice of a village carpenter, — that the total structure is in dignity inferior to Chartres, in sublimity to Beauvais, and in decorative splendour to Rheims, and in loveliness of figure sculpture to Bourges. It has nothing like the artful pointing and moulding of the arcades of Salisbury — nothing of the might of Durham; no Dædalian inlaying like Florence, no glow of mythic fantasy like Verona. And yet, in all, and more than these, ways, outshone or overpowered, the Cathedral of Amiens deserves the name given it by M. Viollet le Duc —

" The Parthenon of Gothic Architecture." . . .

Whatever you wish to see, or are forced to leave unseen at Amiens, if the overwhelming responsibilities of your

THE CATHEDRAL OF AMIENS.

existence, and the inevitable necessities of precipitate locomotion in their fulfilment, have left you so much as one quarter of an hour, not out of breath — for the contemplation of the capital of Picardy, give it wholly to the cathedral choir. Aisles and porches, lancet windows and roses, you can see elsewhere as well as here — but such carpenter's work you cannot. It is late, — fully developed flamboyant just past the Fifteenth Century — and has some Flemish stolidity mixed with the playing French fire of it ; but woodcarving was the Picard's joy from his youth up, and, so far as I know, there is nothing else so beautiful cut out of the goodly trees of the world.

Sweet and young-grained wood it is: oak, *trained* and chosen for such work, sound now as four hundred years since. Under the carver's hand it seems to cut like clay, to fold like silk, to grow like living branches, to leap like living flame. Canopy crowning canopy, pinnacle piercing pinnacle — it shoots and wreathes itself into an enchanted glade, inextricable, imperishable, fuller of leafage than any forest, and fuller of story than any book.[1]

---

[1] Arnold Boulin, master-joiner (*menuisier*) at Amiens, solicited the enterprise, and obtained it in the first months of the year 1508. A contract was drawn and an agreement made with him for the construction of one hundred and twenty stalls with historical subjects, high backings, crownings, and pyramidal canopies. It was agreed that the principal executor should have seven sous of Tournay (a little less than the sou of France) a day, for himself and his apprentice, (threepence a day the two — say a shilling a week the master, and sixpence a week the man,) and for the superintendence of the whole work, twelve crowns a year, at the rate of twenty-four sous the crown ; (i. e. twelve shillings a year). The salary of the simple workman was only to be three sous a day. For the sculptures and histories of the seats, the

I have never been able to make up my mind which was really the best way of approaching the cathedral for the first time. . . .

I think the best is to walk from the Hôtel de France or the Place de Perigord, up the street of Three Pebbles, towards the railway station — stopping a little as you go, so as to get into a cheerful temper, and buying some bon-bons or tarts for the children in one of those charming *patissier's* shops on the left. Just past them, ask for the theatre; and just past that, you will find, also on the left, three open arches, through which you can turn passing the Palais de Justice, and go straight up to the south transept, which has really something about it to please everybody. It is simple and severe at the bottom, and daintily traceried and pinnacled at the top, and yet seems all of a piece — though it is n't — and everybody *must* like the taper and transparent fret-work of the *flèche* above, which seems to bend in the west wind, — though it does n't — at least, the bending is a long habit, gradually yielded into, with gaining grace and submissiveness, during the last three hundred years. And coming quite up to the porch, everybody must like the pretty French Madonna in the middle of it, with her head a little aside, and her nimbus switched a little aside too, like a becoming bonnet. A Madonna in decadence she is, though, for all, or rather by reason of all, her prettiness and her gay soubrette's smile; and she has no business there,

bargain was made separately with Antoine Avernier, image cutter, residing at Amiens, at the rate of thirty-two sous (sixteen pence), the piece. Most of the wood came from Clermont en Beauvoisis, near Amiens; the finest, for the bas-reliefs from Holland, by St. Valery and Abbeville.

neither, for this is Saint Honoré's porch, not her's; and grim and grey Saint Honoré used to stand there to receive you,— he is banished now to the north porch where nobody ever goes in. This was done long ago in the Fourteenth Century days when the people first began to find Christianity too serious, and devised a merrier faith for France, and would have bright glancing soubrette Madonnas everywhere, letting their own dark-eyed Joan of Arc be burnt for a witch. And thenceforward things went their merry way, straight on, *ça allait*, *ça ira* to the merriest days of the guillotine.

But they could still carve in the Fourteenth Century and the Madonna and her hawthorn-blossom lintel are worth your looking at, — much more the field above, of sculpture as delicate and more calm, which tells you Saint Honoré's own story, little talked of now in his Parisian faubourg. . . .

A Gothic cathedral has, almost always, these five great entrances; which may be easily, if at first attentively, recognized under the titles of the Central door (or porch), the Northern door, the Southern door, the North door, and the South door. But when we use the terms right and left, we ought always to use them as in going *out* of the cathedral, or walking down the nave, — the entire north side and aisles of the building being its right side, and the south its left, — these terms being only used well and authoritatively, when they have reference either to the image of Christ on the apse or on the rood, or else to the central statue, whether of Christ, the Virgin, or a saint in the west front. At Amiens, this central statue, on the "*trumeau*" or supporting and dividing pillar of the central porch, is of Christ Immanuel, — God *with* us. On His right hand and His left, occupying the entire walls of the central porch, are the apostles and the four greater prophets. The twelve minor prophets stand side by side on the front, three on each of its great piers.

The northern porch is dedicated to St. Firman, the first Christian missionary to Amiens.

The southern porch to the Virgin.

But these are both treated as withdrawn behind the great foundation of Christ and the Prophets; and their narrow recesses partly conceal their sculpture until you enter them. What you have first to think of, and read, is the scripture of the great central porch and the façade itself.

You have then in the centre of the front, the image of Christ Himself, receiving you: " I am the Way, the truth and the life." And the order of the attendant powers may be best understood by thinking of them as placed on Christ's right and left hand: this being also the order which the builder adopts in his Scripture history on the façade — so that it is to be read from left to right — *i. e.* from Christ's left to Christ's right, as *He* sees it. Thus, therefore, following the order of the great statues: first in the central porch, there are six apostles on Christ's right hand, and six on His left. On His left hand, next Him, Peter; then in receding order, Andrew, James, John, Matthew, Simon; on His right hand, next Him, Paul; and in receding order, James the Bishop, Philip, Bartholomew, Thomas, and Jude. These opposite ranks of the Apostles occupy what may be called the apse or curved bay of the porch, and form a nearly semicircular group, clearly visible as we approach.

But on the sides of the porch, outside the lines of apostles, and not clearly seen till we enter the porch are the four greater prophets. On Christ's left, Isaiah and Jeremiah, on His right, Ezekiel and Daniel.

Then in front, along the whole façade — read in order from Christ's left to His right — come the series of the twelve minor prophets, three to each of the four piers of the temple, beginning at the south angle with Hosea, and ending with Malachi.

As you look full at the façade in front, the statues which fill the minor porches are either obscured in their narrower recesses or withdrawn behind each other so as to be unseen. And the entire mass of the front is seen, literally, as built on the foundation of the Apostles and Prophets, Jesus Christ Himself being the chief corner-stone. Literally *that*; for the receding Porch is a deep " angulus " and its mid-pillar is the " Head of the Corner."

Built on the foundation of the Apostles and Prophets, that is to say of the Prophets who foretold *Christ*, and the Apostles who declared Him. Though Moses was an Apostle of *God*, he is not here — though Elijah was a Prophet of *God*, he is not here. The voice of the entire building is that of the Heaven at the Transfiguration. " This is my beloved Son, hear ye Him."

There is yet another and a greater prophet still, who, as it seems at first, is not here. Shall the people enter the gates of the temple, singing " Hosanna to the Son of *David*; " and see no image of his father, then? — Christ Himself declare, " I am the root and offspring of David ; " and yet the Root have no sign near it of its Earth?

Not so. David and his Son are together. David is the pedestal of the Christ.

We will begin our examination of the Temple front, therefore with this goodly pedestal stone. The statue of David is only two-thirds life-size, occupying the niche in front of the pedestal. He holds his sceptre in his right hand, the scroll in his left. King and Prophet, type of all Divinely right doing, and right claiming, and right proclaiming, kinghood forever.

The pedestal of which this statue forms the fronting or western sculpture, is square, and on the two sides of it are two flowers in vases, on its north side the lily, and on its south the rose. And the entire monolith is one of the noblest pieces of Christian sculpture in the world.

Above this pedestal comes a minor one, bearing in front of it a tendril of vine, which completes the floral symbolism of the whole. The plant which I have called a lily is not the Fleur de Lys, nor the Madonna's, but an ideal one with bells like the crown Imperial (Shakespeare's type of " lilies of all kinds "), representing the *mode of growth* of the lily of the valley, which could not be sculptured so large in its literal form without appearing monstrous, and is exactly expressed in this tablet — as it fulfils, together with the rose and vine, its companions, the triple saying of Christ, " I am the Rose of Sharon, and the Lily of the Valley." " I am the true Vine."

On the side of the upper stone are supporters of a different character. Supporters, — not captives nor victims; the Cockatrice and Adder. Representing the most active evil principles of the earth, as in their utmost malignity;

still Pedestals of Christ, and even in their deadly life, accomplishing His final will.

Both creatures are represented accurately in the mediæval traditional form, the cockatrice half dragon, half cock; the deaf adder laying one ear against the ground and stopping the other with her tail.

The first represents the infidelity of Pride. The cockatrice — king serpent or highest ·serpent — saying that he *is* God, and *will be* God.

The second, the infidelity of Death. The adder (nieder or nether snake) saying that he *is* mud and *will be* mud.

Lastly, and above all, set under the feet of the statue of Christ Himself, are the lion and dragon; the images of Carnal sin, or *Human* sin, as distinguished from the Spiritual and Intellectual sin of Pride, by which the angels also fell.

The Bible of Amiens (Our Fathers Have Told Us), (Sunnyside, Orpington, Kent, 1884).

THE MOSQUE OF SANTA SOFIA.

EDMONDO DE AMICIS.

THE external aspect has nothing worthy of note. The only objects that attract the eye are the four high white minarets that rise at the four corners of the edifice, upon pedestals as big as houses. The famous cupola looks small. It appears impossible that it can be the same dome that swells into the blue air, like the head of a Titan, and is seen from Pera, from the Bosphorus, from the Sea of Marmora, and from the hills of Asia. It is a flattened dome, flanked by two half domes, covered with lead, and perforated with a wreath of windows, supported upon four walls painted in stripes of pink and white, sustained in their turn by enormous bastions, around which rise confusedly a number of small mean buildings, baths, schools, mausoleums, hospitals, etc., which hide the architectural forms of the basilica. You see nothing but a heavy, irregular mass, of a faded colour, naked as a fortress, and not to all appearance large enough to hold within it the immense nave of Santa Sofia's church. Of the ancient basilica nothing is really visible but the dome, which has lost the silvery splendour that once made it visible, according to the Greeks, from the summit of Olympus. All the rest is Mussulman. One summit was built by Mahomet the

THE MOSQUE OF SANTA-SOFIA.

THE MOSQUE OF SANTA SOFIA. 243

Conqueror, one by Selim II., the other two by Amurath III. Of the same Amurath are the buttresses built at the end of the Sixteenth Century to support the walls shaken by an earthquake, and the enormous crescent in bronze planted upon the top of the dome, of which the gilding alone cost fifty thousand ducats.

On every side the mosque overwhelms and masks the church, of which the head only is free, though over that also the four imperial minarets keep watch and ward. On the eastern side there is a door ornamented by six columns of porphyry and marble; at the southern side another door by which you enter a court, surrounded by low, irregular buildings, in the midst of which bubbles a fountain for ablution, covered by an arched roof with eight columns. Looked at from without, Santa Sofia can scarcely be distinguished from the other mosques of Stamboul, unless by its inferior lightness and whiteness; much less would it pass for the "greatest temple in the world after Saint Peter's." . . .

Between the four enormous pilasters which form a square in the middle of the basilica, rise, to the right and left as you enter, eight marvellous columns of green *breccia* from which spring the most graceful arches, sculptured with foliage, forming an elegant portico on either side of the nave, and sustaining at a great height two vast galleries, which present two more ranges of columns and sculptured arches. A third gallery which communicates with the two first, runs along the entire side where the entrance is, and opens upon the nave with three great arches, sustained by twin columns. Other minor galleries.

supported by porphyry columns, cross the four temples posted at the extremity of the nave and sustain other columns bearing tribunes. This is the basilica. The mosque is, as it were, planted in its bosom and attached to its walls. The *Mirab*, or niche which indicates the direction of Mecca, is cut in one of the pilasters of the apse. To the right of it and high·up is hung one of the four carpets which Mahomet used in prayer. Upon the corner of the apse, nearest the *Mirab*, at the top of a very steep little staircase, flanked by two balustrades of marble sculptured with exquisite delicacy, under an odd conical roof, between two triumphal standards of Mahomet Second, is the pulpit where the *Ratib* goes up to read the Koran, with a drawn scimetar in his hand, to indicate that Santa Sofia is a mosque acquired by conquest. Opposite the pulpit is the tribune of the Sultan, closed with a gilded lattice. Other pulpits or platforms, furnished with balustrades sculptured in open work, and ornamented with small marble columns and arabesque arches, extend here and there along the walls, or project towards the centre of the nave. To the right and left of the entrance, are two enormous alabaster urns, brought from the ruins of Pergamo, by Amurath III. Upon the pilasters, at a great height are suspended immense green disks, with inscriptions from the Koran in letters of gold. Underneath, attached to the walls, are large cartouches of porphyry inscribed with the names of Allah, Mahomet, and the first four Caliphs. In the angles formed by the four arches that sustain the cupola, may still be seen the gigantic wings of four mosaic cherubim, whose faces are concealed by gilded rosettes. From the vaults of the domes depend innumerable thick silken cords, to which are attached ostrich eggs, bronze lamps, and globes of crystal. Here and there are seen lecterns, inlaid with mother-of-pearl and copper, with manuscript Korans upon them. The pavement is covered with carpets and mats. The walls are bare, whitish, yellowish, or dark grey, still ornamented here and there with faded mosaics. The general aspect is gloomy and sad.

The chief marvel of the mosque is the great dome. Looked at from the nave below, it seems indeed, as Madame de Staël said of the dome of Saint Peter's, like an abyss suspended over one's head. It is immensely high, has an enormous circumference, and its depth is only one-sixth of its diameter; which makes it appear still larger. At its base a gallery encircles it, and above the gallery there is a row of forty arched windows. In the top is written the sentence pronounced by Mahomet Second, as he sat on his horse in front of the high altar on the day of the taking of Constantinople: " Allah is the light of heaven and of earth;" and some of the letters, which are white upon a black ground, are nine yards long. As every one knows, this aerial prodigy could not be constructed with the usual materials; and it was built of pumice-stone that floats on water, and with bricks from the island of Rhodes, five of which scarcely weigh as much as one ordinary brick. . . .

When you have visited the nave and the dome, you have only begun to see Santa Sofia. For example, whoever has a shade of historic curiosity may dedicate an hour to the columns. Here are the spoils of all the temples in the world. The columns of green *breccia* which support the two great galleries, were presented to Justinian by the magistrates of Ephesus, and belonged to the Temple of Diana that was burned by Erostratus. The eight porphyry columns that stand two and two between the pilasters belonged to the Temple of the Sun built by Aurelian at Balbek. Other columns are from the Temple of Jove at Cizicum, from the Temple of Helios of Palmyra, from the temples of Thebes, Athens, Rome, the Troad, the Ciclades, and from Alexandria; and they present an infinite variety of sizes and colours. Among the columns, the balustrades, the pedestals, and the slabs which remain of the ancient lining of the walls, may be seen marbles from all the ruins of the Archipelago; from Asia Minor, from Africa and from Gaul. The marble of the Bosphorus, white spotted with black, contrasts with the black Celtic marble veined with white; the green marble of Laconia is reflected in the azure marble of Lybia; the speckled porphyry of Egypt, the starred granite of Thessaly, the red and white striped stone of Jassy, mingle their colours with the purple of the Phrygian marble, the rose of that of Synada, the gold of the marble of Mauritania, and the snow of the marble of Paros. . . .

From above can be embraced at once with the eye and mind all the life of the mosque. There are to be seen Turks on their knees, with their foreheads touching the pavement; others erect like statues with their hands before their faces, as if they were studying the lines in their palms; some seated cross-legged at the base of columns, as if they were reposing under the shadow of trees; a veiled woman on her knees in a solitary corner; old men seated before the lecterns, reading the Koran; an *imaum* hearing a group of boys reciting sacred verses; and here and there, under the distant arcades and in the galleries, *imaum*, *ratib*, *muezzin*, servants of the mosque in strange costumes, coming and going silently as if they did not touch the pavement. The vague harmony formed by the low, monotonous voices of those reading or praying, those thousand strange lamps, that clear and equal light, that deserted apse, those vast silent galleries, that immensity, those memories, that peace, leave in the soul an impression of mystery and grandeur which words cannot express, nor time efface.

Constantinople (London, 1878, translation by C. Tilton).

WESTMINSTER ABBEY.

ARTHUR PENRHYN STANLEY.

IT is said that the line in Heber's "Palestine" which describes the rise of Solomon's temple originally ran —

"Like the green grass, the noiseless fabric grew;"

and that, at Sir Walter Scott's suggestion, it was altered to its present form —

"Like some tall palm, the noiseless fabric sprung."

Whether we adopt the humbler or the grander image, the comparison of the growth of a fine building to that of a natural product is full of instruction. But the growth of an historical edifice like Westminster Abbey needs a more complex figure to do justice to its formation: a venerable oak, with gnarled and hollow trunk, and spreading roots, and decaying bark, and twisted branches, and green shoots; or a coral reef extending itself with constantly new accretions, creek after creek, and islet after islet. One after another, a fresh nucleus of life is formed, a new combination produced, a larger ramification thrown out. In this respect Westminster Abbey stands alone amongst the edifices of the world. There are, it may be, some which surpass it in beauty or grandeur; there are others, certainly,

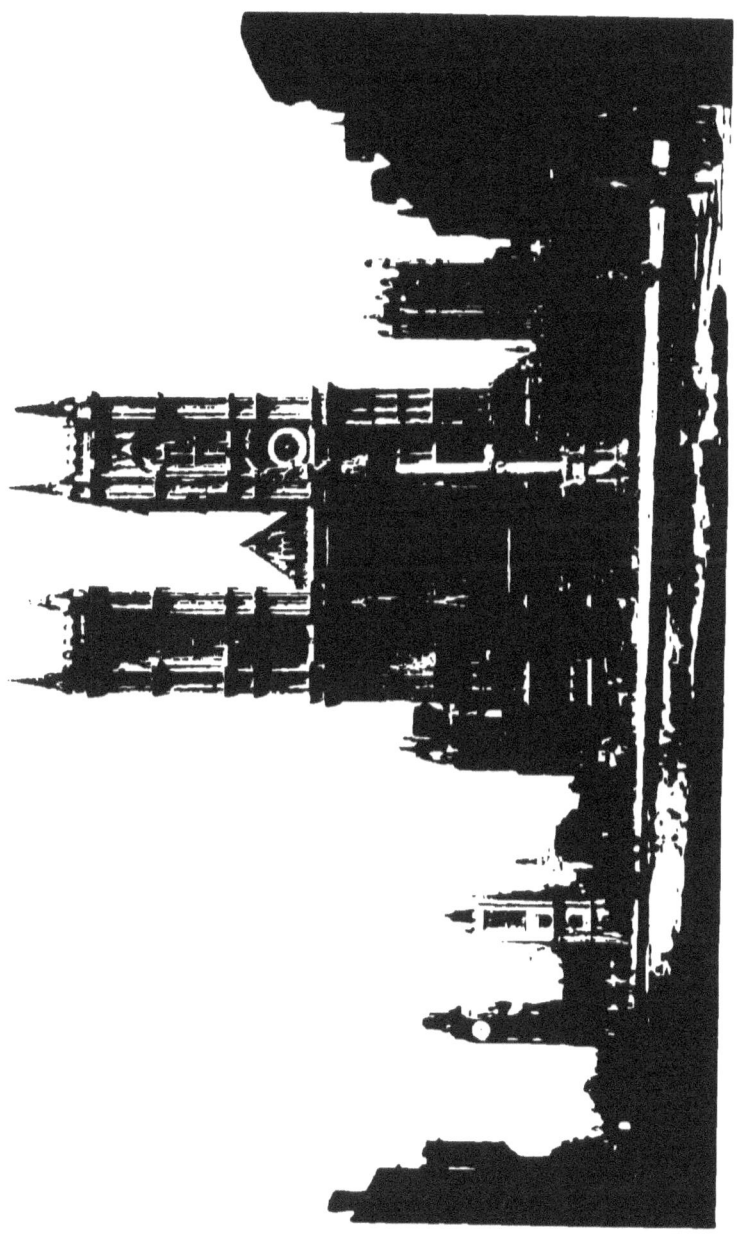

WESTMINSTER ABBEY.

which surpass it in depth and sublimity of association; but there is none which has been entwined by so many continuous threads with the history of a whole nation. . . .

If the original foundation of the Abbey can be traced back to Sebert, the name, probably, must have been given in recollection of the great Roman sanctuary, whence Augustine, the first missionary, had come. And Sebert was believed to have dedicated his church to St. Peter in the Isle of Thorns, in order to balance the compliment he had paid to St. Paul on Ludgate Hill : a reappearance, in another form, of the counterbalancing claims of the rights of Diana and Apollo — the earliest stage of that rivalry which afterwards expressed itself in the proverb of " robbing Peter to pay Paul."

This thin thread of tradition, which connected the ruinous pile in the river-island with the Roman reminiscences of Augustine, was twisted firm and fast round the resolve of Edward; and by the concentration of his mind on this one subject was raised the first distinct idea of an Abbey, which the Kings of England should regard as their peculiar treasure. . . .

The Abbey had been fifteen years in building. The King had spent upon it one-tenth of the property of the kingdom. It was to be a marvel of its kind. As in its origin it bore the traces of the fantastic childish character of the King and of the age, in its architecture it bore the stamp of the peculiar position which Edward occupied in English history between Saxon and Norman. By birth he was a Saxon, but in all else he was a foreigner. Accordingly, the Church at Westminster was a wide sweeping innovation on all that had been seen before. "Destroying the old building," he says in his Charter, "I have built up a new one from the very foundation." Its fame as "a new style of composition" lingered in the minds of men for generations. It was the first cruciform church in England, from which all the rest of like shape were copied — an expression of the increasing hold which the idea of the Crucifixion in the Tenth Century had laid on the imagination of Europe. Its massive roof and pillars formed a contrast with the rude rafters and beams of the common Saxon churches. Its very size — occupying, as it did, almost the whole area of the present building — was in itself portentous. The deep foundations, of large square blocks of grey stone, were duly laid. The east end was rounded into an apse. A tower rose in the centre crowned by a cupola of wood. At the western end were erected two smaller towers, with five large bells. The hard strong stones were richly sculptured. The windows were filled with stained glass. The roof was covered with lead. The cloisters, chapter-house, refectory, dormitory, the infirmary, with its spacious chapel, if not completed by Edward, were all begun, and finished in the next generation on the same plan. This structure, venerable as it would be if it had lasted to our time, has almost entirely vanished. Possibly one vast dark arch in the southern transept — certainly the substructures of the dormitory, with their huge pillars, "grand and regal at the bases and capitals " — the massive low-browed passage leading from the great cloister to Little Dean's Yard — and some portions of the refectory and of the infirmary chapel, remain as specimens of the work which astonished the last age of the Anglo-Saxon and the first age of the Norman monarchy. . . .

In the earliest and nearly the only representation which exists of the Confessor's building — that in the Bayeux Tapestry — there is the figure of a man on the roof, with one hand resting on the tower of the Palace of Westminster, and with the other grasping the weathercock of the Abbey. The probable intention of this figure is to indicate the close contiguity of the two buildings. If so, it is the natural architectural expression of a truth valuable everywhere, but especially dear to Englishmen. The close incorporation of the Palace and the Abbey from its earliest days is a likeness of the whole English Constitution — a combination of things sacred and things common — a union of the regal, legal, lay element of the nation with its religious, clerical, ecclesiastical tendencies, such as can be found hardly elsewhere in Christendom. The Abbey is secular because it is sacred, and sacred because it is secular. It is secular in the common English sense, because it is " sæcular " in the far higher French and Latin sense : a " sæcular " edifice, a " sæcular " institution — an edifice and an institution which has grown with the growth of ages, which has been furrowed with the scars and cares of each succeeding century.

> A million wrinkles carve its skin ;
> A thousand winters snow'd upon its breast,
> From cheek, and throat, and chin.

The vast political pageants of which it has been the theatre, the dust of the most worldly laid side by side with the dust of the most saintly, the wrangles of divines or statesmen which have disturbed its sacred peace, the clash of arms which has pursued fugitive warriors and princes into the shades of its sanctuary — even the traces of Westminster boys who have played in its cloisters and inscribed their names on its walls — belong to the story of the Abbey no less than its venerable beauty, its solemn services, and its lofty aspirations. . . .

The Chapel of Henry VII. is indeed well called by his name, for it breathes of himself through every part. It is the most signal example of the contrast between his closeness in life, and his "magnificence in the structures he had left to posterity" — King's College Chapel, the Savoy, Westminster. Its very style was believed to have been a reminiscence of his exile, being "learned in France," by himself and his companion Fox. His pride in its grandeur was commemorated by the ship, vast for those times, which he built, "of equal cost with his Chapel," "which afterwards, in the reign of Queen Mary, sank in the sea and vanished in a moment."

It was to be his chantry as well as his tomb, for he was determined not to be behind the Lancastrian princes in devotion; and this unusual anxiety for the sake of a soul not too heavenward in its affections expended itself in the immense apparatus of services which he provided. Almost a second Abbey was needed to contain the new establishment of monks, who were to sing in their stalls "as long as the world shall endure." Almost a second Shrine, surrounded by its blazing tapers, and shining like gold with its glittering bronze, was to contain his remains.

To the Virgin Mary, to whom the chapel was dedicated

he had a special devotion. Her "in all his necessities he had made his continual refuge;" and her figure, accordingly, looks down upon his grave from the east end, between the apostolic patrons of the Abbey, Peter and Paul, with " the holy company of heaven — that is to say, angels, archangels, patriarchs, prophets, apostles, evangelists, martyrs, confessors and virgins," to " whose singular mediation and prayers he also trusted," including the royal saints of Britain, St. Edward, St. Edmund, St. Oswald, St. Margaret of Scotland, who stand, as he directed, sculptured, tier above tier, on every side of the Chapel; some retained from the ancient Lady Chapel; the greater part the work of his own age. Around his tomb stand his "accustomed Avours or guardian saints" to whom " he calls and cries " — " St. Michael, St. John the Baptist, St. John the Evangelist, St. George, St. Anthony, St. Edward, St. Vincent, St. Anne, St. Mary Magdalene, and St. Barbara," each with their peculiar emblems, — " so to aid, succour, and defend him, that the ancient and ghostly enemy, nor none other evil or damnable spirit, have no power to invade him, nor with their wickedness to annoy him, but with holy prayers to be intercessors to his Maker and Redeemer." These were the adjurations of the last mediæval King, as the Chapel was the climax of the latest mediæval architecture. In the very urgency of the King's anxiety for the perpetuity of these funeral ceremonies, we seem to discern an unconscious presentiment lest their days were numbered.

But, although in this sense the Chapel hangs on tenaciously to the skirts of the ancient Abbey and the ancient Church, yet that solemn architectural pause between the two — which arrests the most careless observer, and renders it a separate structure, a foundation "adjoining the Abbey" rather than forming part of it — corresponds with marvellous fidelity to the pause and break in English history of which Henry VII.'s reign is the expression. It is the close of the Middle Ages: the apple of Granada in its ornaments shows that the last Crusade was over; its flowing draperies and classical attitudes indicate that the Renaissance had already begun. It is the end of the Wars of the Roses, combining Henry's right of conquest with his fragile claim of hereditary descent. On the one hand, it is the glorification of the victory of Bosworth. The angels, at the four corners of the tomb, held or hold the likeness of the crown which he won on that famous day. In the stained-glass we see the same crown hanging on the green bush in the fields of Leicestershire. On the other hand, like the Chapel of King's College at Cambridge, it asserts everywhere the memory of the "holy Henry's shade"; the Red Rose of Lancaster appears in every pane of glass: and in every corner is the Portcullis — the "Alters securitas," as he termed it, with an allusion to its own meaning, and the double safeguard of his succession — which he derived through John of Gaunt from the Beaufort Castle in Anjou, inherited from Blanche of Navarre by Edmund Crouchback; whilst Edward IV. and Elizabeth of York are commemorated by intertwining these Lancastrian symbols with the Greyhound of Cecilia Neville, wife of Richard, Duke of York, with the Rose in the Sun, which scattered the mists at Barnet, and the Falcon on the Fetterlock, by which the first Duke of York expressed to his descendants that " he was locked up from the hope of the kingdom, but advising them to be quiet and silent, as God knoweth what may come to pass."

It is also the revival of the ancient, Celtic, British element in the English monarchy, after centuries of eclipse. It is a strange and striking thought, as we mount the steps of Henry VII.'s Chapel, that we enter there a mausoleum of princes, whose boast it was to be descended, not from the Confessor or the Conqueror, but from Arthur and Llewellyn; and that round about the tomb, side by side with the emblems of the great English Houses, is to be seen the Red Dragon of the last British king, Cadwallader— " the dragon of the great Pendragonship " of Wales, thrust forward by the Tudor king in every direction, to supplant the hated White Boar of his departed enemy — the fulfilment, in another sense than the old Welsh bards had dreamt, of their prediction that the progeny of Cadwallader should reign again. . . .

We have seen how, by a gradual but certain instinct, the main groups have formed themselves round particular centres of death: how the Kings ranged themselves round the Confessor; how the Prince and Courtiers clung to the skirts of Kings; how out of the graves of the Courtiers were developed the graves of the Heroes; how Chatham became the centre of the Statesmen, Chaucer of the Poets, Purcell of the Musicians, Casaubon of the Scholars, Newton of the Men of Science: how, even in the exceptional details, natural affinities may be traced; how Addison was buried apart from his brethren in letters, in the royal shades of Henry VII.'s Chapel, because he clung to the vault of his own loved Montague; how Ussher lay beside his earliest instructor, Sir James Fullerton, and Garrick at the foot of Shakespeare, and Spelman opposite his revered Camden, and South close to his master Busby, and Stephenson to his fellow-craftsman Telford, and Grattan to his hero Fox, and Macaulay beneath the statue of his favourite Addison.

These special attractions towards particular graves and monuments may interfere with the general uniformity of the Abbey, but they make us feel that it is not a mere dead museum, that its cold stones are warmed with the life-blood of human affections and personal partiality. It is said that the celebrated French sculptor of the monument of Peter the Great at St. Petersburg, after showing its superiority in detail to the famous equestrian statue of Marcus Aurelius at Rome, ended by the candid avowal, " *Et cependant cette mauvaise bête est vivante, et la mienne est morte.*" Perhaps we may be allowed to reverse the saying, and when we contrast the irregularities of Westminster Abbey with the uniform congruity of Salisbury or the Valhalla, may reflect, " *Cette belle bête est morte, mais la mienne est vivante.*"

Historical Memorials of Westminster Abbey (London, 1866).

THE PARTHENON.

THE PARTHENON.

JOHN ADDINGTON SYMONDS.

FROM whatever point the plain of Athens with its semicircle of greater and lesser hills may be surveyed, it always presents a picture of dignified and lustrous beauty. The Acropolis is the centre of this landscape, splendid as a work of art with its crown of temples; and the sea, surmounted by the long low hills of the Morea, is the boundary to which the eye is irresistibly led. Mountains and islands and plain alike are made of limestone, hardening here and there into marble, broken into delicate and varied forms, and sprinkled with a vegetation of low shrubs and brushwood so sparse and slight that the naked rock in every direction meets the light. This rock is grey and colourless; viewed in the twilight of a misty day, it shows the dull, tame uniformity of bone. Without the sun it is asleep and sorrowful. But by reason of this very deadness, the limestone of Athenian landscape is always ready to take the colours of the air and sun. In noonday it smiles with silvery lustre, fold upon fold of the indented hills and islands melting from the brightness of the sea into the untempered brilliance of the sky. At dawn and sunset the same rocks array themselves with a celestial robe of rainbow-woven hues: islands, sea, and mountains, far and near, burn with saffron, violet, and rose, with the tints of beryl and topaz, sapphire and almandine and amethyst, each in due order and at proper distances. The fabled dolphin in its death could not have showed a more brilliant succession of splendours waning into splendours through the whole chord of prismatic colours. This sensitiveness of the Attic limestone to every modification of the sky's light gives a peculiar spirituality to the landscape. . . .

Seen from a distance, the Acropolis presents nearly the same appearance as it offered to Spartan guardsmen when they paced the ramparts of Deceleia. Nature around is unaltered. Except that more villages, enclosed with olive-groves and vineyards, were sprinkled over those bare hills in classic days, no essential change in the landscape has taken place, no transformation, for example, of equal magnitude with that which converted the Campagna of Rome from a plain of cities to a poisonous solitude. All through the centuries which divide us from the age of Hadrian — centuries unfilled, as far as Athens is concerned, with memorable deeds or national activity — the Acropolis has stood uncovered to the sun. The tones of the marble of Pentelicus have daily grown more golden; decay has here and there invaded frieze and capital; war too has done its work, shattering the Parthenon in 1687 by the explosion of a powder-magazine, and the Propylæa in 1656 by a similar accident, and seaming the colonnades that still remain with cannon-balls in 1827. Yet in spite of time and violence the Acropolis survives, a miracle of beauty: like an everlasting flower, through all that lapse of years it has spread its coronal of marbles to the air, unheeded. And now, more than ever, its temples seem to be incorporate with the rock they crown. The slabs of column and basement have grown together by long pressure or molecular adhesion into a coherent whole. Nor have weeds or creeping ivy invaded the glittering fragments that strew the sacred hill. The sun's kiss alone has caused a change from white to amber-hued or russet. Meanwhile, the exquisite adaptation of Greek building to Greek landscape has been enhanced rather than impaired by that "unimaginable touch of time," which has broken the regularity of outline, softened the chisel-work of the sculptor, and confounded the painter's fretwork in one tint of glowing gold. The Parthenon, the Erechtheum, and the Propylæa have become one with the hill on which they cluster, as needful to the scenery around them as the everlasting mountains, as sympathetic as the rest of nature to the successions of morning and evening, which waken them to passionate life by the magic touch of colour. . . .

In like manner, when moonlight, falling aslant upon the Propylæa, restores the marble masonry to its original whiteness, and the shattered heaps of ruined colonnades are veiled in shadow, and every form seems larger, grander, and more perfect than by day, it is well to sit on the lowest steps, and looking upwards, to remember what processions passed along this way bearing the sacred peplus to Athene. The Panathenaic pomp, which Pheidias and his pupils carved upon the friezes of the Parthenon, took place once in five years, on one of the last days of July. All the citizens joined in the honour paid to their patroness. Old men bearing olive branches, young men clothed in bronze, chapleted youths singing the praise of Pallas in prosodial hymns, maidens carrying holy vessels, aliens bending beneath the weight of urns, servants of the temple leading oxen crowned with fillets, troops of horsemen reining in impetuous steeds: all these pass before us in the frieze of Pheidias. But to our imagination must be left what he has refrained from sculpturing, the chariot formed like a ship, in which the most illustrious nobles of Athens sat, splendidly arrayed, beneath the crocus-coloured curtain or peplus outspread upon a mast. Some concealed machinery caused this car to move; but whether it passed through the Propylæa, and entered the Acropolis, admits of doubt. It is, however, certain that the procession which ascended those steep slabs, and before whom the vast gates of the Propylæa swang open with the clangour of resounding bronze, included not only the citizens of Athens and their attendant aliens, but also troops of cavalry and chariots; for the mark of chariot-wheels can still be traced upon the rock. The ascent is so abrupt that this multitude moved but slowly. Splendid indeed, beyond any pomp of modern ceremonial, must have been the spectacle of the well-ordered procession, advancing through those giant colonnades to the sound of flutes and solemn chants — the shrill clear voices of boys in antiphonal chorus rising above the confused murmurs of such a crowd, the chafing of horses' hoofs upon the stone, and the lowing of bewildered oxen. To realise by fancy the many-coloured radiance of the temples, and the rich dresses of the votaries illuminated by that sharp light of a Greek sun, which defines outline and shadow and gives value to the faintest hue, would be impossible. All we can know for positive about the chromatic decoration of the Greeks is, that whiteness artificially subdued to the tone of ivory prevailed throughout the stonework of the buildings, while blue and red and green in distinct, yet interwoven patterns, added richness to the fretwork and the sculpture of pediment and frieze. The sacramental robes of the worshippers accorded doubtless with this harmony, wherein colour was subordinate to light, and light was toned to softness.

Musing thus upon the staircase of the Propylæa, we may say with truth that all our modern art is but child's play to that of the Greeks. Very soul-subduing is the gloom of a cathedral like the Milanese Duomo, when the incense rises in blue clouds athwart the bands of sunlight falling from the dome, and the crying of choirs upborne on the wings of organ music fills the whole vast space with a mystery of melody. Yet such ceremonial pomps as this are but as dreams and shapes of visions, when compared with the clearly defined splendours of a Greek procession through marble peristyles in open air beneath the sun and sky. That spectacle combined the harmonies of perfect human forms in movement with the divine shapes of statues, the radiance of carefully selected vestments with hues inwrought upon pure marble. The rhythms and melodies of the Doric mood were sympathetic to the proportions of the Doric colonnades. The grove of pillars through which the pageant passed grew from the living rock into shapes of beauty, fulfilling by the inbreathed spirit of man Nature's blind yearning after absolute completion. The sun himself — not thwarted by artificial gloom, or tricked with alien colours of stained glass — was made to minister in all his strength to a pomp, the pride of which was a display of form in manifold magnificence. The ritual of the Greeks was the ritual of a race at one with Nature, glorying in its affiliation to the mighty mother of all life, and striving to add by human art the coping-stone and final touch to her achievement.

Sketches in Italy and Greece (London, 1874).

THE CATHEDRAL OF ROUEN.

THOMAS FROGNALL DIBDIN.

THE approach to Rouen is indeed magnificent. I speak of the immediate approach; after you reach the top of a considerable rise, and are stopped by the barriers, you then look down a straight, broad, and strongly paved road, lined with a double row of trees on each side. As the foliage was not thickly set, we could discern, through the delicately clothed branches the tapering spire of the Cathedral and the more picturesque tower of the Abbaye St. Ouen — with hanging gardens and white houses to the left — covering a richly cultivated ridge of hills, which sink as it were into the *Boulevards* and which is called the *Faubourg Cauchoise*. To the right, through the trees, you see the river Seine (here of no despicable depth or breadth) covered with boats and vessels in motion: the voice of commerce and the stir of industry cheering and animating you as you approach the town. I was told that almost every vessel which I saw (some of them two hundred and even of three hundred tons burthen) was filled with brandy and wine. The lamps are suspended from the centre of long ropes, across the road; and the whole scene is of a truly novel and imposing character. But how shall I convey to you an idea of what I experienced, as, turning to the left, and *leaving* the broader streets which flank the quay, I began to enter the *penetralia* of this truly antiquated town? What narrow streets, what overhanging houses, what bizarre, capricious ornaments! What a mixture of modern with ancient art! What fragments, or rather what ruins of old delicately-built Gothic churches! What signs of former and of modern devastation! What fountains, gutters, groups of never-ceasing men, women and children, all occupied, and all apparently happy! The *Rue de la Grosse Horloge* (so called from a huge, clumsy, antiquated clock which goes across it) struck me as being not among the least singular streets of Rouen. In five minutes I was within the court-yard of the Hôtel Vatel, the favourite residence of the English.

It was evening when I arrived in company with three Englishmen. We were soon saluted by the *laquais de place* — the leech-like hangers-on of every hôtel — who begged to know if we would walk upon the Boulevards. We consented; turned to the right; and, gradually rising gained a considerable eminence. Again we turned to the right, walking upon a raised promenade; while the blossoms of the pear and apple trees, within a hundred walled gardens, perfumed the air with a delicious fragrance. As we continued our route along the *Boulevard Beauvoisine*, we gained one of the most interesting and commanding views imaginable of the city of Rouen — just at that moment lighted up by the golden rays of a glorious sun-set — which gave a breadth and a mellower tone to the shadows upon the Cathedral and the Abbey of Saint Ouen. . . .

I have now made myself pretty well acquainted with the

THE CATHEDRAL OF ROUEN.

geography of Rouen. How shall I convey to you a summary, and yet a satisfactory description of it? It cannot be done. You love old churches, old books, and relics of ancient art. These be my themes, therefore: so fancy yourself either strolling leisurely with me, arm in arm, in the streets — or sitting at my elbow. First for the Cathedral: — for what traveller of taste does not doff his bonnet to the Mother Church of the town through which he happens to be travelling — or in which he takes up a temporary abode? The west front, always the *forte* of the architect's skill, strikes you as you go down, or come up, the principal street — La Rue des Calmes, — which seems to bisect the town into two equal parts. A small open space (which, however has been miserably encroached upon by petty shops) called the *Flower-garden*, is before this western front; so that it has some little breathing room in which to expand its beauties to the wondering eyes of the beholder. In my poor judgment, this western front has very few elevations comparable with it — including even those of Lincoln and York. The ornaments, especially upon three porches, between the two towers, are numerous, rich, and for the greater part entire: — in spite of the Calvinists,[1] the French Revolution, and time. Among the lower and smaller basso-relievos upon these porches is the subject

[1] The ravages committed by the Calvinists throughout nearly the whole of the towns of Normandy, and especially in the Cathedrals towards the year 1560, afford a melancholy proof of the effects of *religious animosity*. But the Calvinists were bitter and ferocious persecutors. Pommeraye in his quarto volume Histoire de l'Église Cathedrale de Rouen (1686) has devoted nearly one hundred pages to an account of Calvinistic depredations.

of the daughter of Herodias dancing before Herod. She is manœuvering on her hands, her feet being upwards. To the right, the decapitation of Saint John is taking place.

The southern transept makes amends for the defects of the northern. The space before it is devoted to a sort of vegetable market: curious old houses encircle this space: and the ascent to the door, but more especially the curiously sculptured porch itself, with the open spaces in the upper part — light, fanciful and striking to a degree — produce an effect as pleasing as it is extraordinary. Add to this the ever-restless feet of devotees, going in and coming out, the worn pavement, and the frittered ornaments, in consequence — seem to convince you that the ardour and activity of devotion is almost equal to that of business.

As you enter the Cathedral, at the centre door, by descending two steps, you are struck with the length and loftiness of the nave, and with the lightness of the gallery which runs along the upper part of it. Perhaps the nave is too narrow for its length. The lantern of the central large tower is beautifully light and striking. It is supported by four massive clustered pillars, about forty feet in circumference;[1] but on casting your eye downwards, you are shocked at the tasteless division of the choir from the nave by what is called a *Grecian screen:* and the interior of the transepts has undergone a like preposterous restoration. The rose windows of the transepts, and that at the west end of the nave, merit your attention and commendation. I could not avoid noticing to the right, upon entrance, perhaps the oldest side chapel in the Cathedral: of a date, little

---

[1] M. Licquet says each clustered pillar contains thirty-one columns.

less ancient than that of the northern tower, and perhaps of the end of the Twelfth Century. It contains by much the finest specimens of stained glass — of the early part of the Sixteenth Century. There is also some beautiful stained glass on each side of the Chapel of the Virgin, behind the choir; but although very ancient, it is the less interesting, as not being composed of groups, or of historical subjects. Yet, in this, as in almost all the churches which I have seen, frightful devastations have been made among the stained-glass windows by the fury of the Revolutionists. . . .

As you approach the Chapel of the Virgin, you pass by an ancient monument, to the left, of a recumbent Bishop, reposing behind a thin pillar, within a pretty ornamented Gothic arch. To the eye of a tasteful antiquary this cannot fail to have its due attraction. While, however, we are treading upon hallowed ground, rendered if possible more sacred by the ashes of the illustrious dead, let us move gently onwards towards the Chapel of the Virgin, behind the choir. See, what bold and brilliant monumental figures are yonder to the right of the altar! How gracefully they kneel and how devoutly they pray! They are the figures of the Cardinals D'Amboise — uncle and nephew : — the former minister of Louis XII. and (what does not necessarily follow, but what gives him as high a claim upon the gratitude of posterity) the restorer and beautifier of the glorious building in which you are contemplating his figure. This splendid monument is entirely of black and white marble, of the early part of the Sixteenth Century. The figures just mentioned are of white marble, kneeling upon cushions, beneath a rich canopy of Gothic fret-work. . . .

THE CATHEDRAL OF ROUEN.

The south-west tower remains, and the upper part of the central tower, with the whole of the lofty wooden spire : — the fruits of the liberality of the excellent men of whom such honourable mention has been made. Considering that this spire is very lofty, and composed of wood, it is surprising that it has not been destroyed by tempest or by lightning.[1] The taste of it is rather capricious than beautiful. . . .

Leaving the Cathedral, you pass a beautifully sculptured fountain (of the early time of Francis I.) which stands at the corner of a street, to the right ; and which, from its central situation, is visited the live-long day for the sake of its limpid waters.

A Bibliographical, Antiquarian, and Picturesque Tour in France and Germany (London, 1829).

[1] Within three years of writing it, the spire was consumed by lightning. The newspapers of both France and England were full of this melancholy event ; and in the year 1823 M. Hyacinthe Langlois of Rouen, published an account of it, together with some views of the progress of the burning.

THE CASTLE OF HEIDELBERG.

VICTOR HUGO.

THERE is every style in the Castle of Heidelberg. It is one of those buildings where are accumulated and mingled beauties which elsewhere are scattered. It has some notched towers like Pierrefonds, some jewelled façades like Anet, some fosse-walls fallen into the moat in a single piece like Rheinfels, some large sorrowful fountains, moss-grown and ready to fall, like the Villa Pamfili, some regal chimney-pieces filled with briers and brambles, — the grandeur of Tancarville, the grace of Chambord, the terror of Chillon. . . .

If you turn towards the Palace of Frederick IV. you have before you the two high, triangular pediments of this dark and bristling façade, the greatly projecting entablatures, where, between four rows of windows, are sculptured with the most spirited chisel, nine Palatines, two Kings, and five Emperors.

On the right you have the beautiful Italian front of Otho-Heinrich with its divinities, its chimeræ, and its nymphs who live and breathe velveted by the soft shadows, with its Roman Cæsars, its Grecian demi-gods, its Hebraic heroes, and its porch which was sculptured by Ariosto. On the left you catch a glimpse of the Gothic front of

Louis the Bearded, as savagely dug out and creviced as if gored by the horns of a gigantic bull. Behind you, under the arches of a porch, which shelters a half-filled well, you see four columns of grey granite, presented by the Pope to the great Emperor of Aix-la-Chapelle, which in the Eighth Century went to Ravenna on the border of the Rhine, in the Fifteenth, from the borders of the Rhine to the borders of the Neckar, and which, after having witnessed the fall of Charlemagne's Palace at Ingelheim, have watched the crumbling of the Palatines' Castle at Heidelberg. All the pavement of the court is covered with ruins of flights of steps, dried-up fountains, and broken basins. Everywhere the stones are cracked and nettles have broken through.

The two façades of the Renaissance which give such an air of splendour to this court are of red sandstone and the statues which decorate them are of white sandstone, an admirable combination which proves that the great sculptors were also great colourists. Time has rusted the red sandstone and given a golden tinge to the white. Of these two façades one, that of Frederick IV., is very severe; the other, that of Otho Heinrich, is entirely charming. The first is historical, the second is fabulous. Charlemagne dominates the one, Jupiter dominates the other.

The more you regard these two Palaces in juxtaposition and the more you study their marvellous details, the more sadness gains upon you. Strange destiny for masterpieces of marble and stone! An ignorant visitor mutilates them, an absurd cannon-ball annihilates them, and they were not mere artists but kings who made them. Nobody knows to-day the names of those divine men who built and sculptured the walls of Heidelberg. There is renown there for ten great artists who hover nameless above this illustrious ruin. An unknown Boccador planned this Palace of Frederick IV.; an ignored Primaticcio composed the façade of Otho-Heinrich; a Cæsar Cæsarino, lost in the shadows, designed the pure arches to the equilateral triangle of Louis V.'s mansion. Here are arabesques of Raphael, and here are figurines of Benvenuto. Darkness shrouds everything. Soon these marble poems will perish, — their poets have already died.

For what did these wonderful men work? Alas! for the sighing wind, for the thrusting grass, for the ivy which has come to compare its foliage with theirs, for the transient swallow, for the falling rain, and for the enshrouding night.

One singular thing here is that the three or four bombardments to which these two façades have been subjected have not treated them in the same way. Only the cornice and the architraves of Otho-Heinrich's Palace have been damaged. The immortal Olympians who dwell there have not suffered. Neither Hercules, nor Minerva, nor Hebe has been touched. The cannon-balls and shells crossed each other here without harming these invulnerable statues. On the other hand, the sixteen crowned knights, who have heads of lions on the *grenouillières* of their armour and who have such valiant countenances, on the Palace of Frederick IV. have been treated by the bombs as if they had been living warriors. Nearly every one of them has been wounded. The face of the Emperor Otho has been covered with scars; Otho, King of Hungary, has had his left leg fractured; Otho-Heinrich, the Palatine, has lost his hand; a ball has disfigured Frederick the Pious; an explosion has cut Frederick II. in half and broken Jean Casimir's loins. In the assaults which were levelled at the highest row, Charlemagne has lost his globe and in the lower one Frederick IV. has lost his sceptre.

However, nothing could be more superb than this legion of princes all mutilated and all standing. The anger of Leopold II. and of Louis XIV., the thunder — the anger of the sky, and the anger of the French Revolution — the anger of the people, have vainly assailed them; they all stand there defending their façade with their fists on their hips, with their legs outstretched, with firmly planted heel and defiant head. The Lion of Bavaria is proudly scowling under their feet. On the second row beneath a green bough, which has pierced through architrave and which is gracefully playing with the stone feathers of his casque, Frederick the Victorious is half drawing his sword. The sculptor has put into his face an indescribable expression of Ajax challenging Jupiter and Nimrod shooting his arrow at Jehovah. These two Palaces of Otho-Heinrich and Frederick IV. must have offered a superb sight when seen in the light of that bombardment on the fatal night of May 21, 1693. . . .

To-day the Tower of Frederick the Victorious is called the Blown-up Tower.

Half of this colossal cylinder of masonry lies in the moat. Other cracked blocks detached from the top of the tower would have fallen long ago if the monster-trees had not seized them in their powerful claws and held them suspended above the abyss.

A few steps from this terrible ruin chance has made a ruin of ravishing beauty; this is the interior of Otho-Heinrich's Palace, of which until now I have only described the façade. There it stands open to everybody under the sunshine and the rain, the snow and the wind, without a ceiling, without a canopy, and without a roof, whose dismantled walls are pierced as if by hazard with twelve Renaissance doors, — twelve jewels of *orfèvrerie*, twelve *chefs d'œuvre*, twelve idyls in stone — entwined as if they issued from the same roots, a wonderful and charming forest of wild flowers, worthy of the Palatines, *consule dignæ*. I can only tell you that this mixture of art and reality is indescribable; it is at once a contest and a harmony. Nature, who has a rival in Beethoven, finds also a rival in Jean Goujon. The arabesques form tendrils and the tendrils form arabesques. One does not know which to admire most, the living or the sculptured leaf.

This ruin appears to be filled with a divine order.

It seems to me that this Palace, built by the fairies of the Renaissance, is now in its natural state. All these marvellous fantasies of free and savage art would be out of harmony in these halls when treaties of peace or war were signed here, when grave princes dreamed here, and when queens were married and German emperors created here. Could these Vertumnuses, Pomonas, or Ganymedes have understood anything about the ideas that came into the heads of Frederick IV. or Frederick V., by the grace of God Count Palatine of the Rhine, Vicar of the Holy

Roman Empire, Elector and Duke of Upper and Lower Bavaria? A grand *seigneur* slept in this chamber beside a king's daughter, under a ducal baldaquin; now there is neither *seigneur*, king's daughter, baldaquin, nor even ceiling to this chamber; it is now the home of the bind-weed, and the wild mint is its perfume. It is well. It is better thus. This adorable sculpture was made to be kissed by the flowers and looked upon by the stars. . . .

The night had fallen, the clouds were spread over the sky, and the moon had mounted nearly to the zenith, while I was still sitting on the same stone, gazing into the darkness which had gathered around me and into the shadows which I had within me. Suddenly the town-clock far below me sounded the hour; it was midnight: I rose and descended. The road leading to Heidelberg passes the ruins. At the moment when I arrived before them, the moon, veiled by the diffused clouds and surrounded by an immense halo, threw a weird light upon this magnificent mass of mouldering ruins. . . .

The ruin, always open, is deserted at this hour. The idea of entering it possessed me. The two stone giants, who guard the stone court, allowed me to pass. I crossed the dark porch, upon which the iron portcullis still hangs, and entered the court. The moon had almost disappeared beneath the clouds. There was only a pallid light in the sky.

Nothing is grander than that which has fallen. This ruin, illuminated in such a way, at such an hour, was indescribably sad, gentle, and majestic. I fancied that in the scarcely perceptible rustling of the trees and foliage there was something grave and respectful. I heard no footstep, no voice, no breath. In the court there was neither light, nor shadow; a sort of dreamful twilight outlined everything and veiled everything. The confused gaps and rifts allowed the feeble rays of moonlight to penetrate the most remote corners; and in the black depths of the inaccessible arches and corridors, I saw white figures, slowly gliding.

It was the hour when the façades of old abandoned buildings are no longer façades, but faces. I walked over the uneven pavement without daring to make any noise, and I experienced between the four walls of this enclosure that strange disquietude, that undefined sentiment which the ancients called "the horror of the sacred woods." There is a kind of insurmountable terror in the sinister mingled with the superb.

However, I climbed up the green and damp steps of the old stairway without rails and entered the old roofless dwelling of Otho-Heinrich. Perhaps you will laugh; but I assure you that to walk at night through chambers which have been inhabited by people, whose doors are dismantled, whose apartments each have their peculiar signification, saying to yourself: "Here is the dining-room, here is the bed-room, here is the alcove, here is the mantel-piece, — and to feel the grass under your feet and to see the sky above your head, is terrifying. A room which has still the form of a room and whose ceiling has been lifted off, as it were like the lid of a box, becomes a mournful and nameless thing. It is not a house, it is not a tomb. In a tomb you feel the *soul* of a man; in this place you feel his shadow.

As soon as I passed the Knights' Hall I stopped. Here

there was a singular noise, the more distinct because a sepulchral silence filled the rest of the ruin. It was a weak, prolonged, strident rattle, mingled at moments with a little, dry and rapid hammering, which at times seemed to come from the depths of the darkness, from a far-away copse, or the edifice itself; at times, from beneath my feet between the rifts in the pavement. Whence came this noise? Of what nocturnal creature was it the cry, or the knocking? I am not acquainted with it, but as I listen to it, I cannot help thinking of that hideous, legendary spinner who weaves rope for the gibbet.

However, nothing, nobody, not a living person is here. This hall, like the rest of the Palace, is deserted. I struck the pavement with my cane, the noise ceased, only to begin again a moment afterwards. I knocked again, it ceased, then it began again. Yet I saw nothing but a large frightened bat, which the blow of my cane on the stones had scared from one of the sculptured corbels of the wall, and which circled around my head in that funereal flight which seems to have been made for the interior of ruined towers. . . .

At the moment I descended the flight of stairs the moon shone forth, large and brilliant, from a rift in the clouds; the Palace of Frederick IV., with its double pediment, suddenly appeared, magnificent and clear as daylight with its sixteen pale and formidable giants; while, at my right, Otho's façade, a black silhouette against the luminous sky, allowed a few dazzling rays of moonlight to escape through its twenty-four windows.

I said clear as daylight — I am wrong. The moon upon ruins is more than a light, — it is a harmony. It hides no detail, it exaggerates no wounds, it throws a veil on broken objects and adds an indescribable, misty aureole of majesty to ancient buildings. It is better to see a palace, or an old cloister, at night than in the day. The hard brilliancy of the sunlight is severe upon the ruins and intensifies the sadness of the statues. . . .

I went out of the Palace through the garden, and, descending, I stopped once more for a moment on one of the lower terraces. Behind me the ruin, hiding the moon, made, half down the slope, a large mass of shadow, where in all directions were thrown out long, dark lines, and long, luminous lines, which striped the vague and misty background of the landscape. Below me lay drowsy Heidelberg, stretched out at the bottom of the valley, the length of the mountain; all the lights were out; all the doors were shut; below Heidelberg I heard the murmur of the Neckar, which seemed to be whispering to the hill and valley; and the thoughts which filled me all the evening, — the nothingness of man in the Past, the infirmity of man in the Present, the grandeur of Nature, and the eternity of God, — came to me altogether, in a triple figure, whilst I descended with slow steps into the darkness between this river awake and living, this sleeping town, and this dead Palace.

Le Rhin (Paris, 1842).

THE DUCAL PALACE.

JOHN RUSKIN.

THE charm which Venice still possesses, and which for the last fifty years has rendered it the favourite haunt of all the painters of picturesque subject, is owing to the effect of the palaces belonging to the period we have now to examine, mingled with those of the Renaissance.

The effect is produced in two different ways. The Renaissance palaces are not more picturesque in themselves than the club-houses of Pall Mall; but they become delightful by the contrast of their severity and refinement with the rich and rude confusion of the sea life beneath them, and of their white and solid masonry with the green waves. Remove from beneath them the orange sails of the fishing boats, the black gliding of the gondolas, the cumbered decks and rough crews of the barges of traffic, and the fretfulness of the green water along their foundations, and the Renaissance palaces possess no more interest than those of London or Paris. But the Gothic palaces are picturesque in themselves, and wield over us an independent power. Sea and sky, and every other accessory might be taken away from them, and still they would be beautiful and strange. They are not less striking in the loneliest streets of Padua and Vicenza (where many were built during the period of the Venetian authority in those cities) than in the most crowded thoroughfares of Venice itself; and if they could be transported into the midst of London, they would still not altogether lose their power over the feelings.

The best proof of this is in the perpetual attractiveness of all pictures, however poor in skill, which have taken for their subject the principal of these Gothic buildings, the Ducal Palace. In spite of all architectural theories and teachings, the paintings of this building are always felt to be delightful; we cannot be wearied by them, though often sorely tried; but we are not put to the same trial in the case of the palaces of the Renaissance. They are never drawn singly, or as the principal subject, nor can they be. The building which faces the Ducal Palace on the opposite side of the Piazzetta is celebrated among architects, but it is not familiar to our eyes; it is painted only incidentally, for the completion, not the subject, of a Venetian scene; and even the Renaissance arcades of St. Mark's Place, though frequently painted, are always treated as a mere avenue to its Byzantine church and colossal tower. And the Ducal Palace itself owes the peculiar charm which we have hitherto felt, not so much to its greater size as compared with other Gothic buildings, or nobler design (for it never yet has been rightly drawn), as to its comparative isolation. The other Gothic structures are as much injured by the continual juxtaposition of the Renaissance palaces, as the latter are aided by it; they exhaust their own life by breathing it into the Renaissance coldness: but the Ducal Palace stands comparatively alone, and fully expresses the Gothic power. . . .

The Ducal Palace, which was the great work of Venice, was built successively in the three styles. There was a Byzantine Ducal Palace, a Gothic Ducal Palace, and a Renaissance Ducal Palace. The second superseded the first totally; a few stones of it (if indeed so much) are all that is left. But the third superseded the second in part only, and the existing building is formed by the union of the two.

We shall review the history of each in succession.

1st. The BYZANTINE PALACE.

The year of the death of Charlemagne, 813, — the Venetians determined to make the island of Rialto the seat of the government and capital of their state. Their Doge, Angelo or Agnello Participazio, instantly took vigorous means for the enlargement of the small group of buildings which were to be the nucleus of the future Venice. He appointed persons to superintend the rising of the banks of sand, so as to form more secure foundations, and to build wooden bridges over the canals. For the offices of religion he built the Church of St. Mark; and on, or near, the spot where the Ducal Palace now stands, he built a palace for the administration of the government.

The history of the Ducal Palace therefore begins with the birth of Venice, and to what remains of it, at this day, is entrusted the last representation of her power. . . .

In the year 1106, it was for the second time injured by fire, but repaired before 1116, when it received another emperor Henry V. (of Germany), and was again honoured by imperial praise. Between 1173 and the close of the

THE DUCAL PALACE.

century, it seems to have been again repaired and much enlarged by the Doge Sebastian Ziani. . . .

2nd. The GOTHIC PALACE.

The reader, doubtless, recollects that the important change in the Venetian government which gave stability to the aristocratic power took place about the year 1297, under the Doge Pietro Gradenigo, a man thus characterized by Sansovino : — " A prompt and prudent man, of unconquerable determination and great eloquence, who laid, so to speak, the foundations of the eternity of this republic, by the admirable regulations which he introduced into the government." . . .

We accordingly find it recorded by Sansovino, that " in 1301 another saloon was begun on the Rio del Palazzo *under the Doge Gradenigo,* and finished in 1309, *in which year the Grand Council first sat in it."* In the first year, therefore, of the Fourteenth Century, the Gothic Ducal Palace of Venice was begun ; and as the Byzantine Palace, was, in its foundation, coeval with that of the state, so the Gothic Palace, was, in its foundation, coeval with that of the aristocratic power. Considered as the principal representation of the Venetian school of architecture, the Ducal Palace is the Parthenon of Venice, and Gradenigo its Pericles. . . .

Its decorations and fittings, however, were long in completion; the paintings on the roof being only executed in 1400. They represented the heavens covered with stars, this being, says Sansovino, the bearings of the Doge Steno. . . . The Grand Council sat in the finished chamber for the first time in 1423. In that year the Gothic Ducal

Palace of Venice was completed. It had taken, to build it, the energies of the entire period which I have above described as the central one of her life.

3rd. The RENAISSANCE PALACE.

I must go back a step or two, in order to be certain that the reader understands clearly the state of the palace in 1423. The works of addition or renovation had now been proceeding, at intervals, during a space of a hundred and twenty-three years. Three generations at least had been accustomed to witness the gradual advancement of the form of the Ducal Palace into more stately symmetry, and to contrast the works of sculpture and painting with which it was decorated,—full of the life, knowledge, and hope of the Fourteenth Century,—with the rude Byzantine chiselling of the palace of the Doge Ziani. The magnificent fabric just completed, of which the new Council Chamber was the nucleus, was now habitually known in Venice as the "Palazzo Nuovo;" and the old Byzantine edifice, now ruinous, and more manifest in its decay by its contrast with the goodly stones of the building which had been raised at its side, was of course known as the "Palazzo Vecchio." That fabric, however, still occupied the principal position in Venice. The new Council Chamber had been erected by the side of it towards the Sea; but there was not the wide quay in front, the Riva dei Schiavoni, which now renders the Sea Façade as important as that of the Piazzetta. There was only a narrow walk between the pillars and the water; and the *old* palace of Ziani still faced the Piazzetta, and interrupted, by its decrepitude, the magnificence of the square where the nobles daily met. Every increase of the beauty of the new palace rendered the discrepancy between it and the companion building more painful; and then began to arise in the minds of all men a vague idea of the necessity of destroying the old palace, and completing the front of the Piazzetta with the same splendour as the Sea Façade. . . . The Great Council Chamber was used for the first time on the day when Foscari entered the Senate as Doge,—the 3rd of April, 1423, . . . and the following year, on the 27th of March, the first hammer was lifted up against the old palace of Ziani.

That hammer stroke was the first act of the period properly called the " Renaissance." It was the knell of the architecture of Venice,— and of Venice herself. . . .

The whole work must have been completed towards the middle of the Sixteenth Century. . . . But the palace was not long permitted to remain in this finished form. Another terrific fire, commonly called the great fire, burst out in 1574, and destroyed the inner fittings and all the precious pictures of the Great Council Chamber, and of all the upper rooms on the Sea Façade, and most of those on the Rio Façade, leaving the building a mere shell, shaken and blasted by the flames. . . . The repairs necessarily undertaken at this time were however extensive, and interfere in many directions with the earlier work of the palace: still the only serious alteration in its form was the transposition of the prisons, formerly at the top of the palace, to the other side of the Rio del Palazzo; and the building of the Bridge of Sighs, to connect them with the palace, by Antonio da Ponte. The completion of this work brought the whole edifice into its present form. . . .

The traveller in Venice ought to ascend into the corridor, and examine with great care the series of capitals which extend on the Piazzetta side from the Fig-tree angle to the pilaster which carries the party wall of the Sala del Gran Consiglio. As examples of graceful composition in massy capitals meant for hard service and distant effect, these are among the finest things I know in Gothic Art; and that above the fig-tree is remarkable for its sculptures of the four winds; each on the side turned towards the wind represented. Levante, the east wind; a figure with rays round its head, to show that it is always clear weather when that wind blows, raising the sun out of the sea: Hotro, the south wind; crowned, holding the sun in its right hand: Ponente, the west wind; plunging the sun into the sea: and Tramontana, the north wind; looking up at the north star. This capital should be carefully examined, if for no other reason than to attach greater distinctness of idea to the magnificent verbiage of Milton:

> " Thwart of these, as fierce,
> Forth rush the Levant and the Ponent winds,
> Eurus, and Zephyr; with their lateral noise,
> Sirocco and Libecchio."

I may also especially point out the bird feeding its three young ones on the seventh pillar on the Piazzetta side; but there is no end to the fantasy of these sculptures; and the traveller ought to observe them all carefully, until he comes to the great pilaster or complicated pier which sustains the party wall of the Sala del Consiglio; that is to say, the forty-seventh capital of the whole series, counting from the pilaster of the Vine angle inclusive, as in the series of the lower arcade. The forty-eighth, forty-ninth, and fiftieth are bad work, but they are old; the fifty-first is the first Renaissance capital of the lower arcade; the first new lion's head with smooth ears, cut in the time of Foscari, is over the fiftieth capital; and that capital, with its shaft, stands on the apex of the eighth arch from the Sea, on the Piazzetta side, of which one spandril is masonry of the Fourteenth and the other of the Fifteenth Century. . . .

I can only say that, in the winter of 1851 the "Paradise" of Tintoret was still comparatively uninjured, and that the Camera di Collegio, and its antechamber, and the Sala de' Pregadi were full of pictures by Veronese and Tintoret, that made their walls as precious as so many kingdoms, so precious indeed, and so full of majesty, that sometimes when walking at evening on the Lido, whence the great chain of the Alps, crested with silver clouds, might be seen rising above the front of the Ducal Palace, I used to feel as much awe in gazing on the building as on the hills, and could believe that God had done a greater work in breathing into the narrowness of dust the mighty spirits by whom its haughty walls had been raised, and its burning legends written, than in lifting the rocks of granite higher than the clouds of heaven, and veiling them with their various mantle of purple flower and shadowy pine.

Stones of Venice (London, 1851-'3).

THE MOSQUE OF CORDOVA.

EDMONDO DE AMICIS.

THE Mosque of Cordova, which was converted into a cathedral when the Moors were expelled but which has, notwithstanding, always remained a Mosque, was built on the ruins of the primitive cathedral not far from the Guadalquiver. Abd-er-Rahman began to build it in the year 785 or 786. "Let us build a Mosque," said he, "which will surpass that of Bagdad, that of Damascus, and that of Jerusalem, which shall be the greatest temple of Islam and become the Mecca of the Occident." The work was begun with ardour; and Christian slaves were made to carry the stones of razed churches for its foundation. Abd-er-Rahman, himself, worked an hour every day; in a few years the Mosque was built, the Caliphs who succeeded Abd-er-Rahman embellished it, and it was completed after a century of continuous labour.

"Here we are," said one of my hosts, as we suddenly stopped before a vast edifice. I thought it was a fortress; but it was the wall that surrounded the Mosque, in which formerly opened twenty large bronze doors surrounded by graceful arabesques and arched windows supported by light columns; it is now covered with a triple coat of plaster.

A trip around the boundary-wall is a nice little walk after dinner: you can judge then of the extent of the building.

The principal door of this enclosure is at the north, on the spot where Abd-er-Rahman's minaret rose, from whose summit fluttered the Mohammedan standard; I expected to see the interior of the Mosque at once, and I found myself in a garden full of orange-trees, cypresses, and palms, enclosed on three sides by a very light portico, and shut in on the fourth side by the façade of the Mosque. In the time of the Arabs there was a fountain in the centre for their ablutions, and the faithful gathered under the shade of these trees before entering the temple. I remained there for some moments looking around me and breathing the fresh and perfumed air with a very lively sensation; my heart was beating rapidly at the thought of being so near the famous Mosque, and I felt myself impelled with a great curiosity and yet held back by an indescribable childish trembling. "Let us go in!" said my companions. "Another moment!" I replied. "Let me taste the pleasure of anticipation." Finally I stepped forward, and without glancing at the marvellous door, which my companions showed me, I entered.

I do not know what I did, or said when I entered; but certainly some strange exclamation must have escaped me, or I must have made some extraordinary gesture, for several people who were near me at that moment began to laugh and turned around to look about them, as if they wanted to discover what caused the excitement I manifested.

Imagine a forest, and imagine that you are in the depths of this forest, and that you can see nothing but the trunks of the trees. Thus, no matter on what side of the Mosque you look, the eye sees nothing but columns. It is a limitless forest of marble. Your glance wanders down the long rows of columns, one by one, which every now and then are intersected by other interminable rows, until it reaches a twilight background where you seem to see the white gleam of still other columns. Nineteen naves extend before the visitor; they are intersected by thirty-three other naves, and the whole building is supported by more than nine hundred columns of porphyry, jasper, *breccia*, and marbles of every colour. The central nave, much larger than the others, leads to the Maksurah, the most sacred spot in the temple, where they read the Koran. A pale ray of light falls from the high windows here and shines upon a row of columns; beyond, there is a dark spot; and, still further away, another ray of light illuminates another nave. It is impossible to describe the mystical feeling and admiration that this sight evokes in your soul. It is like the sudden revelation of an unknown religion, nature, and life, which carries your imagination to the delights of that Paradise, so full of love and voluptuousness, where the blessed ones seated under the shadow of thick-leaved plane-trees and thornless rose-bushes drink from crystal vases that wine, sparkling like jewels, which is mixed by immortal virgins, and sleep in the arms of houris with large black eyes. All these pictures of eternal pleasure, which the Koran promises to the faithful, rush upon the mind at this first sight of the Mosque in such a vital, intense, and bewildering manner that for an instant they give you a sweet intoxication which leaves your heart

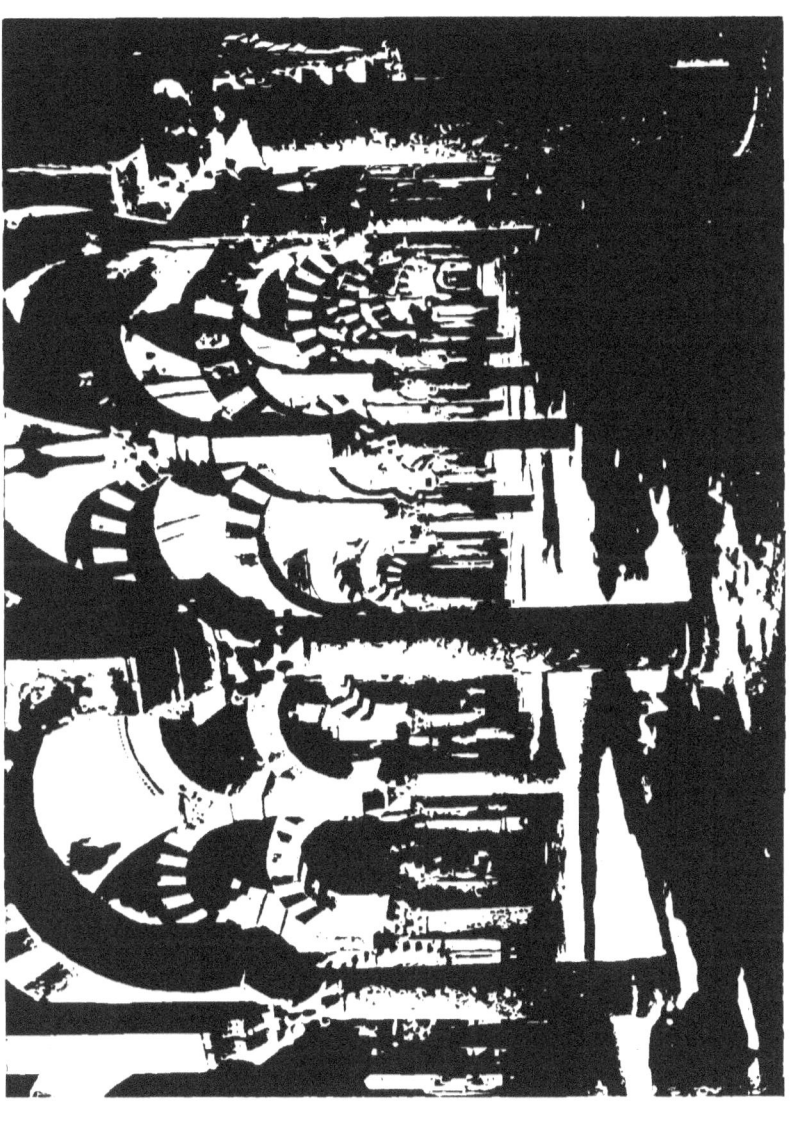

THE MOSQUE OF CORDOVA.

THE MOSQUE OF CORDOVA. 289

in a state of indescribable and gentle melancholy. Confusion in the mind and a rushing fire through the veins — that is your first sensation on entering the Cathedral of Cordova.

We begin to wander from nave to nave, observing everything in detail. What variety there is in this edifice, which seemed all alike at the first glance! The proportions of the columns, the designs of the capitals and the forms of the arches, change, so to speak, at every step you take. Most of the columns are ancient and were brought by the Arabs from Northern Spain, Gaul, and Roman Africa; and some of them, it is said, belonged to a temple of Janus on whose ruins was built the church which the Arabs destroyed in order to erect this Mosque. On many of the capitals you can still distinguish the cross, which was carved upon them and which the Arabs erased with their chisels. In some of the columns pieces of curved iron are fixed, to which it is said the Arabs chained the Christians; one, particularly, is exhibited, to which, according to popular tradition, a Christian was chained for many long years, and during this time he dug at the stone with his nails to make a cross, which the guides show you with deep veneration.

We stood before the Maksura, the most complete and marvellous example of Arabian Art of the Tenth Century. There are three adjacent chapels in front of it, with vaulted ceilings of dentelated arches and walls covered with superb mosaics in the form of large bunches of flowers and inscriptions from the Koran. The principal Mihrab, the holy place where the spirit of God dwells, is at the back of the central chapel. It is a niche with an octagon base and arched at the top by an enormous shell of marble. In the Mihrab, and fastened on a stool of aloe-wood, was kept the Koran, copied by the hand of the Caliph Othman, covered with gold and ornamented with pearls; and the faithful made the tour of it seven times on their knees. On approaching the wall, I felt the pavement sink under my feet: the marble is hollowed out!

Coming out of the niche, I stopped for a long time to look at the ceiling and the walls of the principal church, the only portion of the Mosque which is almost intact. It is a dazzling array of crystal of a thousand colours, an interlacing of arabesques which confounds the imagination, a complication of bas-reliefs, of gold-work, of ornaments, and of details of design and hues of a delicacy, a grace, and a perfection to drive the most patient painter to despair. It is impossible to recall clearly that prodigious work; you might return a hundred times to look at it, yet it would only be remembered as an aggregation of blue, red, green, golden, and luminous points, or a complicated embroidery whose patterns and colours are continually changing. Such a miracle of art could only emanate from the fiery and indefatigable imagination of the Arabs.

Again we wandered about the Mosque, examining here and there on the walls the arabesques of the ancient doors, of which you get glimpses from beneath the detestable Christian paint. My companions looked at me, laughed, and whispered to each other.

"You have not seen it yet?" asked one.

"What?"

They looked at each other again and smiled.

"Do you think you have seen the entire Mosque?" said the one who had first spoken.

"I? Yes," I replied, looking around me.

"Well, you have not seen it all: what remains to be seen is a church — nothing more!"

"A church!" I cried, stupefied, "where is it?"

"Look!" said the other companion, pointing it out, "it is in the very centre of the Mosque."

"Good heavens! And I had not noticed it at all!"

By that you may judge of the size of the Mosque. We went to see the church. It is very beautiful and very rich, with a magnificent high altar and a choir worthy of ranking with those of Burgos and Toledo; but, like all things which do not harmonize with their surroundings, it annoys you instead of exciting your admiration. Even Charles V., who gave the Chapter permission to build it here, repented when he saw the Mussulman temple. Next to the church there is a kind of Arabian chapel, admirably preserved and rich in mosaics not less beautiful and varied than those of the Maksura; it is said that the doctors of this religion met there to read the Book of the Prophet.

Such is the Mosque of to-day.

What must it have been in the time of the Arabs! It was not enclosed then by a surrounding wall, but it was open in such a way that the garden could be seen from every one of its parts, while from the garden you could see the entire length of the long naves, and the breeze carried the perfume from the orange-trees and flowers to the very arches of the Maksura. Of the columns, which to-day number less than a thousand, there were fourteen hundred; the ceiling was of cedar and larch sculptured and incrusted with the most delicate work; the walls were of marble; the light of eight hundred lamps filled with perfumed oil made the crystals in the mosaics sparkle like diamonds and caused a marvellous play of colour and reflection on the floor, on the arches, and on the walls. "An ocean of splendours," a poet said, "filled this mysterious enclosure, the balmy air was impregnated with aromas, and the thoughts of the faithful strayed until they became lost in the labyrinth of columns which glimmered like lances in the sunlight."

La Spagna (Florence, 1873).

THE CATHEDRAL OF THRONDTJEM.

THE CATHEDRAL OF THRONDTJEM.

AUGUSTUS J. C. HARE.

ON July 25 we left Kristiania for Throndtjem — the whole journey of three hundred and sixty miles being very comfortable, and only costing thirty francs. The route has no great beauty, but endless pleasant variety — rail to Eidswold, with bilberries and strawberries in pretty birchbark baskets for sale at all the railway stations; a vibrating steamer for several hours on the long, dull Miosem lake; railway again, with some of the carriages open at the sides; then an obligatory night at Koppang, a large station, where accommodation is provided for every one, but where, if there are many passengers, several people, strangers to each other, are expected to share the same room. On the second day the scenery improves, the railway sometimes running along and sometimes over the river Glommen on a wooden causeway, till the gorge of mountains opens beyond Stören, into a rich country with turfy mounds constantly reminding us of the graves of the hero-gods of Upsala. Towards sunset, beyond the deep cleft in which the river Nid runs between lines of old painted wooden warehouses, rises the burial place of S. Olaf, the shrine of Scandinavian Christianity, the stumpy-towered Cathedral of Throndtjem. The most northern railway station, and the most northern cathedral in Europe.

Surely the cradle of Scandinavian Christianity is one of the most beautiful places in the world! No one had ever told us about it, and we went there only because it is the old Throndtjem of sagas and ballads, and expecting a wonderful and beautiful cathedral.

But the whole place is a dream of loveliness, so exquisite in the soft silvery morning light on the fyord and delicate mountain ranges, the rich nearer hills covered with bilberries and breaking into steep cliffs — that one remains in a state of transport, which is at a climax while all is engraven upon an opal sunset sky, when an amethystine glow spreads over the mountains, and when ships and buildings meet their double in the still transparent water. Each wide street of curious low wooden houses displays a new vista of sea, of rocky promontories, of woods dipping into the water; and at the end of the principal street is the grey massive Cathedral where S. Olaf is buried, and where northern art and poetry have exhausted their loveliest and most pathetic fancies around the grave of the national hero.

The "Cathedral Garden," for so the graveyard is called, is most touching. Acres upon acres of graves are all kept — not by officials, but by the families they belong to — like gardens. The tombs are embowered in roses and honeysuckle, and each little green mound has its own vase for cut flowers daily replenished, and a seat for the survivors, which is daily occupied, so that the link between the dead and the living is never broken.

Christianity was first established in Norway at the end of the Tenth Century by King Olaf Trygveson, son of Trygve and of the lady Astrida, whose romantic adventures, when sold as a slave after her husband's death, are the subject of a thousand stories. When Olaf succeeded to the throne of Norway after the death of Hako, son of Sigurd, in 996, he proclaimed Christianity throughout his dominions, heard matins himself daily, and sent out missionaries through his dominions. But the duty of the so-called missionaries had little to do with teaching, they were only required to baptize. All who refused baptism were tortured and put to death. When, at one time, the estates of the province of Throndtjem tried to force Olaf back to the old religion, he outwardly assented, but made the condition that the offended pagan deities should in that case be appeased by human sacrifice — the sacrifice of the twelve nobles who were most urgent in compelling him; and upon this the ardour of the chieftains for paganism was cooled, and they allowed Olaf unhindered to demolish the great statue of Thor, covered with gold and jewels, in the centre of the province of Throndtjem, where he founded the city then called Nidaros, upon the river Nid. . . .

Olaf Trygveson had a godson Olaf, son of Harald Grenske and Asta, who had the nominal title of king given to all sea captains of royal descent. From his twelfth year, Olaf Haraldsen was a pirate, and he headed the band of Danes who destroyed Canterbury and murdered S. Elphege — a strange feature in the life of one who has been himself regarded as a saint since his death. By one of the strange freaks of fortune common in those times, this Olaf Haraldsen gained a great victory over the chieftain Sweyn, who then ruled at Nidaros, and, chiefly through the influence of Sigurd Syr, a great northern landowner, who had become the second husband of his mother, he became seated in 1016 upon the throne of Norway. His first care was for the restoration of Christianity, which had fallen into decadence in the sixteen years which had elapsed since the defeat of Olaf Trygveson. The second Olaf imitated the violence and cruelty of his predecessor. Whenever the new religion was rejected, he beheaded or hung the delinquents. In his most merciful moments he mutilated and blinded them: " he did not spare one who refused to serve God.". . .

However terrible the cruelties of Olaf Haraldsen were in his lifetime, they were soon dazzled out of sight amid the halo of miracles with which his memory was encircled by the Roman Catholic Church. . . .

It was when the devotion to S. Olaf was just beginning that Earl Godwin and his sons were banished from England for a time. Two of these, Harold and Tosti, became vikings, and, in a great battle, they vowed that if they were victorious, they would give half the spoil to the shrine of S. Olaf; and a huge silver statue, which they actually gave, existed at Throndtjem till 1500, and if it existed still would be one of the most important relics in archæology. The old Kings of Norway used to dig up the saint from time to time and cut his nails. When Harold Hardrada was going to England, he declared that he must see S. Olaf once again. " I must see my brother once more," he said, and he also cut the saint's nails. But he also thought that from that time it would be better that no one should see his brother any more — it would not be for the good of the Church — so he took the keys of the shrine and threw them into the fyord; at the same time, he said, it would be good for men in after ages to know what a great king was like, so he caused S. Olaf's measure to be engraved upon the wall in the church at Throndtjem — his measure of seven feet — and there it is still.

Around the shrine of Olaf in Throndtjem, in which, in spite of Harald Hardrada, his "incorrupt body" was seen more than five hundred years after his death, has arisen the most beautiful of northern cathedrals, originating in a small chapel built over his grave within ten years after his death. The exquisite colour of its green-grey stone adds greatly to the general effect of the interior, and to the delicate sculpture of its interlacing arches. From the ambulatory behind the choir opens a tiny chamber containing the Well of S. Olaf, of rugged yellow stone, with the holes remaining in the pavement through which the dripping water ran away when the buckets were set down. Amongst the many famous bishops of Throndtjem, perhaps the most celebrated has been Anders Arrebo, "the father of Danish poetry" (1587–1637), who wrote the "Hexameron," an extraordinarily long poem on the Creation, which nobody reads now. The Cathedral is given up to Lutheran worship, but its ancient relics are kindly tended and cared for, and the building is being beautifully restored. Its beautiful Chapter House is lent for English service on Sundays.

Sketches in Holland and Scandinavia (London, 1885).

LEANING TOWER OF PISA.

CHARLES DICKENS.

FROM the summit of a lofty hill beyond Carrara, the first view of the fertile plain in which the town of Pisa lies — with Leghorn a purple spot in the flat distance — is enchanting. Nor is it only distance that lends enchantment to the view; for the fruitful country, and rich woods of olive-trees through which the road subsequently passes, render it delightful.

The moon was shining when we approached Pisa, and for a long time we could see, behind the wall, the Leaning Tower, all awry in the uncertain light; the shadowy original of the old pictures in school-books, setting forth "The Wonders of the World." Like most things connected in their first associations with school-books and school-times, it was too small. I felt it keenly. It was nothing like so high above the wall as I had hoped. It was another of the many deceptions practised by Mr. Harris, Bookseller, at the corner of St. Paul's Church-yard, London. *His* Tower was a fiction, but this was reality — and, by comparison, a short reality. Still, it looked very well, and very strange, and was quite as much out of the perpendicular as Harris had represented it to be. The quiet air of Pisa, too; the big guard-house at the gate,

THE LEANING TOWER OF PISA.

with only two little soldiers in it; the streets, with scarcely any show of people in them; and the Arno, flowing quaintly through the centre of the town; were excellent. So, I bore no malice in my heart against Mr. Harris (remembering his good intentions), but forgave him before dinner, and went out, full of confidence, to see the Tower next morning.

I might have known better; but, somehow, I had expected to see it casting its long shadow on a public street where people came and went all day. It was a surprise to me to find it in a grave, retired place, apart from the general resort, and carpeted with smooth green turf. But, the group of buildings clustered on and about this verdant carpet; comprising the Tower, the Baptistery, the Cathedral, and the Church of the Campo Santo; is perhaps the most remarkable and beautiful in the whole world; and, from being clustered there together away from the ordinary transactions and details of the town, they have a singularly venerable and impressive character. It is the architectural essence of a rich old city, with all its common life and common habitations pressed out, and filtered away.

SIMOND compares the Tower to the usual pictorial representations in children's books of the Tower of Babel. It is a happy simile, and conveys a better idea of the building than chapters of laboured description. Nothing can exceed the grace and lightness of the structure; nothing can be more remarkable than its general appearance. In the course of the ascent to the top (which is by an easy staircase), the inclination is not very apparent; but, at the summit, it becomes so, and gives one the sensation of being in a ship that has heeled over, through the action of an ebb tide. The effect *upon the low side*, so to speak — looking over from the gallery, and seeing the shaft recede to its base — is very startling ; and I saw a nervous traveller hold on to the Tower involuntarily, after glancing down, as if he had some idea of propping it up. The view within, from the ground — looking up, as through a slanted tube — is also very curious. It certainly inclines as much as the most sanguine tourist could desire. The natural impulse of ninety-nine people out of a hundred, who were about to recline upon the grass below it to rest, and contemplate the adjacent buildings, would probably be, not to take up their position under the leaning side ; it is so very much aslant.

Pictures from Italy (London, 1845).

THE CATHEDRAL OF CANTERBURY.

THE CATHEDRAL OF CANTERBURY.

W. H. FREMANTLE.

THE foundation of St. Martin's Church and the lower part of its walls, which are Roman, stood in 598 as they stand to-day; and they were the walls of the little church which had been given to the Christian Queen Bertha and her chaplain Bishop Luithart, by her pagan husband King Ethelbert. When Augustine passed towards the city, as described by the Venerable Bede, with his little procession headed by the monk carrying a board on which was a rough picture of Christ, and a chorister bearing a silver cross, his heart, no doubt, beat high with hope: but his hope would have grown into exultation could he have looked forward through the centuries, and beheld the magnificent Cathedral which was to spring up where his episcopal throne was fixed, and the energetic and varied Christian life which has issued from this first home of Anglo-Saxon Christianity. To us the scene is full of historical recollections. Between the place where we are standing and the Cathedral are the city walls, on the very site which they occupied in the days of Ethelbert, and the postern-gate through which Queen Bertha came every day to her prayers; in the nearer distance, a little to the right of the Cathedral, are the remains of the great abbey which Augustine founded; to our left is the Pilgrims' Way, by which, after Becket's canonization, those who landed at Dover made their way to the shrine of St. Thomas.

The eye glances over the valley of the Stour, enclosed between the hill on which we are placed and that of St. Thomas, crowned by the fine buildings of the Clergy Orphan School; and ranges from Harbledown (Chaucer's " little town under the Blean ycleped Bob-up-and-down ") on the left to the Jesuit College at Hale's Place farther to the right; and thence down the valley to Fordwich, where formerly the waters of the Stour joined those of the Wantsome, the estuary separating Thanet from the mainland. This town at the Domesday epoch was a port with flourishing mills and fisheries. There the Caen stone was landed to build the Cathedral, and the tuns of wine from the monks' vineyards in France were lifted out of the ships by the mayor's crane. . . .

But it is time that we go into the Cathedral precincts. Making use of a canon's key, we pass, by Queen Bertha's Postern, through the old city walls, along a piece of the ancient Queningate lane—a reserved space between the walls of the city and the precincts, along which the citizens and troops could pass freely for purposes of defence: through the Bowling Green, where the tower of Prior Chillenden is seen to have been used as a pigeon-house, into the Cathedral Yard. In so doing we pass under a Norman archway of the date of Lanfranc and the Conqueror, which formerly stood in a wall separating the cemetery of the monks from that of the laity; then along the south side of the Cathedral, passing Anselm's chapel, and the beautiful Norman tower attached to the south-eastern transept, with its elaborate tracery, which shows how delicate Norman work could be; past the south porch, over which is a bas-relief of the altar where the sword of Becket's murderer was preserved; and round, past the western door, into the cloister.

The cloister occupies the same space as the Norman cloister built by Lanfranc, but of the Norman work only a doorway remains at the north-east corner; there is some Early English arcading on the north side, but the present tracery and fan-worked roof belong to the end of the Fourteenth Century, when Archbishops Sudbury, Arundell, and Courtenay, and Prior Chillenden (1390–1411) rebuilt the nave, the cloister and the chapter-house. The later work cuts across the older in the most unceremonious way, as is seen especially in the square doorway by which we shall presently enter the "Martyrdom," which cuts into a far more beautiful portal of the decorated period. . . .

If from the place at which we have in imagination been standing, at the north-west corner of the cloister, we look for a moment behind us, we see in the wall a blocked-up door, with a curious door at the side of it. The hole is said to have been made in order to pass bottles and other articles through from the cellarer's lodgings, which were on the other side of the wall. The doorway was the entrance from the Archbishop's Palace, which occupied the space a little further to the west; and through it Becket passed out to his death, on the 29th of December, 1170. . . .

Henry had to do penance, and practically to concede the clerical immunities for which Becket had contended; and Becket became a saint, "the holy, blissful martyr," himself the worker of a thousand miracles, and his shrine the goal of pilgrimages from all parts of England and of Europe. But, whatever we may think of this, his death was certainly the making of Canterbury and its Cathedral. Four years after Becket's death the choir was burned down (1174): but the treasure which was poured into the martyr's church enabled the monks to rebuild it in its present grander proportions; and the city, which before was insignificant, became wealthy, populous, and renowned.

The crypt was the first place of Becket's interment, and into the crypt we now pass. . . . The pavement in the centre of the Trinity Chapel (the part east of the screen) is very rough, being composed of the stones which formed the steps and pavement of the shrine; but the marble pavement around it is still as it was when the shrine was standing, and a perceptible line marks the impress of the pilgrims' feet as they stood in a row to see the treasures. The shrine stood upon a platform approached by three marble steps, some stones of which, grooved by the pilgrims' knees, are still seen in the flooring. The platform was paved with mosaic and medallions, specimens of which may still be seen in the present pavement. Above this platform was the chased and gilded coffin of the saint, supported by three arches, which were hung with votive offerings of extreme richness, and between two of which sick persons were allowed to pass, so that by rubbing themselves against the stones they might draw forth virtue from the relics of the saint. The whole was covered with an oaken case richly decorated, which at a given signal from the monk whom Erasmus styles the mystagogus, or master of the mysteries, was drawn up and revealed the riches within to the wondering gaze of the pilgrims. In the painted windows of the chapel are the records of the miracles wrought by the intercession of St. Thomas: here, a dead man being carried out to burial is raised; there, the parents of a boy who has been drowned in the attempt to catch frogs in the river are informed of their loss by his companions with eager gestures, and he too is restored to life; and in each case offerings of gold and silver are poured upon the shrine; the madman is seen coming back in his right mind; "Amens accedit, sanus recedit:" and on several occasions the saint himself comes on the scene to heal the sick man on his bed, in one case flying forth from the shrine in his episcopal robes. The worship of Becket was the favourite cultus of the unreformed Church of England; yet, strange to tell, from the day when Henry gave orders to demolish the shrine, and to expunge his name from all the service books and his memorials from all the churches, no one seems to have thought anything more about him. The blow which, to adapt the language of the Old Testament, "destroyed Becket out of Israel," though violent, was timely.

The Black Prince, whose wife was the Fair Maid of Kent, was especially attached to Canterbury, and founded two chantries in the crypt or undercroft. These now form the entrance to the French Church, where the descendants of the Walloon and Huguenot refugees still worship in the forms of their ancestors. The Prince had desired to be buried below; but, partly from the special devotion which he had to the Trinity, partly that so great a man might have the place of honour, his tomb was erected at the side of Becket's shrine. He left to the Church of Canterbury his velvet coat embroidered with lions and lilies, his ornamental shield, his lion-crested helmet, his sword and his gauntlets, all of which still hang above his bronze effigy, except the sword, which is said to have been removed by Cromwell, and of which only part of the scabbard remains. The effigy is believed to be a good likeness. It was placed upon the tomb where the body lies soon after his death, which occurred on the 8th of June, 1376, the feast of the Trinity, as recorded in the inscription in the French of his own Aquitaine. The Prince of Wales's feathers and the lions and lilies, with the Prince's two mottoes, "Ich diene," (I serve), and "Houmout," (High Courage), form the ornaments of the tomb, which is also surrounded by some French verses chosen by the Prince himself, and describing the vanity of earthly glory. . . .

And now we leave the Cathedral, and pass out of the precincts by the Christ Church Gate, still beautiful even in its defacement, and through the narrow Mercery Lane, where stood in old times the booths for the sellers of relics and of the little leaden bottles supposed to contain in their water some drops of St. Thomas's blood; where also stood the Chequers of the Hope, at which Chaucer's pilgrims regaled themselves, and of which one fragment, marked by the Black Prince's emblem of the lion with protruding tongue, may still be seen at the corner of the lane; down the High Street, where we pass the old East Bridge Hospital, founded by Lanfranc, endowed by Becket, and saved from confiscation by Cranmer, with its low Norman doorway and the crypt under its hall; and leave the city by the West Gate, which was erected by Archbishop Sudbury on the line where the eastern wall ran along the Stour; and past the Falstaff Inn, where the sign of the roystering old knight hangs out on some beautiful ancient ironwork, and welcomes the cyclists who specially affect his inn; and so on to the South Eastern Railway Station.

We entered Canterbury on foot with Augustine, we leave it by a modern railway.

Farrar, *Our English Minsters* (London, 1893).

THE ALHAMBRA.

THÉOPHILE GAUTIER.

HAVING passed through the gate, you enter a large square called *Plaza de las Algives* in the centre of which you find a well whose curb is surrounded by a kind of wooden shed covered with spartium matting and where, for a *cuarto*, you can have a glass of water, as clear as a diamond, as cold as ice, and of the most delicious flavour. The towers of Quebrada, the Homenaga, the Armeria, and of the Vela, whose bell announces the hours when the water is distributed, and stone-parapets, on which you can lean to admire the marvellous view which unfolds before you, surround one side of the square; the other is occupied by the Palace of Charles V., an immense building of the Renaissance, which you would admire anywhere else, but which you curse here when you remember that it covers a space once occupied by a portion of the Alhambra which was pulled down to make room for this heavy mass. This Alcazar was, however, designed by Alonzo Berruguete; the trophies, the bas-reliefs, and the medallions of its façade have been accumulated by means of a proud, bold, and patient chisel; the circular court with its marble columns, where, in all probability, the bull-fights took place, is certainly a magnificent piece of architecture, but *non erat hic locus*.

You enter the Alhambra through a corridor situated in an angle of the Palace of Charles V., and, after several windings, you arrive in a large court, designated indifferently under the names of *Patio de los Arraynes* (Court of Myrtles), of the *Alberca* (of the Reservoir), or of the *Mezouar* (an Arabian word signifying bath for women).

When you issue from these dark passages into this large space flooded with light, the effect is similar to that produced by a diorama. You can almost fancy that an enchanter's wand has transported you to the Orient of four or five centuries ago. Time, which changes everything in its flight, has altered nothing here, where the apparition of the Sultana *Chaine des cœurs* and of the Moor *Tarfe* in his white cloak would not cause the least surprise. . . .

The antechamber of the Hall of the Ambassadors is worthy of the purpose for which it was intended: the boldness of its arches, the variety and interlacing of its arabesques, the mosaics of its walls, and the work on its stuccoed ceiling, crowded like the stalactite roof of a grotto and painted with azure, green, and red, traces of which colours are still visible, produce an effect both charming and bizarre.

On each side of the door which leads to the Hall of the Ambassadors, in the jamb of the arch itself and where the facing of glazed tiles, whose triangles of glaring colours adorn the lower portion of the walls, are hollowed out, like little chapels, two niches of white marble sculptured with an extreme delicacy. It was here that the ancient

Moors left their Turkish slippers before entering, as a mark of deference, just as we remove our hats in places that demand this respect.

The Hall of the Ambassadors, one of the largest in the Alhambra, fills the whole interior of the tower of Comares. The ceiling, composed of cedar, shows those mathematical combinations so common to the Arabian architect: all the bits are arranged in such a way that all their converging or diverging angles form an infinite variety of designs; the walls disappear under a network of ornaments, so packed together and so inextricably interwoven that I can think of no better comparison than pieces of lace placed one above the other. Gothic architecture, with its stone lace-work and its perforated roses, cannot compare with this. Fish-slices and the paper embroidery cut out with a punch, which the confectioners use to decorate their sweets, can alone give you any idea of it. One of the characteristics of the Moorish style is that it offers very few projections and profiles. All the ornamentation is developed on flat surfaces and is hardly ever more than four or five inches in relief; it is really like a kind of tapestry worked on the wall itself. One feature in particular distinguishes it — the employment of writing as a motive of decoration; it is true that Arabian letters, with their mysteriously winding forms, lend themselves remarkably to this use. The inscriptions, which are almost always *suras* of the Koran, or eulogies to various princes who have built and decorated these halls, unfold upon the friezes, on the jambs of the doors, and round the arches of the windows interspersed with flowers,

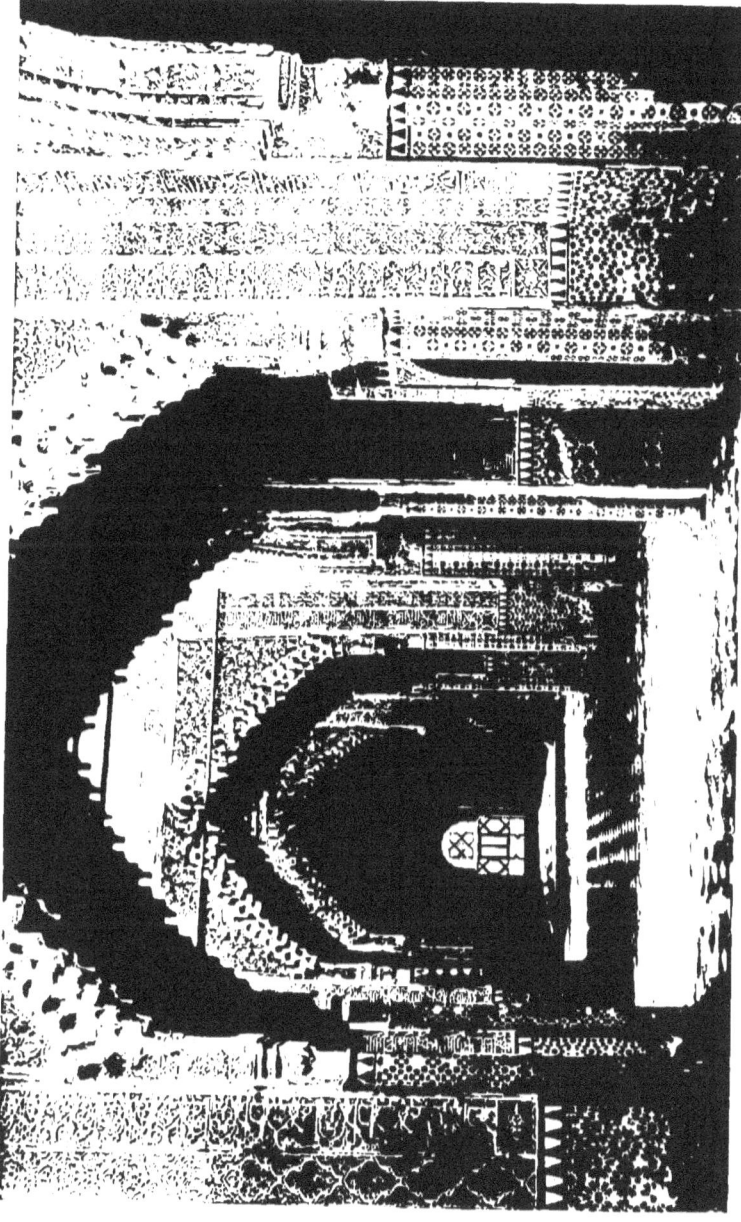

THE ALHAMBRA.

boughs, network, and all the wealth of Arabian caligraphy. Those in the Halls of the Ambassadors signify " Glory to God, power and wealth to believers," or consist of praises to Abu Nazar, who, " if he had been taken into Heaven while living, would have diminished the brightness of the stars and planets," a hyperbolical assertion which seems to us a little too Oriental.

Other bands are filled with eulogies to Abu Abd Allah, another Sultan who ordered work upon this part of the Palace. The windows are bedizened with verses in honour of the limpid waters of the reservoir, of the freshness of the shrubbery, and the perfume of the flowers which ornament the Court of the *Mezouar*, which in fact is seen, from the Hall of the Ambassadors through the doors and little columns of the gallery.

The loop-holes of the interior balcony, pierced at a great height from the ground, and the ceiling of wood-work, devoid of ornaments except the zig-zags and the interlacings formed by the joining of the pieces, give the Hall of the Ambassadors a more severe aspect than any other halls in the Palace, and more in harmony with its purpose. From the back window you can enjoy a marvellous view over the ravine of the Darro. . . .

From the Hall of the Ambassadors you go down a corridor of relatively modern construction to the *tocador*, or dressing-room of the queen. This is a small pavilion on the top of a tower used by the sultanas as an oratory, and from which you can enjoy a wonderful panorama. You notice at the entrance a slab of white marble perforated with little holes in order to let the smoke of the perfumes burned beneath the floor to pass through. You can still see on the walls the fantastic frescoes of Bartholomew de Ragis, Alonzo Perez, and Juan de la Fuente. Upon the frieze the ciphers of Isabella and Philip V. are intertwined with groups of Cupids. It is difficult to imagine anything more coquettish and charming than this room, with its small Moorish columns and its surbased arches, over-hanging an abyss of azure, the bottom of which is studded with the roofs of Grenada and into which the breeze brings the perfumes from the Generalife, — that enormous cluster of oleanders blossoming in the foreground of the nearest hill, — and the plaintive cry of the peacocks walking upon the dismantled walls. How many hours have I passed there in that serene melancholy, so different from the melancholy of the North, with one leg hanging over the precipice and charging my eyes to photograph every form and every outline of this beautiful picture unfolded before them, and which, in all probability, they will never behold again! No description in words, or colours, can give the slightest hint of this brilliancy, this light, and these vivid tints. The most ordinary tones acquire the worth of jewels and everything else is on a corresponding scale. Towards the close of day, when the sun's rays are oblique, the most inconceivable effects are produced: the mountains sparkle like heaps of rubies, topazes, and carbuncles; a golden dust bathes the ravines; and if, as is frequent in the summer, the labourers are burning stubble in the field, the wreaths of smoke, which rise slowly towards the sky, borrow the most magical reflections from the fires of the setting sun. . . .

The Court of Lions is 120 feet long and 73 feet wide, while the surrounding galleries do not exceed 20 feet in height. These are formed by 128 columns of white marble, arranged in a symmetrical disorder of groups of fours and groups of threes; these columns, whose highly-worked capitals retain traces of gold and colour, support arches of extreme elegance and of a very unique form. . . .

To the left and midway up the long side of the gallery, you come to the Hall of the Two Sisters, the *pendant* to the Hall of the Abencerrages. The name of *las Dos Hermanas* is given to it on account of two immense flag-stones of white Macael marble of equal size and exactly alike which you notice at once in the pavement. The vaulted roof, or cupola, which the Spanish very expressively call *media naranja* (half an orange), is a miracle of work and patience. It is something like a honey-comb, or the stalactites of a grotto, or the soapy grape-bubbles which children blow through a pipe. These myriads of little vaults, or domes, three or four feet high, which grow out of one another, intersecting and constantly breaking their corners, seem rather the product of fortuitous crystallization than the work of human hands; the blue, the red, and the green still shine in the hollows of the mouldings as brilliantly as if they had just been laid on. The walls, like those in the Hall of the Ambassadors, are covered from the frieze to the height of a man with the most delicate embroideries in stucco and of an incredible intricacy. The lower part of the walls is faced with square blocks of glazed clay, whose black, green, and yellow angles form a mosaic upon the white background. The centre of the room, according to the invariable custom of the Arabs, whose habitations seem to be nothing but great ornamental fountains, is occupied by a basin and a jet of water. There are four fountains under the Gate of Justice, as many under the entrance-gate, and another in the Hall of the Abencerrages, without counting the *Taza de los Leones*, which, not content with vomiting water through the mouths of its twelve monsters, tosses a jet towards the sky through the mushroom-cap which surmounts it. All this water flows through small trenches in the floors of the hall and pavements of the court to the foot of the Fountain of Lions, where it is swallowed up in a subterranean conduit. Certainly this is a species of dwelling which would never be incommoded with dust, but you ask how could these halls have been tenanted during the winter. Doubtless the large cedar doors were then shut and the marble floors were covered with thick carpets, while the inhabitants lighted fires of fruit-stones and odoriferous woods in the *braseros*, and waited for the return of the fine season, which soon comes in Grenada.

We will not describe the Hall of the Abencerrages, which is precisely like that of the Two Sisters and contains nothing in particular except its antique door of wood, arranged in lozenges, which dates from the time of the Moors. In the Alcazar of Seville you can find another one of exactly the same style.

The *Taza de los Leones* enjoys a wonderful reputation in Arabian poetry: no eulogy is considered too extravagant for these superb animals. I must confess, however, that it would be hard to find anything which less resembles lions than these productions of Arabian fantasy; the paws are simple stakes like those shapeless pieces of wood which one thrusts into the bellies of pasteboard dogs to make them keep their equilibrium; their muzzles streaked with transverse lines, very likely intended for whiskers, are exactly like the snout of a hippopotamus, and the eyes are so primitive in design that they recall the crude attempts of children. However, if you consider these twelve monsters as chimeræ and not lions, and as a fine caprice in ornamentation, producing in combination with the basin they support a picturesque and elegant effect, you will then understand their reputation and the praises contained in this Arabian inscription of twenty-four verses and twenty-four syllables engraved on the sides of the lower basin into which the waters fall from the upper basin. I ask the reader's pardon for the rather barbarous fidelity of the translation:

"O thou, who lookest upon the lions fixed in their place! remark that they only lack life to be perfect. And you to whom will fall the inheritance of this Alcazar and Kingdom, take them from the noble hands of those who have governed them without displeasure and resistance. May God preserve you for the work, which you will accomplish, and protect you forever from the vengeance of your enemy! Honour and glory be thine, O Mohammed! our King, endowed with the high virtues, with whose aid thou hast conquered everything. May God never permit this beautiful garden, the image of thy virtues, to be surpassed by any rival. The material which covers the substance of this basin is like mother-of-pearl beneath the shimmering waters; this sheet of water is like melted silver, for the limpidity of the water and the whiteness of the stone are unequalled; it might be called a drop of transparent essence upon a face of alabaster. It would be difficult to follow its course. Look at the water and look at the basin, and you will not be able to tell if it is the water that is motionless, or the marble which ripples. Like the prisoner of love whose face is full of trouble and fear when under the gaze of the envious, so the jealous water is indignant at the marble and the marble is envious of the water. To this inexhaustible stream we may compare the hand of our King which is as liberal and generous as the lion is strong and valiant."

Into the basin of the Fountain of Lions fell the heads of the thirty-six Abencerrages, drawn there by the stratagem of the Zegris. The other Abencerrages would have shared the same fate if it had not been for the devotion of a little page who, at the risk of his own life, ran to warn the survivors from entering the fatal court. Your attention will be attracted by some large red spots at the bottom of the basin — an indelible accusation left by the victims against the cruelty of their murderers. Unfortunately, the learned declare that neither the Abencerrages nor the Zegris existed. Regarding this fact, I am entirely guided by romances, popular traditions, and Chateaubriand's novel, and I solemnly believe that these crimson stains are blood and not rust.

We established our headquarters in the Court of the Lions; our furniture consisted of two mattresses which were rolled up in a corner during the day, a copper lamp, an earthenware jar, and a few bottles of sherry which we placed in the fountain to cool. Sometimes we slept in the Hall of the Two Sisters, and sometimes in that of the Abencerrages, and it was not without some slight fear that I, stretched out upon my cloak, looked at the white rays of the moon which fell through the openings of the roof into the water of the basin quite astonished to mingle with the yellow, trembling flame of a lamp.

The popular traditions collected by Washington Irving in his *Tales of the Alhambra* came into my memory; the story of the *Headless Horse* and of the *Hairy Phantom* solemnly related by Father Echeverria seemed very probable to me, especially when the light was out. The truth of legends always appears much greater at night when these dark places are filled with weird reflections which give a fantastic appearance to all objects of a vague outline: Doubt is the son of day, Faith is the daughter of the night, and it astonishes me to think that St. Thomas believed in Christ after having thrust his finger into his wounds. I am not sure that I did not see the Abencerrages walking through the moonlit galleries carrying their heads under their arms: anyhow the shadows of the columns always assumed forms that were diabolically suspicious, and the breeze as it passed through the arches made me wonder if it was not a human breath.

Voyage en Espagne (Paris, new ed., 1865).

www.ingramcontent.com/pod-product-compliance
Lightning Source LLC
Chambersburg PA
CBHW032142010526
44111CB00035B/923